Rebecca's Revival

JON F. SENSBACH

Rebecca's Revival

Creating Black Christianity
in the Atlantic World

HARVARD

UNIVERSITY PRESS

Cambridge, Massachusetts

London, England

2005

Library of Congress Cataloging-in-Publication Data

Sensbach, Jon F.
Rebecca's revival : creating Black Christianity in the Atlantic world / Jon F. Sensbach.
p. cm.
Includes bibliographical references (p.) and index.
ISBN 0-674-01689-0 (alk. paper)
1. Protten, Rebecca, 1718–
2. African-American evangelists—Biography.
3. African-American women—Biography.   I. Title.
BV3785.P74S46 2005
269′.2′092—dc22
[B]   2004054021

FOR MY PARENTS

CONTENTS

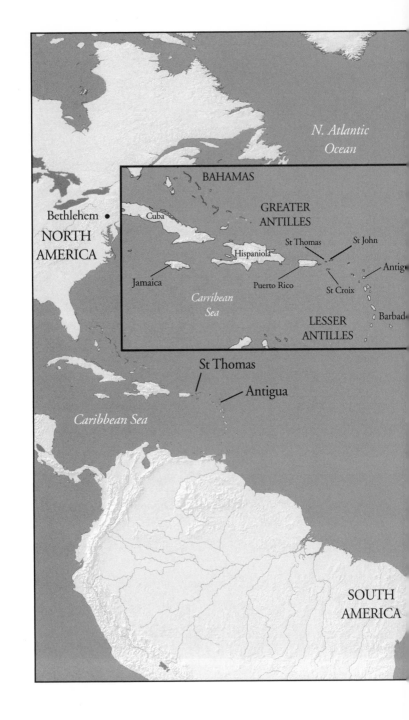

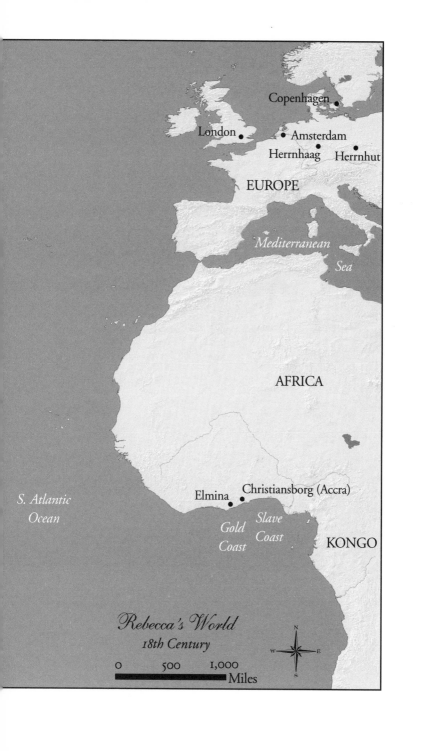

Copenhagen

London • Amsterdam
Herrnhaag Herrnhut

EUROPE

Mediterranean

Sea

AFRICA

S. Atlantic
Ocean

Elmina Christiansborg (Accra)

Gold *Slave*
Coast *Coast* KONGO

Rebecca's World
18th Century

0   500   1,000
■■■■■■■■■■■■■Miles

Prologue

A green line of trees stretches along the coast, broken only by the white towers of a fort clinging to a promontory. From here, on the rim of the continent, the old woman can watch the ships skim west to melt in the horizon. She knows what they carry, their destination, how long they stay at sea, and what happens when they arrive, two months later and five thousand miles away. Perhaps her own mother was carried away on such a ship, like the thousands herded aboard every year bound for the slave markets of America. Still, the vessels are going back there, back to the place she knows best, and it has probably crossed her mind to board one and return too. She lives in the shadow of Fort Christiansborg, on Africa's Gold Coast, where the merchants make their money buying the men, women, and children who march, to an incongruous serenade of birds, out of putrid holding pens and onto the ships. Nobody has time any more for the feeble widow, forgotten in the mulatto village among the other outcast children of the slave trade.

Perhaps Rebecca Protten is surprised, then, when the ship owners make her an offer: the *Ada* will sail for the Caribbean in August 1776, and they will pay her passage. The ship is going home.

An ocean away, bands of turquoise-green water surround the West Indian island of St. Thomas, about forty miles east of Puerto Rico.

Famous today as one of the U.S. Virgin Islands, this string of volcanic mountains is among the most popular holiday destinations in the Caribbean. Two million visitors each year come to bask under palm trees on the white sand, to sail and snorkel in the sparkling translucence of the sea; they pour out of cruise ships docked in the harbor to shop and wander the colorful streets and alleys of town, stopping to admire the colonial-era red fort presiding over the bay.

Back in the hills outside of town, down a dirt road far from the resorts and beaches, is a hidden side of St. Thomas rarely seen by anyone but local people—a simple whitewashed church, unobtrusively tucked onto a wooded slope. Built on the site of a former plantation, it is home to an Afro-Caribbean congregation whose ancestors began holding services there in 1737. On Sunday mornings when worshippers fill the wooden benches inside and begin to sing, the music floats out of the windows and drifts on a warm breeze toward former fields where slaves once worked. Such sounds have drifted over the hills for a long time, because the singers who gather here week after week belong to the oldest black Protestant church in the Americas.

Their congregation dates from a time when the island was a Danish colony, a small Atlantic outpost of an aspiring European power and a busy international maritime crossroads for pirates, smugglers, and traders. Plantation owners eagerly awaited ships bearing Africans from the Gold Coast because, as on virtually every Caribbean island, the economy of St. Thomas depended on slavery. Unfree workers—about nine of every ten inhabitants—did almost everything. Gangs of slaves cultivated sugar cane on terraced slopes, hacked down the stalks with machetes, and hauled them off to be boiled down to molasses, from which rum and sugar would be refined and sent out to world markets. Enslaved Africans built and cleaned houses, loaded and unloaded ships, tanned leather, sewed garments, fired bricks, picked and spun cotton, tended gardens and animals, cooked the food they raised, hauled in fish, caned chairs, and wove the mats they lay down on to sleep. On St. Thomas, as in South Carolina, Virginia, Jamaica, Martinique, and Brazil, black people produced the wealth that vaulted Europe to worldwide supremacy.[1]

But it was here on St. Thomas, in the 1730s, that something else happened, when a solitary young woman began trudging daily along rugged roads through the hills in the sultry evenings after the slaves had returned from the fields. Known then only as Rebecca, she was not yet twenty years old, and she had made herself an apostle for Christ. She was a preacher and a mentor, a provocateur and a prophet, determined to take what she regarded as the Bible's liberating grace to people of African descent. She broadcast her message the only way an evangelist can: by carrying it directly to the people. Her long peregrinations took her to the slave quarters deep in the island's plantation heartland, where she proclaimed salvation to the domestic servants, cane boilers, weavers, and cotton pickers whose bodies and spirits were strip-mined every day by slavery.

Rebecca's light brown skin was the product of mixed African and European parentage. Once a slave herself, she had gained freedom while still quite young, but the experience of bondage gave her a passport to travel and speak with authority among the slaves. Though neither an incendiary nor a soaring orator, she was direct and persuasive, and enslaved people turned out to listen when the teenage preacher testified that Jesus loved them. They responded to her appeals. In what became one of the great social and religious movements of modern history, black women and men began to blend Christianity with the religions they had brought with them from Africa, creating a faith to fortify themselves against slavery. Though hardly anyone knows her name today, Rebecca helped ignite the fires of a new kind of religion that in subsequent centuries has given spiritual sustenance to millions.[2]

A surge of energy from Africans themselves fueled this movement. They needed courage to face violent opposition from planters terrified that Christianity, with its promise of spiritual equality and universal salvation, would promote rebellion among the slaves. Inspired by the belief that Jesus died for them, black people took to the roads, walking miles over the mountains to teach the Scriptures, lead each other in prayer and song, and—in a time when slaveowners considered literacy dangerous for slaves—school each other to read and write. Worshippers built "praise houses" and jammed into them by the hundreds to get baptized and dunk their feet in tubs of holy water. Men whose hands were raw from chopping sugar cane held titles like "keeper of the alms" and "blessed and accomplished teacher of the heathen"; women who spent their days scrubbing chamberpots and cooking meals for plantation mistresses transformed themselves into "faithful helpers" and "venerated evangelical elders" when they passed over the church threshold. They carried on their teaching even after angry whites stormed their meetings and thrashed them with swords and whips. They persisted when planters set fire to their Bibles and beat out the flames on their slaves' faces; or chained them to the ground to keep them away from meetings; or flogged their skin to a pulp; or dumped them in jail; or sold their families apart. The slaves sent petitions to the king and queen of Denmark politely asking that the abuse stop and that they be allowed to worship in peace. The persecution didn't end, but neither did the worship. In time, the movement that in key ways began on this small island caught hold and spread through the Caribbean and North America, changing African-American culture forever. Much that we associate with the black church in subsequent centuries—anchor of community life, advocate of social justice, midwife to spirituals and gospel music—in some measure derives, however distantly, from those early origins.[3]

Though she was not alone in fostering this movement, Rebecca was a principal alchemist in it. Her tenacity was rooted in the certainty of faith; standing trial once on charges of sedition and immorality, she refused to back down when a magistrate ordered her to testify in a way she thought blasphemous, and she declared herself willing to return to slavery instead. She held meetings late into the night, teaching people to read and to find lessons in the Scriptures that fit their own lives. She would talk any time to anybody about Jesus, but she reached out especially to African-American women, pulling many into the church with her words. Her instigation was vital, for women formed a majority in these early congregations, where they emerged from the shadows to preach, recruit, and organize. The Bible was a coded incantation, a talisman for action. Women used it to declare their own value, some fearlessly spitting verses like magic words to silence their masters. Far more than anonymous plantation workers cast adrift in the tides of captivity, these enslaved and free women of color galvanized a new form of thought against white claims that they were damned by a God who sanctioned their bondage.[4]

Only the feverish swirl of people, money, and ideas in the Atlantic world of the early modern age could have produced a person like Rebecca. The Caribbean where she spent her early years, like the rest of the Americas, was a siphon for European colonizers and unfree Africans, a polyglot jostle of adventurers, fortune-seekers, preachers, scoundrels, and captives, always mingling, forever measuring one another. Chafing cultures gave off the spark of something new, melded and fused, picked up new cadences, then spun off into something different again. Even by those norms, however, the young preacher was unusual. Rebecca was a mixed-race native of a British colony who was transplanted to a Danish island; her primary language was Dutch, but she spoke at least four other languages. Mobility defined her world, whether in the labored footsteps of the itinerant preacher or the ship crossings of the serial voyager. Her ability to move vast distances between places and to slide easily between groups of people was extraordinary for a free woman of color in the eighteenth century. Born in the West Indies, she traveled thousands of miles as an early disciple in the black international evangelical movement. She lived on two islands, on two continents, and in two hemispheres. Near the end of her life, she arrived by a twist of fate on Africa's western coast, from where the slave ships departed for the Caribbean she had long since left behind.[5]

Rebecca moved, too, in and around the complicated spaces where people lived as "black" or "white" in the eighteenth century. She spent years almost entirely among Africans or Europeans, or a mix of both, but never fitting into either group. She was willing to surrender her freedom for the sake of Christianity, but she believed that Africans should surrender their own religions for that cause as well. She belonged to a religious order founded by Europeans that denied the importance of physical differences among the redeemed, but among white coreligionists she always stood out as different— "Rebecca the mulatto," they called her.

A handful of better-known black voyagers—all of them men, such as Olaudah Equiano, James Gronniosaw, and Ottobah Cugoano—crossed the ocean in captivity at the height of the eighteenth-century slave trade and eventually wrote dramatic memoirs of bondage and redemption. Their narratives—survivors' depositions, really—proclaimed to a largely skeptical European world the humanity and intelligence of all people of African descent.[6] Rebecca left no journal, no autobiography, no sermons or thick body of correspondence, no affidavit of trials endured and transcended. Her life's work was talking. But she was literate, and could read and write at least two languages. A few of her letters have survived, including a testimonial to Jesus in Dutch and a letter in German to her husband. It is unusual that written testimony from any black woman in that century should have survived to our own time, so her few letters are precious indeed. Among the millions of Afro-Atlantic women during the era of the slave trade, only a scant few are known to us beyond the barest biographical outlines, if even that much. Like them, Rebecca remains in many ways an enigma, a name in someone else's journal or in a church ledger, a shadow darting across a court document—her life seemingly no more than the sum of scattered fragments.

On the other hand, the fragments are far more numerous than we might expect. Rebecca's life and travels can be tracked down in a surprising array of manuscripts in German, Danish, and West Indian archives—documentary echoes of her far-flung voyages around the Atlantic.[7] She had a way of turning up in unexpected places at important times to help conduct social experiments that challenged strictures of race, religion, and gender. The same woman who preached to the slaves later became a spiritual leader for white women in Germany and, apparently, the first black woman ordained in western Christianity. Rebecca's story is the unique record of one person steering her way through the worlds of slavery and religious faith in the eighteenth century, with their limited possibilities and ambiguous choices. But her own fortunes are also a mirror on a larger narrative—the origins of the black church itself.

As the *Ada* waited at anchor off the Gold Coast in August of 1776, Rebecca would look west toward the hillside church on St. Thomas and choose once again.

CHAPTER ONE

A Baptism of Blood

Picking their way through the darkness, a dozen men climbed a path uphill to a fort overlooking Coral Bay, a small harbor on the Caribbean island of St. John. It was three o'clock in the morning on November 23, 1733. The men, all natives of West Africa, were held as slaves of the Danish West India and Guinea Company, known simply as "the Company," a slave-trading firm that operated sugar and cotton plantations in Denmark's West Indian colonies. It was their job to supply the fort with firewood, so the Africans lugged bundles of kindling and logs up the path. But on this night the bundles served another purpose, for inside them the men had hidden knives and *Kapmesser,* long blades used for cutting sugar cane.

The group arrived at the entrance to the fort, which was guarded by a garrison of six soldiers.

"Who's there?" called the sentry.

"Company Negroes with wood."

Apparently satisfied that there was nothing unusual about such a delivery in the early morning hours, the sentry asked no further questions and opened the gate. Inside the fort, the Africans dropped their wood, withdrew their weapons, and slashed the sentinel and four other soldiers to death; the sixth was wounded but escaped by

hiding under a bed. The attackers fired the fort's cannon to an-
nounce to other Africans on the island that a rebellion had begun.

At the signal, slaves at the nearby plantation of the local magistrate, John Reimert Soedtman, burst into his room, forced him to
strip, and ordered him to sing and dance naked. Perhaps they had
once been told to dance on the slave auction block for prospective buyers, or to perform for the judge's amusement. Now, they
watched him desperately pirouette and sing by candlelight in the
darkness; then they jabbed a sword through him, sheared off his
head, gutted his body, and, in an apparent ritual of purification or
cleansing, they "washed themselves in his blood." Soedtman's wife
was on the nearby island of St. Thomas and so eluded the massacre,
but the rebels killed his thirteen-year-old stepdaughter and dumped
her body on his eviscerated corpse. Then they fanned out into the
early dawn.[1]

Let us begin by talking about the missing body parts of enslaved
men and women. Curious visitors to the Danish West Indies who
noticed the many amputees hobbling along the roads on crutches or
trying to do their fieldwork with one hand would learn that they
had been penalized for defying the *Blancken,* or white colonists.
These insubordinates left a frightening inventory of extremities on
the chopping block. A slave without a foot had run away; one missing both feet had run away twice. A one-legged former rebel had escaped and remained free for half a year before being captured. A
one-handed field worker had raised the other hand to strike a white
person. A black West Indian who could not speak had once shouted
at a *Blancke,* and his tongue had been cut out.[2]

"If one has a slave, how much more a slave is he than the one he
purchased! He must be fed, clothed, and screamed and cursed at to
make him do his task. And finally, one has to sleep always with the
fear that domestic enemies will slit one's throat at night to end our

days as thanks for the care you have taken to sustain them." Such was the master's lament—how my slaves tyrannize me!—expressed by one Pierre Pannet, a planter from the neighboring Danish colony of St. Thomas, whose *Report on the Execrable Conspiracy Carried Out by the Amina Negroes on the Danish Island of St. John in America in 1733* was written eleven days after the massacre of the garrison. The revolt cast a glaring light on the truth of Pannet's observation: Denmark's modest imperial holdings in the south Atlantic—a couple of Caribbean colonies, two forts in West Africa, and one slave-trading company—depended on African laborers who wanted to slit their masters' throats.[3]

In the year of the great rebellion there were five people of African descent—the great majority of them enslaved—for every European in the Danish colonies. On St. Thomas, blacks outnumbered whites by 3,741 to about 650, and on St. John 1,087 to 208. To control this captive population, planters staged an elaborate choreography of terror. They punished minor acts of theft or insolence on the plantation with a few lashes, after which a slave was expected to say, "Thank you, master!" But with more serious insubordination, reprisals became public spectacles of vengeance. An enslaved person who looked defiantly at a white was tied to a pillory and whipped by another slave 100 times; one who ran away for three months was lashed 500 times with a whip made of dried, braided strips of cowhide that ripped away the flesh, and then salt or Spanish pepper was smeared on the wounds. Slaves were strung up by the arms to posts and flailed with red-hot firebrands. Those who continually ran away or who committed arson or murder were beheaded in the square by the fort in Charlotte Amalie, the St. Thomas harbor.[4]

The fort was supposed to protect the colony from foreign invaders by sea and from slave rebels on land. But the soldiers stationed there, most of them poor farmers and indentured servants from Denmark, were not always skilled in the arts of deference either. Wretchedly paid and treated, they were forced by order of the governor to eat rye bread, which they hated, deriding it as the "governor's ca-ca." A slave at the fort once hollowed out a loaf of bread and stuffed it with human excrement in ridicule. The governor executed him by having him strung up by the feet from the gallows, alongside a dog hanging by the neck. A man could survive this torture a few hours before strangling.[5]

In the confusing hours after the first assault on Coral Bay, bands of rebels, now numbering about eighty and armed with guns, powder, shot, swords, and axes from the fort's arsenal, moved across St. John raiding plantations and killing white men, women, and children. The island is only about six miles long and three miles wide, but its mountainous interior and ragged, inlet-dented coastline kept news of the uprising from spreading quickly, adding further surprise to the Africans' attack. They had divided their forces into several units—one to occupy the fort, another to move west along the northern coast, and a third to seize plantations along the main road through the middle of the island, and eventually to rendezvous in the west with the second group. By the middle of the following day they had gained control of much of the island, setting fire to cane fields but taking care to preserve the sugar refineries. Still, some planters were able to elude them, in more than one case because they were warned by their own slaves, many of whom did not join the rebellion. One slave told a group of rebels approaching his plantation that he had already killed his master, then he "pretended to fall in with them, but as soon as he found the opportunity, he returned to warn his master and help him and his family to flee" to St. Thomas.[6]

On another plantation, black defenders met the attackers with gunfire, killing several before retreating to the western end of the island where they joined a group of whites holding out at the plantation of Pieter Durlo, under the command of militia captain Johannes van Beverhout. The rebels charged, but driven back by gunshot and fire from a few small cannon, they fell back to besiege the defensive position overnight from the cover of the forest, cutting off the plantation's water supply and "promising to return in the morning to bring to completion the destruction of all the planters." The next morning, the exhausted and thirsty defenders repulsed another charge, although, as Pierre Pannet put it, "they would have been defeated had the attackers acted as courageously as their great numbers should have allowed."[7]

More than twenty-four hours had now passed since the capture of the fort, and word of the uprising had gotten to St. Thomas, only three miles to the west, as a few frantic whites managed to make their way into boats and flee. Shocked colonists there could find no shortage of scapegoats for the debacle—namely, each other. The governor, Philip Gardelin, "blamed the causes of this calamity on our disunity and exhorted us as Christians to look among ourselves for the means to a solution," citing a lack of food and supplies for his inability to relieve the besieged *Blancken* of St. John. Others blamed the governor for the colony's disorganization and excoriated his apparent indifference to the struggle on St. John. One critic "objected sharply to Governor Gardelin that it was shameful to abandon in this manner the interests of his government's children to the barbarism of their disloyal slaves, and that he was the one responsible for these events." The exasperated governor exclaimed: "What do you want me to do? If you have any remedies for the situation, then act. I authorize you to do so." Finally spurred by the criticism, the governor sent sixteen soldiers as well as about fifty other volunteers, including white citizens and free blacks from St. Thomas, across the straits along with provisions. Not impressed, Pannet accused Gardelin of sending "a few barrels of biscuits and several of salted Irish mutton, which stank; he said that there was no other meat to be had, although in fact the island was well supplied with good beef. They had to take those provisions along, though even the Negroes would not take a bite of it." Nevertheless, reinforcements relieved the besieged defenders at Durlo's plantation while another force assaulted and retook the fort, capturing ten of the African rebels. The rest disappeared into the woods, their power still far from broken.[8]

Tiny, seafaring Denmark, with a population of less than half a million, was no major world power in 1733, but it had ambitions to be one, and its Caribbean colonies, about forty miles east of Puerto Rico, existed because of that desire. These two small islands formed part of the Leeward archipelago, the long crescent that, together with the Windward Islands, defined the eastern rim of the Caribbean Sea. Sailing between these islands in 1493, Christopher Columbus, mesmerized by their beauty, called them "Las Virgenes"—the Virgin Islands, which he naturally claimed for Spain. The Spanish made no serious effort to plant settlements there, and over the next century and a half the islands remained uncolonized, although the Spanish, English, Dutch, and French contested the entire Leeward and Windward chain. In the seventeenth century the English colonized Tortola, Virgin Gorda, and Anegada in the Virgin cluster, but not their close neighbors, St. Thomas and St. John. All these islands, like the rest of the West Indies, became pawns in the European rivals' gambit for imperial power. Those competitors took a generation to master the formula, but eventually they realized that colonies laid out with sugar plantations worked by African slaves would produce immense profits. Denmark, though entering this colonizing race somewhat late, likewise coveted Caribbean wealth to nourish its larger imperial hopes.

The Danish pushed their way into the slave-trading market by buying one fort, Frederiksberg, in 1659 from the kingdom of Fetu and building another, Christiansborg, in 1661 on the Gold Coast of West Africa. The Danish king, Frederick III, chartered the Danish West India and Guinea Company in 1671 to take over Denmark's slaving and colonizing ventures in Africa and the south Atlantic. In early 1672, the Company sent two ships loaded with men to take possession of St. Thomas. The island was still occupied by a tiny number of Caribs who had survived the diseases introduced by European settlers, and whom the Danish sought to convert to Christianity. The colonizers may have wanted to save the Indians' souls, but while they were at it they also put a claim on their labor, either as slaves or as some kind of indentured servants, thus making them trial balloons for the massive use of captive workers that would soon follow. The records tell of one "John Indian" who repeatedly tried to run away and finally had a leg chopped off as a reward. Here was the original sin of Danish colonialism—the last of the Caribs lurching around one-legged in his own land.[9]

The earliest colonizers were a jumble of adventurers, soldiers, indentured servants, and convicts dredged from Danish prisons, whom the governor derided as "lazy, shiftless louts" and "uncontrollable fellows whom neither the workhouse nor the penitentiary could improve." A dreadful mortality rate culled most of these first recruits—ninety percent died either en route to the West Indies or soon after arriving, devoured by tropical fevers. The bulk of the early colonists, in fact, soon became the Dutch, French, German, and English settlers who migrated to St. Thomas from other Caribbean outposts, quickly outnumbering the Danish in their own colony. As the largest European group on the island, the Dutch dominated culture, politics, and the economy almost from the outset. Their language became the colony's lingua franca.[10]

Denmark, embarking on the business of empire long after England, France, and Holland, followed their examples for its blueprint of St. Thomas. Those nations had fumbled about for years in their early American colonies, experimenting with Indian and indentured European labor before importing enslaved African workers wholesale. Displaying none of the anxieties over "race" and slavery that their predecessors had struggled to resolve, the Danish knew from the beginning that St. Thomas was to be a sugar colony worked by

Africans. Within a year, the first shipment of 103 Africans arrived in St. Thomas and went to work clearing land and laying out plantations. As was true of so many Caribbean colonies, an enslaved African majority became the settlement's dominant feature.[11]

The colony grew, slowly, and mostly because the slave ships kept coming. By 1715, when the white population had increased to only 555, there were 160 plantations and 32 sugar mills on St. Thomas operated by 3,042 Africans. But unlike larger plantation colonies like Barbados or Jamaica, where miles of fertile coastal plains made an ideal landscape for sugar cane, the mountains of St. Thomas offered few level stretches for planting. The image of vast tracts lorded over by stately mansions seldom applied in this rugged landscape. Nudged into narrow valleys or sculpted onto hillside terraces, plantations were less profitable; many planters raised more cotton than sugar, and most held far fewer slaves, about twenty per plantation. Only a handful found business lucrative, and even the West India and Guinea Company failed to make much money from either its plantations or its African voyages.[12]

Both the demand for and supply of slaves were unreliable. The Company, ill-financed and managed, operated only a few ships which delivered cargoes only sporadically and not always when needed. Vessels put in at Christiansborg, where Danish merchants contracted with African slave dealers to supply them with captives. Those traders worked along the Gold Coast and inland as much as a hundred miles, buying slaves from African rulers and delivering them to holding pens inside the Danish forts, where they waited to be shipped to America. In the 1680s the Danes even gave their slave-trading concession to a German company from Brandenburg, but reclaimed it for their own company in 1717. To augment these erratic sources, the Danes also relied on Dutch merchants, who were among the major suppliers of African slave labor in the New World through the end of the eighteenth century. From their base at Elmina on the Gold Coast, Dutch traders roamed the coast from

Dahomey to Kongo, scooping up unfortunate captives from African civil wars and interethnic slaving raids. Several thousand of these were sold in the Danish West Indies. As a result, enslaved Africans from at least a two-thousand-mile stretch between Senegambia and Kongo poured into St. Thomas. They represented many cultures and spoke diverse languages, but the greatest number came from various branches of the Akan peoples on the Gold Coast.[13]

The Danish occupied nearby St. John in 1717. Settlers migrating from St. Thomas, where much of the land had been exhausted by decades of sugar cultivation, overspread the island with plantations in fifteen years. Though hardly challenging Britain or France, Denmark and its colonies were immersed in the classic overseas triangle trade between Europe, West Africa, and America, and its ships carried the goods well known to most European and African traders, including muskets, gunpowder, sugar, rum, gold, ivory, and slaves, to a growing circuit of international markets. At the heart of the system were those who wielded the *Kapmesser*.[14]

On St. Thomas, Governor Gardelin and the military were learning more about the St. John rebels from the first prisoners taken in the Danish counterattack. They were all countrymen and women from the same African group known in America as "Amina" because they inhabited the vicinity of the Dutch fort of Elmina on the Gold Coast, though Europeans applied the term loosely to many Akan-speaking peoples spread across a very large region. More precisely, the insurgents belonged to the Akwamu kingdom that had gained ascendancy during the early eighteenth century and dominated trade and politics along the Gold Coast. Later estimates put the number of Amina, or Akwamu, rebels on St. John at about 150, a substantial core of people whose shared culture enabled them to organize such an ambitious uprising.

The kingdom of Akwamu had risen to power through the aggressiveness of its merchants and by the use of new forms of warfare made possible by European firearms, which enabled its fighters to overrun many other kingdoms on the Gold and Slave Coasts by about 1710. "Their land is quite big, full of large villages," wrote a European. "These people are terrifying to their neighbors due to their might and their cruelty. They wage almost constant war against" the neighbors to gain captives for the slave trade. "They trade in gold, ivory, and slaves. In return, they receive iron, guns, and the like from the Europeans. As is the practice of several African nations, the Amina are served by slaves, who, according to their opinion, however, are not treated as harshly as those in the West Indies." Thousands of the slaves brought to America during these decades were captives taken by the Akwamu and sold to European traders, including the Danish and Dutch.[15]

Fed up with these slaving practices, a group of rebels launched a civil war, aided by a coalition of nearby states who invaded and overthrew the Akwamu empire in 1730. They sold into slavery many Akwamu captives to the same Danish buyers who had once bought slaves from the Akwamu themselves. Between 1730 and 1733, Danish ships delivered more than 350 Akwamu captives to St. John, where they worked alongside Africans from other nations whom they had conquered and sold into American slavery years earlier.[16]

The Akwamus, or Aminas, already had a reputation among West Indian planters as the most difficult of Africans to control, in part because of their persistence in trying to escape. They were considered "the most unruly and barbaric of the nations," "wilder, more murderous and devil-like in their nature than others, practicing magic and devil-fantasies," wrote a European several years after the St. John Rebellion, which only solidified the Amina reputation. "They are unfaithful and warlike to all the other nations." They were said to be "headstrong and tyrannical," the "strongest of all the Negroes, able to pull and carry loads just like the mules," but also "so wicked and lazy that they must always be driven before the whip."[17]

The Aminas were credited by both Europeans and other Africans with possessing ferocious supernatural powers. "There are witch doctors among them who are so powerful that they can bewitch a person to the size of a cat. They can put a hex on a person by means of a strand of hair, fingernail clippings, sharp, thin pieces of rusty iron, the thickness and size of a musket ball, which results in the person's death. They can both conceal a firearm and guide a bullet where they want it to go when they see someone shooting a gun." They believed the world was created by a high god named Borriborri, whose son was named Jacompo, and whose duty was to intercede with his father for mankind. When they prayed to Jacompo for luck in war or other favors, the Aminas knelt in front of a pan of water, drank from it, and spat the water back in the pan as they said the prayer. They may have used this method to summon divine support for their assault on Coral Bay.[18]

As the Danish tortured their prisoners to learn more about the inner workings of the rebellion, it became clear that this was no spontaneous uprising, no effort to simply escape slavery and retreat into the hills, but a systematic plot to overturn the slave masters' order and replace it with one controlled by the Aminas themselves. The plan required careful organization, as Pierre Pannet noted: "The Negroes were meeting at night to plot at their ease, without anyone being able to stop them or to imagine that these meetings would lead to their [the planters'] ruin, until the fatal day of the execution of their plans would reveal the horrible success of their plotting." Evidently modeling their insurgency on familiar Akwamu political forms, the participants elected a king, queen, and chief officers. The main organizer was identified as "King June," a foreman on the Soedtman estate on St. John. This rebel, whose Akwamu name was Jama, had been an important member of the royal court on the Gold Coast who served as tribute collector, trading agent, and military commander. Other important leaders of the plot included men called Kanta, Claes, King Bolombo, Prince Aquashie,

Abedo, Kofi, and Apinda. Many of them appear to have come from royal families in Africa or to have had strong connections to various Akwamu courts and were thus accustomed to exerting authority. All were enslaved and sold to Danish traders working out of Christiansborg between 1730 and 1732, after the final collapse of their empire. Some even held important positions as "bombas," or drivers, on plantations in St. John. The queen of the rebel court was not identified, but at least some of the planners and an estimated one-third of the participants were women, and the insurrection offered them possibilities for frontline military action that they had been denied in Africa.[19]

The rebels devised a bold plan, powerful in its implications for Amina dominion in that quarter of the West Indies. They "plotted to retain the island and they had divided the plantations among themselves, according to the rank and position which each was to hold," wrote Pannet. "The Negroes from other nations were to be provided to them to do their labors and were to belong to them as slaves. This is the reason why they preserved all the sugar factories and other buildings." Nor did they envision their rebellion stopping at the coastline of St. John. "They had additionally resolved that, after succeeding with the St. John revolt, they in concert with the Amina Negroes of this island [St. Thomas], would have brought our complete ruin and would have then worked on that of Tortola. It is easy to see how grand was the design of these wretches and to understand how much more wretched are those who are unable to do without their labor and their help."[20]

Here was the audacity of the scheme and its flaw as well. In their own numbers and cultural solidarity, the Aminas easily saw the means to overthrow the Europeans and re-create in American miniature the glory of their deposed Gold Coast empire. It appears they found ways to communicate covertly with their countrymen and women across the narrow waters between the islands to bring them into the conspiracy. But in envisioning their own freedom, the

Aminas operated out of old antagonisms and the desire to rule their former African subjects again. This was no pan-African coalition united in racial accord against a common white enemy, but a master plan born of one people's exclusive sense of superiority. Small wonder that West Africans once sold into slavery by the Aminas wanted nothing to do with the plot. Despite their numbers, the Aminas were still a minority among the more than one thousand enslaved people on the island. Many of their enemies preferred to fight alongside the *Blancken* rather than serve the Aminas again.

Into St. John and St. Thomas they poured during the 1720s, new shipments of African-born captives to terrace the hills for planting. "Bussals," the white masters called them, a demeaning term that conveyed all the invented reasons why Europeans enslaved Africans: "A Bussal is a person whose faculty of reasoning has not at all been developed and who is also lacking in physical dexterity because he has grown up in his homeland in ignorance and inactivity." Africans learned a new protocol and harsh rules on the plantation. "Usually, a newly acquired slave is given a new name by his master. On the larger islands, his skin is branded with his master's mark. He is now the property of his master, whose command he is obliged to obey with all the strength of his body. This is soon learned by the Bussals, and they become, for the most part, accustomed to subjugation and obedience without resistance, for, in spite of their ignorance and savagery, they recognize that there is nothing else to do but submit to the yoke."[21]

Many did not submit, however, including those who escaped through suicide. "'I am a prince,' said a Negro to his master, who expected him to work. 'For the time being, I am in your power, but nothing will ever persuade me to serve you; I would rather end my life by voluntary death.'" Likewise, an African woman refused to obey her white mistress, saying, "'I was much greater in Guinea than you are here. I had many more slaves in my service than you have. Now you expect me to be your slave? I would much rather die of starvation.'" Both did so. Many Africans believed they would return to their homeland after death. As a deterrent, slave masters chopped off the hands and head of suicides and publicly displayed the grisly trophies in cages. But the urge to escape could not be quelled. One woman "would take no regular food, and when she was force fed, she ate earth and stones until she wasted away and died. Even though her master had her provided with a muzzle, she found it possible to get earth and sand into her mouth, thereby effecting her own death."[22]

Africans arriving in the Danish islands entered a world stratified by far more than a jarring disparity between "white" and "black" islanders. Afro-Caribbean inhabitants themselves were fragmented by a variety of social and occupational ranks. "Bussals" were generally thrown in with the largest group, the so-called kamina folk, or enslaved field hands. Africans also served occasionally as house servants, warehouse laborers, and artisans such as masons, carpenters, coopers, smiths, or tailors. However, the smaller number of Creoles, or black folk born in the West Indies, were much more likely to fill those positions because whites regarded them as more "civilized," trustworthy, and receptive to training. A small number of freed blacks, generally Creole, also worked in some of these trades. Apart from their common oppression by whites, about the only thing unifying most of these groups was the Dutch Creole language, a mixture of Dutch and African tongues concocted by the first Africans to arrive in the late seventeenth century, which all subsequent generations learned, and which black and white islanders spoke to each other. *Mij dodte mij loppe in myn lande:* so ran the Amina expression in Dutch Creole that at death the soul escapes to Africa—"When I die, I shall return to my own land."[23]

Eager for profits, planters used most of the arable land on St. John for sugar and cotton. They provided no food for their workers, instead forcing them to raise their own crops on small patches, or "provision grounds," at the edge of plantations. The slaves tended these gardens in the evenings after the day's fieldwork was done, and on Sundays. The fragility of this system was exposed when droughts and hurricanes periodically devastated crops, as they did with particular severity in 1725–26. Many slaves actually starved to death, while others tried to escape, stole food from masters, and challenged their authority in other ways. The planters responded with force, executing seventeen slaves in 1726.

In the spring of 1733 the awful cycle returned: a drought, two hurricanes, and a swarm of insects destroyed virtually everything. As black West Indians faced famine again, the Governor, Philip Gardelin, issued a new slave code on September 5, 1733, to warn them of harsh penalties for resisting. Leaders of runaway slaves, the code announced, would be pinched three times with red-hot irons and then hanged. Other runaways would lose a leg or, if pardoned by the owner, an ear, and receive 150 lashes. Slaves failing to reveal the intention of others to run away would be burned on the forehead and receive 150 lashes. Those who stole the equivalent of four dollars or more would be pinched and hanged; anyone stealing less than four dollars' worth would be branded and whipped 150 times. Slaves who failed to step aside to wait for a white to pass, or who practiced witchcraft, would be flogged, while anyone attempting to poison a master would be pinched three times with irons and then broken on the wheel.[24]

Instead of preventing uprisings, the new laws quickly produced the opposite effect. In one of the most violent slave societies of the New World, made worse by famine and even harsher crackdowns, the arithmetic of Gold Coast rivalries and the slave trade added up. It was then that the recently enslaved Aminas, contemptuous of other Africans as well as Creoles, and strangely resistant to having their limbs amputated by Europeans, decided that rebellion was their only option.

By March 1734, more than three months after the first attack, the rebels still controlled much of the island. The Danes had retaken the fort in the east and reinforced their stronghold at Durlo's plantation in the west. They had even captured and executed a number of Aminas, at least thirty-two by early December, according to one count, and the rebels were running out of powder and ammunition. Still, they were determined fighters, and they held most of the interior of St. John. Tracking parties failed to root them out, and the Danish lacked sufficient manpower to retake the island systematically. Abandoning their practice of preserving sugar works, the rebels raided and destroyed nearly fifty plantations. In February, the English captain of a man-of-war visiting nearby Tortola sent sixty soldiers in pursuit, but the rebels ambushed them at night, wounding four, and the soldiers mutinied rather than go on. A similar expedition led by an English captain from St. Kitts was also attacked with the loss of three dead, including the captain's own two sons, and five wounded. The survivors fled the island.[25]

The rebels had stripped away the prosperous veneer of Danish colonialism to reveal its vulnerabilities. Slaves had staged plenty of rebellions in American plantation societies and would carry out many more, but few thwarted the planters and their troops as long and insistently as those on St. John. Word was circulating around the Caribbean that a small, poorly armed band of rebels had taken an entire island and was taunting the colonizers. In South Carolina, the only North American colony in which enslaved blacks outnumbered whites, anxious readers attuned to the threat of slave unrest could follow the progress of the revolt in the *South Carolina Gazette*. The paper reported on March 2, 1734, that the St. John rebels "had entirely massacred all the white People on that Island, consisting of about 200 Families, and were inhuman in the Execution of their Murders." Forces sent from St. Thomas had been "beaten off by the Negroes, who have fortified themselves." According to a follow-up story just a week later, a combined expedition from St. Kitts and St. Thomas had "landed on the Island of St. John on four several places, surrounded all the Negroes, and fell upon them with such vigour, that in less than one hour they cut them all to pieces, some were taken as Prisoners, and afterward hang'd and quarter'd as they deserved, and not one of 'em escaped." The *Gazette* had gotten it wrong; in fact, the insurgents had driven the St. Kitts force away in humiliation.[26]

Embarrassed and desperate as the standoff wore on, Governor Gardelin appealed to the French governor on Martinique for help. "No doubt you will have learned of the cruel catastrophe which we have suffered on our island of St. John, caused by a rebellion of our Mina Negroes, who [have] massacred forty of our Whites of both sexes," he wrote on March 21, 1734. "I feel that we are on the verge of some terrible happening unless you have the kindness to honor me with your assistance. Not only are you bound to save us because we are allies, friends, and neighbors, but also because, as Christians, you cannot allow slaves to triumph over our weakness and to render us victims of their rebellion." Ordinarily the French would have had little interest in helping a colonial rival, especially a Protestant one, but they needed money and friends, and they agreed to help when the Danish negotiated to buy the island of St. Croix from them as part of the deal. Besides, as a French official wrote in April: "It is in the interest of all the islands that slaves who dare revolt against Whites be punished; if the St. John rebels are allowed to escape, it would constitute an example which might inspire the spirit of revolt among the Negroes of all the islands."[27]

Martinique's governor quickly put together a force of 60 French and Swiss soldiers and 140 militia, including a detachment of 34 free blacks, and sent them off, instructing the commander, Chevallier de Longueville, that "it is important for the honor of the French nation that not one of these Negroes, regardless of age or sex, escape from our midst." Arriving at St. John on April 23, the force waited out a storm before heading into the mountains to hunt the rebels. "The four detachments split up in the belief that each by itself was strong enough to deal with the rebels should they attack vigorously, as we had been assured in St. Thomas they would do, although now it appeared that there were no more than 55 or 60 of them armed with guns," Longueville later wrote. The Aminas had separated into several small groups, evidently counting on being able to disappear into secret places in the interior. But two French detachments quickly rousted about a dozen rebels from their encampment in a ravine of 26 huts, which Longueville destroyed. Over the next month, the French chased the rebels into the fastnesses. The drought that had done so much to provoke the uprising had ended momentously, and both quarry and hunters slogged through a ceaseless downpour up and down the thickly forested ridges.[28]

The insurgents largely eluded their pursuers, but by early May they seem to have concluded that flight before this relentless and better-armed opponent was hopeless. Following a plume of smoke on a distant hill, the French arrived at a rebel camp to find them gone but for two corpses—one whom the Aminas themselves had slain the day before and another who hanged himself as the enemy approached. Three days later the French captured a wounded boy who had survived a stabbing by his companions, and who led them to a point on the southern side of the island where they found eleven bodies, including two women—all suicides.

That method of escape proved to be the best of several dreadful choices. In his report on the hunt, Longueville described the alternative: "On Sunday, May 16, six Negroes and two Negro women surrendered at the appeal of their master who spared their lives. He then informed me of the matter. I ordered him to bring them to me, since they were identified as rebels. I had them put into chains. Three of them were burned at the stake on three different plantations on St. John." The five others were sent to St. Thomas to serve as public examples. "One was burned to death slowly, another was sawed in half and the third was impaled. The two Negro women had their hands and heads cut off after all five had been tortured with hot pincers in the town." A week later, a free black detachment from St. Thomas, which was aiding in the chase, discovered another group of twenty-five dead rebels, including six women, their broken guns scattered around them. They were estimated to have killed themselves a week to ten days earlier.[29]

Satisfied that their pursuit was over, the French left St. John in elation at the end of May 1734. Two months later, a last band of fourteen rebels was reported still at large under the leadership of Prince Aquashie. To avoid another manhunt, the Danish tricked them into surrendering with promises of a pardon, then seized them. They beheaded Prince Aquashie; his companions were sentenced to be worked to death or to suffer execution in the familiar agonizing ways.[30]

Men and women trapped by slavery in other American colonies noticed: the rebels had held St. John for more than six months. The revolt became a centerpiece among dozens of uprisings throughout the Caribbean and North America during the 1730s. The rebellions fed on each other—news of one inspired another hundreds of miles away, and veterans of some plots recycled themselves to help organize others. One St. John participant named Will resurfaced, almost incredibly, again and again. Captured during the Danish counterattack, he somehow escaped execution, perhaps by turning evidence, and was deported to Antigua. There in 1736, he was implicated in a huge plot organized by an alliance of Akan and Creole slaves, but again he saved himself by testifying against fellow rebels, helping to send dozens to be burned, broken, and hanged. Sold to New York, he was arrested a third time for taking part in the conspiracy there in 1741, to which he was said to have lent his experience from the two earlier revolts, and again he tried to save himself by giving evidence. This time the authorities sent him to the stake.[31]

It is ironic that the St. John rebels, in their war against European colonialism, had no intention of providing an inspiring example to so many enslaved people in the Americas. As the St. John rebellion shows, in the Atlantic world that slavery made, the oppressed did not always make common cause against the master class. Old enmities lingered; coalitions were fragile; and the rulers coaxed betrayals from the vulnerable. For all the boldness, creativity, and careful planning that shaped dozens of slave revolts during nearly four centuries in the Americas, it was almost impossible to make them succeed, and in their wake the enslaved were left with the same urgent problem of daily survival.

As with any failed slave revolt, this uprising raises the question of what happened after the last rebel was captured, after every score was settled. On St. John, where more than two hundred people were dead, European and African survivors now faced each other every day with raw memories of the violence, and the rebellion's repercussions would not fade soon. There and on St. Thomas, its sister colony across the narrow water, Danish colonial power reemerged as more dominant; the slaves were intimidated more fiercely than ever. But all parties now had to redefine the terms by which they would live together, and Afro-Caribbean people were forced to weigh anew their responses to the crushing psychological and punitive burdens of captivity. If rebellion would not work, was freedom by some other means a realistic possibility? How could the unfree maintain dignity in a society designed to deprive them of it? Such were the questions the slaves grappled with as an adolescent girl named Rebecca came of age on St. Thomas in the shadow of rebellion.

CHAPTER TWO

Rebirth and Remembrance

Ships arriving at port in St. Thomas with their slaves from West Africa, their linen and iron from Denmark, or their grain from Pennsylvania entered a harbor that was admired as "one of the finest in all the American islands." Here the southern coast of the island opens into a great arcing bay nearly enclosed by two long arms of land. On old maps, the harbor looks like a keyhole. Mountains rising sharply out of the glassy water ring the bay; in front of them the town of Charlotte Amalie straddles a strip of land about one hundred yards wide by the shore. "There is firm, sandy anchor ground all along the bay so that all kinds of vessels can lie safely at anchor under all wind conditions," wrote an eighteenth-century visitor. "The water's depth is such that all vessels and ships can anchor most anywhere and lie safely at anchor from their bridges, loading and unloading goods there." From one of those ships in the mid-1720s a young girl, six or seven years old, disembarked and was rowed to land. From there she was probably taken to the slave market, in a square near the edge of town, and sold at auction. Her name was Shelly, and she had been stolen from home. Alone and frightened, she was just one more of the hundreds of men, women, and children who arrived every year in chains to be fed into the flesh bazaar on St. Thomas. Though they came from different places and spoke many languages, all of them had a story to tell of a capture, a ship, a nightmare. Shelly had her own tale.[1]

What would she have witnessed there, in the slave market? Perhaps no more than a few people like herself, gathered singly or in small groups from various traders working the Caribbean circuit. But if a slave ship had just arrived from Africa, she would have seen lines of survivors—men, women, and children, dozens of them, maybe as many as two hundred—just emerged from the foul hold after a voyage of up to six weeks, herded into the square to await sale. Their skin shone with palm oil rubbed on by the slavers before landing to make their weakened bodies look strong and healthy, and they wore coarse cotton wraps. In the square they were separated into groups, probably according to ethnic origin, as one European speculated. Dejected expressions were brightened by a "ray of hope" when countrymen already on the island approached them in the market to explain what was happening, thus giving new arrivals the sense that it was "possible to be a slave without at the same time being quite unhappy and without hope." They received a bowl of sweetened rice, which they ate with their hands, and men were given a pipe filled with tobacco while white planters gathered to look.

"Before the sale begins, they are subjected to a thorough examination to determine the condition of their bodies, which is usually performed by a surgeon," wrote the observer. "Since these poor people are not yet rightly certain about the implications of the auction in which they are involved, they are usually quite apprehensive about it all and await the outcome with trembling and shaking." But many remained alert and sharp-witted even after enduring the physical and mental battering of the transatlantic voyage. Some, tipped off by their countrymen, tried with "friendly gestures and motions" to attract the attention of buyers with a reputation as sympathetic masters. "Their sale is not different from the auction of any other commodity. They go to the highest bidder. Once the strong and healthy ones have been sold, then comes the turn of the sick and weak." Strong men drew the highest prices, but buyers paid highly for mothers with several children as well and for women graced with "youth and good body build." Such was the welcome these unwilling immigrants received in America.[2]

Unlike most captives in the slave mart, Shelly's point of origin was not Africa but another Caribbean island, Antigua, one of the British Leeward islands about two hundred miles to the east. There, according to documents, she was born in about 1718. She lived her first six or seven years in Antigua, meaning that—although we know virtually nothing else about her upbringing—she would have been raised in a plantation colony defined by slavery, where disparities between black and white inhabitants were even more stark than on St. Thomas. Antigua, a small place, was still about twice the size of the Danish colony; it had more arable land, and thus supported a lucrative sugar industry that demanded many more slave workers—about 19,000 in 1720, some 86 percent of the population—who were controlled by a punitive system every bit as draconian as that in the Danish islands. Shelly would have witnessed Africans being bought and sold in even greater numbers every day there. She would have seen thousands of black men and women slashing sugar cane in broad fields, and hundreds of African women toting baskets on their heads and selling produce in the street markets of Antigua. Not everything, then, was strange about her surroundings in St. Thomas, but the bleakly familiar sights of this new home could scarcely have been comforting to a young child taken forcibly from her family.[3]

From what sort of home she had come, and who her parents were, are unknown. She left no memoir, and most of what we know about her childhood was reported by a German missionary and historian, Christian Oldendorp, who visited St. Thomas years later (though long after she had left) and probably knew her well during both of their subsequent travels. He described the details of her early life in his history of evangelical missions in the Danish West Indies, published in 1777 as *History of the Mission of the Evangelical Brethren on the Caribbean Islands of St. Thomas, St. Croix, and St. John.* Oldendorp consulted manuscripts left by missionaries for his history, but some of the particulars of her early life, such as her Antiguan origin, could only have come from Shelly herself, as she was the only witness. These she must have told him directly much later, but much was left unsaid or unreported in her account. Either she did not tell him, or he did not document, the identity of her parents. Throughout Shelly's life, Oldendorp and other white diarists and record-keepers, following the protocol of eighteenth-century European racial classification, identified her as "mulatto." It is likely that her mother or grandmother was black and enslaved and her father or grandfather a white planter, since such unions produced most members of that growing class of mixed ancestry found in all the New World slave societies. It was also possible that she was the daughter of a white mother and a black father, since those liaisons also took place, although they accounted for only a small handful of children of mixed descent. Neither do we know whether she was enslaved or free in Antigua. Children of planter fathers and slave women were generally raised in slavery, but they and their mothers could gain freedom through various means, and it is entirely possible that she came from the small class of free blacks on the island.[4]

What she did remember, and told Oldendorp or someone else, was that as a child she had been "kidnapped" from Antigua. The story is plausible. Slave traders and thieves were known to steal free blacks from their homes and neighborhoods, hustling them aboard ships that plied Caribbean ports with contraband goods. Smugglers carried on all sorts of illegal traffic out of Antigua for years, particularly with the Dutch and Danish West Indies, and St. Thomas was known as a friendly place for illicit trade. If Shelly ended up there in that fashion, the case for her having been raised in freedom becomes stronger. But it is also conceivable that she was a slave whose master actually sold her to "legitimate" traders, and that years later the young woman, recalling her terror as a six-year-old being separated from her mother by thugs, believed she had been kidnapped. Whatever the truth was, she surely never lost the memory of that violent trauma or her sense of having been a victim of robbery.[5]

On St. Thomas, she was "sold to a family of high-standing." That was the family of Lucas van Beverhout, a prominent Dutch-speaking planter. It is not certain whether van Beverhout emigrated from the Netherlands or whether he was a Creole—that is, a colonist whose parents or grandparents emigrated to the West Indies from Europe, but who was born in the Caribbean and considered it home. He might have been related to the van Beverhout clan that had been among the earliest settlers on the island in the 1670s. According to fragmentary census records, Lucas seems to have migrated to St. Thomas in 1691 from the Dutch colony of Saba, in the Leeward islands, and married one Margaretha Ronnel on St. Thomas in 1692. The couple had two sons and three daughters by 1710. By 1707 Lucas owned 23 slaves, and by the mid-1720s his holdings had increased to two plantations and about 170 slaves on the eastern end of St. Thomas, making him one of the largest slaveholders there. Intermarrying through several generations with other Creole families, particularly those of Dutch, but also of Danish, ancestry, the van Beverhout family was among a small handful of elites who consolidated an oligarchic hold on the economic and political life of the Danish colonies.[6]

Planters like van Beverhout were among the first generation of *Blancken* in the Danish West Indies to accept as completely natural, and to expand, the plantation regime installed by their foreparents in the 1670s and 1680s. Even if he had been born in the Netherlands, van Beverhout would essentially have creolized himself during his nearly forty years on St. Thomas through his complete immersion in a life, and an entire web of assumptions, built on African slavery. Although their wealth and power generally did not match those of their counterparts in major sugar colonies like Jamaica and

Barbados, planters in the Danish islands grew accustomed to a certain ease of life-style in the tropics. While few built great mansions, their houses were certainly comfortable, generally two stories high, solidly made of brick and expensive woods, many of them imported. Money was spent less on furniture than on ornamentation such as hangings, leather panels, china, and silver and gold settings. Many planters owned a house in the country but lived for months each year in a town house to be near the port action. Their daily schedule could not be said to be taxing. They slept late each morning, rose for a bit of light work—women sewed, men tended to business—then, exhausted after the midday meal, they napped for an hour in their hammocks, fanned to sleep by a slave waving a palm branch. Afternoon tea was followed by card games lasting long into the night, the men often repairing as well to a tavern for extended bouts of billiards.[7]

Observing this routine, some European writers concluded that planters, particularly Creoles, were a feeble lot, enervated by climate and luxury, torpid of spirit and physical energy except in sexual excess, indolent and cruel. "Since the native Whites, or Creoles, have been accustomed from childhood onward to be served by slaves, as well as to give those same slaves orders, they, therefore, become aware quite early of their external superiority over those poor creatures," wrote one traveler. "From there, the transition to pride and a domineering character is quick and easy. Neither does the example which they witness on all sides in the treatment of slaves by others lead to the development of humanitarian sentiments."[8]

"By nature they are arrogant people, as well as unbecomingly proud," agreed another writer.

> They are greedy in the extreme for praise, fame, honor, high rank and an abundance of worldly things. They do not appear to chase after money simply to hoard it and avoid spending it. No, their greed for wealth focuses on their obsession for possessing numerous slaves and being able to own large tracts of land. They rely on

what they own, and with that they ingratiate themselves with those whose association they value. They are quite vindictive, ill-tempered, quarrelsome and quick to anger. They give orders with great authority so that their underlings tremble and shake every time they are called and asked to do something. They are ill-tempered, harsh, sour-looking and quite severe toward anyone subordinate to them. They are nasty and lazy, which is why they call anyone a slave whom they observe being industrious.[9]

The Creoles' "dissolute inclinations" were most evident in their belief in "unlimited rights over the bodies of . . . slaves of both sexes." In this critique, both tyrannical slave masters and chattel women were to blame for a sexual carnival on the Danish islands. Eager to advertise the benefits of Christianity, the missionary Oldendorp described African women as morally corrupt, "accustomed to follow only the impulses generated by their passions." "Since chastity is not a common virtue of the Negro women, it does not trouble their conscience at all—indeed they even consider it an honor—to submit to the indecent demands of their masters. In the case, however, that a female slave might wish to resist such advances, she is nonetheless subject to the power of her master, who can do with her as he pleases." Oldendorp both downplayed the violence of the exploitation and misrepresented African women's sexuality, since many sought relationships with masters as the only way to gain favors and advancement in the plantation regime. Still, he and others saw the masters' behavior as simply more evidence of their degeneracy; another writer, singling out the van Beverhouts for criticism of the circular intermarriage and inbreeding among white Creoles, also implied that the family had absorbed African ancestry into its lines.[10]

An elite planter like Lucas van Beverhout stockpiled slaves for domestic work as a mark of status—the wealthiest Creoles had as many as two dozen in their households, by one count—so Shelly, even as a small girl, was put to work as yet another servant on his staff. Whites preferred mixed-race, or at least black Creole, West Indians over Africans for such work because they were regarded as more trustworthy and loyal, with a "reputation for brave and steady courage" and a "nobler disposition" than Bussals. They were said to admire and emulate whites and to wish to associate with them whenever possible. The reality, of course, was rather more complicated.[11]

Whites often overstated the adulation they believed their domestic workers felt for them. While it is true they sometimes betrayed other slaves' plans for uprisings and other kinds of resistance to whites, domestics also relayed information about the masters to so-called kamina slaves, or field hands. Cooks, housekeepers, nursemaids, gardeners, and footmen received more privileges and generally better treatment than field slaves, but those advantages came at a price, for household workers, constant prisoners to the whim and scrutiny of their masters, often had little personal autonomy. Workloads varied; one observer later in the eighteenth century wrote that "all work consists of fetching meat, fish, and greens at the marketplace, the cleaning of the house, the preparation of the food and serving at the table, all of which is distributed among so many hands that it can better be described as a diversion rather than work." But servants in other households often bore heavy workloads and were not immune from beatings and other punishments. And some among them got stuck with highly undesirable tasks. "When their masters or mistresses answer nature's call by going to defecate in their private room, a slave—a male slave serving his master, a female, her mistress—must accompany them with a whisk brush for comfort's sake. This whisk brush is made from a thrashed corn stalk with a long, rounded, soft tassel on one end. When nature has been satisfied in these proceedings, the slave then wipes and cleans his master." Here, in the master so besotted with his own power that a vassal performed his most basic personal hygiene, was the perfect image of white Creole decadence.[12]

It is impossible to know whether Shelly was given this choice assignment, or whether the van Beverhouts displayed all the unflattering characteristics attributed to planters. The same writer who so thoroughly criticized white Creoles as a class moderated his remarks by observing that individual planters he knew during a six-year stay on St. Thomas were generous, thoughtful, and modest. It was, of course, possible for planters to exhibit both kindness toward their families and other whites and tyranny toward their slaves, without perceiving a contradiction. Whatever the personal characteristics of the van Beverhouts may have been, they seem to have absorbed Shelly into their household and to have become quite fond of her. As a result, she developed close ties with the family and put them to good advantage. She learned to read and write during her years there. The records do not say who instructed her—perhaps an older domestic worker, or a van Beverhout family member. Although it was uncommon for house slaves to gain literacy, they did so occasionally, and in Shelly's case, if the van Beverhouts approved of her reading and writing, or even taught her, this suggests that they held her in relatively high favor. Moreover, the language that she learned to speak, read, and write was Dutch. She had spoken English, or an Afro-English mixture, in Antigua, but in St. Thomas, immersed in a Dutch-speaking household, she must have picked up the language quickly. Her surviving letters from a few years later were written in standard Dutch rather than the Afro-Dutch Creole language spoken by most of the enslaved population on the island. She certainly would have learned that dialect as well, since it was the principal language of the Danish colonies, used by anyone wishing to speak to a black person. But her primary grounding in Dutch indicates that she associated with, learned from, and identified with her master's family—probably to a greater extent than with the kamina folk in the fields and the slave quarters.[13]

This evident closeness with the van Beverhouts, and the skills in literacy it brought, resulted in two important changes during Shelly's childhood and early adolescence: she became interested in

Christianity, and she gained her freedom. It is not clear which came first, but they were probably connected. One possibility is that she was manumitted first and then, since it was more common to teach Christianity to freed people than to slaves, she began receiving lessons in religion. Alternatively—and the more likely prospect—it may have been her conversion to Christianity that led to emancipation. There would have been no particular reason for the van Beverhouts to have freed her at such a young age—anywhere from ten to fifteen, roughly—had not religion provided that crucial opening.

What we do know from the scanty record is this: Shelly, a later court document said, was "brought up in this island in the Reformed religion." A plausible scenario is that her earliest exposure to the Gospels came with lessons in reading. When she showed interest, the family might have encouraged her by taking her to the Reformed Church in town, where the Dutch colonists, as well as a few slaves and free people of color, worshipped. Reformed Church policy in the Dutch Caribbean urged that "the poor and blind pagans," including Africans and Indians, "be led to the knowledge of God and their salvation." Few slaves converted, in part because planters feared that bringing slaves into the church would diminish the social distance between them. But some planters did allow slaves to worship, as did the van Beverhouts, although no records indicate whether Shelly attended school at the church, sat with the family or separately during services, or participated in devotions.[14]

She was interested enough in what she was learning to continue studying, perhaps on her own or under the tutelage of family members or clergy. Her reading, reported the historian Oldendorp, "was useful to her in attaining a sound knowledge of the Holy Scriptures and other books. She had been profoundly impressed by the stories of the martyrs and by the joy with which so many of Christ's witnesses had gone to their violent deaths." It is difficult to say precisely what it was that intrigued her about the martyrs' lives, and what parallels she might have drawn to her own life—fortitude in the face of oppression, perhaps, or freedom in death. But her interest in the subject and her desire to discuss it left an imprint on those around her. Many years later, when Oldendorp visited St. Thomas, he interviewed a black woman who had served with Shelly on the van Beverhout domestic staff, and who recalled that she had obtained a copy of a Dutch *Martelaers-Boek,* or Book of Martyrs. She found much pleasure therein, remembered the woman, and spoke about it often to other women on the staff.[15]

As the anecdote suggests, Shelly was stirred by her lessons to try her hand at teaching others. Her first "pupils" were the people nearest her, the domestic servants with whom she worked. "She endeavored to be of help to the Negro women who served in the same household, admonishing them often to love God and the Savior." Whether, at her young age, she made an explicit spiritual connection between the Bible and African women, or simply spoke to them because they were close at hand, is hard to know. Did she try to teach them after hours or as they scrambled to complete their chores, and did the women regard the fourteen- or fifteen-year-old instructor as a help or as a hectoring annoyance? The records do not say, at least for this early period, but she continued to regard these women as the logical audience for her blossoming pedagogy. She had, on a small scale, started her own mission on St. Thomas.[16]

Shelly was not baptized yet, however, nor did she consider herself to be fully awakened. There remained a spiritual hungering, by Oldendorp's account—and, presumably, by her own telling—that reading and speaking, and even the church, could not fill. "She had hoped for a long time that a teacher might come, one who would point out the true path to salvation to her and others. In fact, she felt certain that God would send them someone for that very purpose. When, during her youth, a Roman Catholic priest baptized some Negroes on St. Thomas, she hastened to him with her heartfelt desires to become a Christian and was baptized by him at her request." Why she did not go to the Reformed minister for baptism is unknown; it is possible that she started attending church only after she was baptized. From time to time Catholic priests from Puerto Rico visited St. Thomas to minister to the colony's small white Catholic population, and on occasion the priests "instructed some Negroes as well in the fundamentals of their religion and baptized some of them." Thus, Shelly gained early exposure to Christianity from a variety of sources, including Catholicism. She was still not satisfied she had found the right direction, but it was evidently the priest who christened her with a new name: Rebecca.[17]

This religious turn in the young girl's life was perhaps the crucial factor in steering her to freedom. Lucas van Beverhout died in 1730, when Rebecca was about twelve, and she was inherited by his son, Adrian, who took his father's place among the planter elite on St. Thomas. At some point, the van Beverhout family set her free at the behest of Adrian's mother and sister. Records do not explain why they did so; perhaps the emancipation took place during the settlement of the inheritance, for later court records described her as being "freed by the heirs of Lucas van Beverhout." Whether she took her former master's name, or any other surname, upon liberation is unknown. In all the available records from those years, she is simply called Rebecca. She fit a common profile of many enslaved girls and women throughout the Caribbean who gained freedom through manumission—she was young, of mixed African and European descent, worked in domestic service, had personal contact with a planter and his family, and thus benefited from opportunities to form a sympathetic attachment. Sometimes women parlayed sexual relationships with planters into freedom, but since the van Beverhout women were instrumental in liberating Rebecca, it seems more likely that they did so because they were fond of this eager, bright, religious young person. There had once been a legal obligation in the Danish islands for slaveowners to emancipate bondpersons who converted to Christianity, but as more slaves took that easy route to freedom, the loophole was closed, or ignored, as in other Protestant colonies. Still, some planter families, like the van Beverhouts, might have continued to believe that Christians should not enslave one another, and freed her as a result of her conversion. Even if most slaves could no longer gain freedom through conversion, some also continued to seek baptism because masters were not permitted to sell enslaved Christians, a factor which may also have influenced Rebecca in pursuing Christianity.[18]

Thus, Rebecca evidently played a central role in winning her freedom. There is no clue whether she actually lobbied or cajoled the van Beverhouts to emancipate her; she may have done nothing of the sort, and the family's decision might have been of their own initiative. But perhaps she had, by her presence in the house—always studying, praying, and teaching—reminded the family daily that it was ungodly to enslave another Christian. Whatever the case, Rebecca parlayed her interest in religion to advance her own social position. She owed part of this triumph to good fortune, certainly, but she was also keen enough to perceive how to manipulate the system. To say that she did so does not necessarily mean her religious interest was insincere, or that she prayed merely to become free, or even that freedom had been her original goal. But of the very few avenues to liberty available to enslaved people, she hit upon one, understood its implications shrewdly, and followed it well.

In 1733, when Rebecca was about fifteen and probably at some intermediate point in her quest for faith and freedom, the St. John rebellion reverberated across the strait, shocking planters on St. Thomas, many of whom, including the van Beverhouts, had holdings on the smaller nearby island. All around her, planters seemed dispirited as the rebel hold on St. John continued into the spring of 1734, while the black population of St. Thomas was becoming bolder. "Our planters, weary from a continued vigil and chase, have become infirm and incapable of serving further," wrote Governor Philip Gardelin of St. Thomas, whose draconian slave code of 1733 had helped precipitate the rebellion. "Our Negroes on this island, witnesses to our visible weakness, refuse tacitly their fruitless assistance and seem to aspire only to occasions on which to express themselves." A French official involved in the manhunt on St. John wrote that French forces aimed to "subdue the rebel Negroes of the island of St. John . . . and to contain the Negroes of St. Thomas who seem disposed to revolt." But after the uprising had been suppressed by June, he noted that white planters had returned to their homes on St. John while "the St. Thomas Negroes, frightened by this expedition, have become more manageable and more submissive than they had ever been."[19]

There is no record of Rebecca's reaction to these events, but given her Christian leanings and her identification with her master's family, it seems likely she would have strongly disapproved of the uprising. Though she might have empathized with the plight of the slaves, she would have had nothing at all to gain from supporting the St. John rebels or the enslaved on St. Thomas who cheered them. Indeed, the St. John revolt, coming at such a crucial juncture in her maturation, might well have influenced the sense of her own life course. Watching the slaves' confidence on St. Thomas turn to fear as the revolt was crushed could have sharpened her desire to preach and to educate black women. By those methods, perhaps she saw a model by which black people, slave and free, could think, hope, and act in a slave society while eschewing violent means.

Such concerns would have been much on her mind, for she now belonged to that small class of free people of color, found in every New World slave society, dangling between slavery and freedom. On St. Thomas their numbers were tiny—118 in 1755, no doubt even fewer in the early 1730s—and most were quarantined by law in a small free black neighborhood of Charlotte Amalie called the Free Guts. Many, like Rebecca, were mixed-race people who had gained freedom through their master's wills and other private acts of manumission. Others were liberated by the government for meritorious service, as in the case of Mingo Tameryn, who participated in the tracking and defeat of the St. John rebels and was appointed captain of a freedmen's paramilitary corps that hunted runaway slaves with trained dogs. Freed people struggled to earn a living on the margins of plantation society, the men working as craftsmen or sailors, or as sellers of bread and fruit drinks, while women served as domestics in white households. Though classified legally as free, this intermediate group never enjoyed the same rights and legal protection as white colonists, who regarded them as dangerous models for the slaves. They were required to have their legal status registered in a document called a *fribrev*, and Governor Gardelin's slave code of 1733 made almost no distinction between slaves and freed people in its prescribed punishments and restrictions on the black populace. In subsequent years, additional laws forbade freed people from buying rum after dark, owning rum shops, holding "dances and drinking assemblies" after ten o'clock in the evening, and wearing jewelry and lavish clothing. Distrusted as they were by whites, however, their tenuous free identity also depended on separating themselves socially from slaves, creating similarly uneasy relations with that group.[20]

In her new freedom, Rebecca fit much of this pattern. As a young adolescent, she had nowhere else to go—there is no record that she had any connection with the free black enclave in town—so she continued on in wage service with the van Beverhout family. At some point she was promoted to manager of the household, a duty she carried out with "great loyalty." Her new position would have offered important advantages—respect, authority, income. She probably had a room in the van Beverhout house and wore better clothing provided by the family, including a linen shift and blouse, a sash around her head, and most likely shoes—unlike the slaves, who went barefoot. To the missionary Oldendorp, it appeared as though her cultural blackness had disappeared, which he regarded as a positive thing. "She was free and was treated by her employer not as a

servant but as a member of the household," he wrote. "In her outward behavior, she was not to be distinguished from a white person." Writing more than thirty years later, Oldendorp might have
overstated the social equality of the bond between the free house
manager and her employers, perhaps to create an ideal of racial har-
mony in the Christian family. Perhaps she herself even chose to recall it that way. But another diarist who knew both Rebecca and the
van Beverhouts well looked at their relationship in 1738 and noted:
"They like her very much but are ashamed of considering her an
equal." No matter how close the members of an elite planting family
considered themselves to a mixed-race person whom they had set
free, certain barriers of race and caste, it seems, would always remain.[21]

Still, in the very years when the Amina rebels on St. John were
planning and executing their war of liberation, a young adolescent
girl of color fortified herself in the only ways open to her. There is
a providential air in Oldendorp's narrative of Rebecca's early life,
which in key respects is a reflection of her own memory, her own
form of autobiography. She had a knack for gaining every advantage
her position afforded—her master's patronage, literacy, freedom,
managerial status, higher social standing. The threads of her life
story—personal advancement marred by unfulfilled spiritual yearning—were intertwined but lay loosely askew, waiting for a firm hand
to tie them together for some higher calling. Why she might recall
her life in those terms would be framed more clearly by the passage
of years.

Perhaps the most important characteristics we can discern in
Rebecca's young life, apart from the sense of destiny permeating that
account, are her own ability to study the world around her, perceiving its possibilities and limitations, and her aggressiveness in seeking
out sources of learning to help her control that world. In her time
and place, people of African descent—even those fortunate enough
to be free—found few encouragements to express their intellectual

or emotional desires, or anything that might hint of independent thought. Yet, in her restlessness, Rebecca apparently found it hard to wait for answers or to keep quiet. Pursuing religion, and teaching it, was how she measured her station in life. In the eighteenth-century Caribbean, no freed person ever took that place for granted.

CHAPTER THREE

A Priestly Woman

Freedom was precious in a society defined by its absence, and Rebecca was lucky and clever enough to have gained it—or earned it—early in life. Still, despite her ties with a prominent planting family, freedom offered no glittering necklace of possibilities, no magic for evading racism and discrimination. Free people of color, as their small number attested, endured the contempt and distrust of the *Blancken* and, often, of the largely African slave majority, and Rebecca found herself suspended between the two groups. Drawn to study and teach the Bible's mysteries to navigate life's perils, she had found promise but few conclusive answers there.

At the age of eighteen, in 1736, Rebecca discovered a way to twist these threads together when she met a German missionary named Friedrich Martin, who arrived on St. Thomas in March of that year to preach the Gospel. On the busy docks of Charlotte Amalie, white men came and went all the time—traders, planters, seamen, and hustlers, selling and buying in Dutch, Danish, English, French, and German, all eager to exploit the opportunities of the Caribbean frontier. Ordinarily none of them would have caught the eye of Rebecca, with her bookish interests and her insulated life, but Martin was different. He was a member of the Moravian Church, a pietistic Protestant sect based in Germany that had recently begun an ambitious quest to convert the world's non-Christians and had chosen the black men and women of St. Thomas as its first target audience. Rebecca, in turn, saw Martin as a vehicle to increase her own knowledge, and she pursued his acquaintance vigorously. Hearing of his presence on the island, she asked him to call on her, and when he did so, the two impressed each other. "I spoke with a mulatto woman who is very accomplished in the teachings of God," was the preacher's simple diary notation at the time. "Her name is Rebecca."[1]

Two years later, in 1738, Martin wrote another account of that first meeting, in which, perhaps influenced by subsequent events, he described the encounter in grander terms. "As she had taken pleasure in God's word and had expressed a longing to speak with me, I went to her place on September 26 and spoke with her," Martin recalled. The conversation was short, he noted, but "when I left, I believed that she could be a witness for Jesus." In the second account, the preacher claimed to have recognized a disciple at once, as though both were following divinely scripted parts. In his enhanced remembrance of the story, Rebecca seems to have found in Martin the mentor she had long awaited, and she became determined to seek out his instruction. She paid him occasional visits for a time, but when Martin and another missionary rented a house in town from her employer, Adrian van Beverhout, "she came to see us almost daily with the permission of her master and mistress." The narrative momentum of Martin's new recollection pointed in one direction: he was already concocting big plans for Rebecca. "She has done the work of the Savior by teaching the Negro women and speaking about that which the Holy Spirit himself has shown her. I have found nothing in her other than a love of God and his servants. She is modest, honest, and chaste before God, and has served her master and mistress with loyalty and sincerity." Rebecca's demeanor and devotion, Martin believed, made her an ideal spokesperson for Christ.[2]

Moravian evangelists had already begun preaching on the island in late 1732; Friedrich Martin was a relative latecomer to the effort. Curiously, the Moravians were at once one of the oldest and youngest churches in the Protestant world. They began as a pacifist, early Reformation church from central Europe called the *Unitas Fratrum,* or Unity of Brethren, in fifteenth-century Bohemia and Moravia. Driven underground during centuries of religious warfare and persecution, a few scattered believers emerged in the early eighteenth century in southeastern Saxony. There they gained asylum on the feudal estate of a charismatic German nobleman, Count Nikolaus Ludwig von Zinzendorf, where they built a new congregational village called Herrnhut, meaning "Under the Lord's care." Raised in the tradition of Lutheran Pietism, the count was intrigued by the refugees' emphasis on emotion and spirituality rather than religious formalism, and under his leadership the group reorganized in 1727 as the Renewed Unity of Brethren, though most people soon began referring to them in shorthand as Herrnhuters or Moravian Brethren.[3]

Adherents were known for their Christ-centered beliefs and their strict obedience to the New Testament. They were expected to undergo a profound conversion experience and to cultivate a heartfelt relationship with Christ, whose blood emancipated mankind from sin and religious dogmatism. They also abided by a strict Christian code of conduct, including a ban on swearing oaths and bearing arms. The Brethren made many decisions by drawing lots, which they considered the decisive word of God, and they organized themselves into semi-communal towns, governed by a council of elders and patterned after the example of the earliest Christians. Thus covenanted together, the Brethren considered themselves a chosen people assigned to live by God's word and follow his plan.[4]

Women held a central place in the identity of the church. In Moravian doctrine, women were considered spiritually equal to men. "With Him, none comes up short, and He also does not prefer one person to another," wrote the Moravian leader, Count Zinzendorf. "He loves with an inexpressible and inimitable egality." Although the church did not completely discount the notion of the social subordination of women, the Brethren exalted women's spirituality, referring to their congregations in the feminine as the "bride" of Christ (an analogy drawn from Ephesians 5:22–24) and worshipping the Holy Spirit as the "mother" of the church. Church doctrine held that although men and women were joined in Christ and created in spiritual equality, they had different religious experiences and led inner lives that should be nurtured separately. Marriage was encouraged in the church, but Moravian congregations were divided into groups by gender, age, and marital status that worshipped apart from one another; single men and women even lived in sex-segregated dormitories. Because of their different needs and outlooks, men were assigned to encourage and guide one another, while women did the same. This belief created the basis for an elaborate architecture of leadership by a fleet of male and female supervisors and teachers, a command structure that gave women power and responsibility for order, worship, and pedagogy over their half of the congregation.[5]

Such female leaders were the Moravians' response to Paul's command for women to keep silence in devotions. They were too respectful of the New Testament to ignore the order altogether, but their scriptural exegesis found ample flexibility in the language (particularly 1 Corinthians 11:5) to allow women to "teach themselves amongst each other": "Now the sisters belong to the class of those whom the Saviour has declared to his heavenly Father as priests just as much as the men," wrote Count Zinzendorf. "Hence there is no question that the whole band . . . are not only priestesses but also priestly women." Hundreds of women were consecrated as acolytes, deacons, and presbyters, and though they did not formally preach to the entire congregation, they led prayer groups, counseled women, and served in church governance. It is true that the male Moravian perception—by no means unique to the church in the eighteenth century—was that women were intellectually inferior to men. When "the Scripture calls the female person a weak worktool, it means by this that she cannot think as broadly, deeply, and continuously as the Brothers," lectured Zinzendorf. "Therefore one finds many fewer among you than among us who have the gift of governing." Still, the Brethren gave women wide latitude to express themselves and exercise spiritual leadership while technically obeying Paul's injunction. It was precisely such a role that Friedrich Martin and the other Brethren forecast for Rebecca when he met the eager young scholar in 1736.[6]

Only a fortuitous inspiration of Afro-Caribbean origin had brought the Moravians to St. Thomas in the first place. In 1731, Count Zinzendorf and several other Brethren went to Copenhagen to attend the coronation of the Danish king, Christian VI. There they met a black man named Anthony, or Anton Ulrich, who had been born enslaved on St. Thomas and taken back to Denmark as a personal servant to the Count of Laurwig, a director of the Danish West India and Guinea Company. In Copenhagen, Anton Ulrich had been schooled in Christianity and baptized, and he used his chance meeting with the Moravians to tell them not only about the awful conditions under which the slaves labored on St. Thomas but about their need for Christianity as well. His own sister, Anna, he explained, was still enslaved on the Company plantation there and unable to worship, and he urged the Brethren to take the Gospel to the slaves.

Amazed by the story, the Moravians invited Anton Ulrich to Germany, where he repeated his plea to the congregation. Two young men, David Nitschmann and Leonhard Dober, were so inspired that they volunteered for a West Indian mission, even being willing, as Ulrich urged, to make slaves of themselves to gain better access to black plantation workers. That moment marked the beginning of the Brethren's realization that their destiny lay in following Jesus' command to "teach all nations" (Matthew 28:19). Christ's martyrdom, they believed, opened the doors of salvation to all the world's people, regardless of culture, ethnicity, or physiognomy.[7]

The Brethren drew inspiration for these ideas from the example of Lutheran Pietism, which had begun a mission in Tranquebar, the Danish colony in India, in 1705. During his boyhood training in the early eighteenth century at the Pietist academy in the eastern German town of Halle, Count Zinzendorf had been impressed by the emphasis taught there on charity and education, which included evangelical outreach to non-Christians. The Pietists, in turn, had been influenced by American Puritans such as Cotton Mather regarding the benefits of mission to indigenous or colonized peoples. Of particular fascination to Pietist leaders was John Eliot's mission to Indians in seventeenth-century Massachusetts, especially his use of techniques such as translating biblical texts into native languages, empowering native leaders to conduct prayer groups, and separating communities of native converts from the unconverted.[8]

Adopting Pietist philosophy and techniques, the Moravian Brethren embarked on what they considered their divine mission to preach among indigenous and enslaved people of color wherever they could. As transitional figures in the continuum of global Protestant evangelism, they achieved a global reach attained by few others during the eighteenth century: by the end of the century they had put mission stations in the Caribbean, Pennsylvania, Ohio, Georgia, Greenland, South Africa, Russia, Ceylon, and elsewhere. It all began when the first pair of missionaries, Nitschmann and Dober, left Germany in the fall of 1732 and arrived in St. Thomas in December.

The odds did not favor them. Despite their eagerness, they were completely naive about the brutalities of West Indian slavery and had no experience as missionaries, or even any effective way to communicate with the slaves. They quickly learned that white men were not allowed to become enslaved, as they had hoped. The principal barriers against them were a long-standing antipathy to mission work in American Protestant colonies and a record of failure by well-intentioned churchmen.

Roman Catholicism had long been entrenched in West Africa, introduced by Portuguese missionaries in the mid-fifteenth century. Thousands of enslaved Kongolese sold to the Americas in subsequent centuries brought their Catholic faith with them, and many more Africans converted in Portuguese, Spanish, and French colonies, fusing native religions with Christianity to create complex, vibrant forms of worship to sustain them in slavery.[9] In contrast, few blacks made their way into Protestant churches in America. Since the mid-seventeenth century, small numbers of black Christians had joined Anglican, Congregational, and Dutch Reformed churches from New England to the Carolinas. In the early eighteenth century, missionaries from the Church of England's Society for the Propagation of the Gospel, or SPG, had tried hard to convert enslaved Africans in South Carolina, but achieved only limited success. Many planters opposed the idea of black spiritual equality that the baptism of slaves implied, fearing it might lead to a desire for social equality and freedom as well. Many Africans and African Americans themselves had no interest in Protestant Christianity, which seemed austere and formal, while plantation masters used biblical teachings to justify African slavery. In Barbados, likewise, the SPG owned a plantation and slaves, whom missionaries sought to convert, with scant results.[10]

It was this unimpressive record that the two Moravian Brethren sought to overturn when they arrived in another Protestant colony, St. Thomas, in 1733. Like other missionaries, however, they encountered difficult challenges at once. They immediately sought out Anton Ulrich's sister, Anna, on the Company plantation, told her they were there at her brother's behest, and asked her to convert. Anna—along with her husband, Gerd, and a second brother, Abraham—was initially surprised and pleased at the attention, but the three were unable to give the Brethren their full commitment to the cause and resisted the missionaries' entreaties to become Christian. In the following months, Dober and Nitschmann struggled with the Dutch Creole language; other black islanders with whom they managed to speak seemed mildly interested but perplexed by it all. Some welcomed the Germans, including a few literate slaves already familiar with Christianity and the Dutch Bible. Others resented the Brethren's constant harping about sin, pointing out that the *Blancken* did plenty of things the missionaries defined as sinful. "'You wish to forbid everything,' a Negro once told them in anger. 'Who can become such as you would have people be?'"[11]

White colonists too were bemused by the Germans. Some found them eccentric oddballs, with their pious ways and their constant chatter about converting blacks. Such talk offended the Reformed or Lutheran sensibilities of many planters who considered blacks to be devils who could never be saved. A few planters sympathized with the mission, believing that Christianity would be a good "civilizing" influence on their enslaved African workers. One supporter was Adrian van Beverhout, who briefly employed Dober as an overseer on one of his plantations, though there is no record that Rebecca knew of him there. Another was a Danish Creole planter named Johann Lorentz Carstens, who invited the preachers to speak to his slaves. But during the tense months after the Amina rebels captured St. John in 1733, most planters came to despise the Brethren, terrified that their message would inflame the slaves even more. "We must always keep the Negroes down, because we are only a handful of whites," one planter scolded a missionary. "If one said to the Negroes that all men are equal before God, their respect for the whites would be weakened." After gaining only a few converts, Nitschmann was recalled to Germany in 1733 and Dober in 1734. The mission then languished for more than a year.[12]

Things changed with the arrival of Martin. A native of Silesia, he had joined the Brethren in the early 1730s, went to the Moravian congregation town of Herrnhut in 1734, and quickly came to believe that his calling was the conversion of Africans in the Caribbean. He was sent into the field in 1736. He had little formal education, as attested by the ragged handwriting and phonetic spelling in his many journals. But he was an irresistible salesman, combining an energetic personality and superb organizational skills with deep respect for black West Indians. In Christian Oldendorp's 1777 history of the mission, an aura of destiny surrounds Martin's arrival. On the preacher's second day on the island, according to Oldendorp, Martin was walking to the company plantation, and "just as he was yearning to be fortunate enough to lead one lost sheep to the Good Shepherd, he met a young Negro named Emanuel."

> "Would you," he asked him, "like to come to know your Savior, who, as the Lamb of God, has taken on the sins of the world?" "With great pleasure," answered the young man, and he then offered the missionary two chickens, apparently his entire fortune, as a sign of gratitude, for introducing him to God. Overjoyed that divine providence had provided him with such a willing pupil, he arranged to meet with him in his dwelling that evening.

The sense of divine fate in the account derives also from the implication that black spiritual seeker and missionary reached out to each other with equal enthusiasm. Of course Martin's, and the other missionaries', belief that Christianity was superior to African religions now seems patronizing and culturally offensive, but to him it was a religion of human spiritual liberation and equality that should be open to everyone without regard to race, culture, or social status. He tenaciously advocated the humanity of the enslaved. Martin is not known to have opposed slavery itself, at least openly; indeed, the Moravians, like many Europeans, accepted servitude, even the hereditary bondage of racial slavery, as part of the divine natural order. Whatever his feelings about the institution may have been, Martin was shrewd enough to know that his mission depended on discretion.[13]

But he and other Brethren were privately aghast at the atrocities they saw committed by the *Blancken*. "They treat the Negroes so

Friedrich Martin with his godchild Oly Carmel, baptized Josua, by Johann Valentin Haidt, c. 1734. Courtesy of Unity Archives, Herrnhut, Germany.

cruelly it would make a stone wail," lamented one of his companions in the mission. To convince Africans that Christianity was a religion of warm empathy, Martin sought to gain their confidence by becoming their friend and ally. Early on he struggled with the Dutch Creole language, but over time he improved enough to make himself understood. He visited the slave quarters to shake the workers' hands and hold searching conversations, addressing them as "Brother" and "Sister." Aware that slaves were quick to pick up on the sexual hypocrisy of many white Christians, he shunned women and instead found release by being bled every eight days. When a famine struck St. Thomas in late 1736, he saved two blacks from starvation by giving them bread and flour.[14]

Little by little, these efforts paid off, and the number of black followers grew steadily. Early on, Martin adopted the canny strategy of linking literacy with his religious message. To many Africans in the Danish West Indies, as throughout the Americas, learning to read was like cracking a mysterious code that would surrender the knowledge and power Europeans had used to enslave them. At the plantations of several sympathetic whites, Martin passed out copies of the Dutch Bible and other texts (of which a few blacks already claimed some knowledge) and held classes in reading and writing that became increasingly popular. "The book will make me wise," said one man. Martin converted a room in his town house into a classroom, and by the end of September 1736, just six months after his arrival, so many students were attending lessons that they crowded the room to overflowing. Pupils were said to be so eager to learn that they pulled their books out of their pockets or knapsacks and read whenever they had a few spare minutes. "In addition to the fact that their newly acquired reading skills enabled the Negroes to read the Bible, it also induced many of those who had come to the meetings with the sole purpose of learning to read to partake of the desire to get to know Christ and to share in his grace," wrote Oldendorp.[15]

Most slaveowners opposed literacy among the enslaved, with better reason than they even suspected. The particular kind of knowledge that Martin encouraged in his eager listeners was an explicit biblical critique of the slaveholders themselves. "When they learn to read the testimony of the Scriptures the Negroes can see for themselves how to avoid the false teachings and wicked life of the so-called Christians under whom they live," explained August Spangenberg, a Moravian church bishop who visited St. Thomas for two months in September and October of 1736 to observe Martin's work. "They can also investigate questions for themselves and can teach others what they have learned from the Savior." Spangenberg was appalled, for example, when he learned that by law a male slave who slept with a white woman would be executed, while a white man who slept with many black women went unpunished, even though the Bible prescribed double punishment for those who knew the Lord's will and defied it. He also accused the planters of promoting promiscuity among their bondmen and women in order to expand their workforce, and he condemned them for denying baptism to slaves: "Damned are the authorities who want to take that honor from the Lord and rule over the conscience of the people." The Moravian preachers did not, of course, advertise their criticism to the planters; their strategy was to encourage the enslaved to set themselves apart from the "so-called Christians" who purported to rule them.[16]

The pacifist Brethren were not urging their pupils to develop a biblical attack on slavery. Spiritual transcendence, not social revolution, was their goal. Still, the slaves' ability to read the Scriptures posed a potentially serious challenge to the plantation society. Unfree workers now could summon scriptural authority to show that the masters' power, and its supposed sources, their religion and their lighter skin color, were irrelevant in the eyes of the Lord. The slaveowners were unmasked as violent, cruel, whoring, swearing, immoral, degraded imposters—a characterization that had some appeal in the slave community. And the opposition of many planters only gave the mission even greater allure for the slaves; one woman who was repeatedly beaten to keep her away from meetings "came to the conclusion that there had to be something very important about the lessons," and was determined all the more to attend them. On another occasion, "the Negroes came to us and wanted to learn," Martin reported in his diary. "They said the whites told them we would make them worse than when they were heathens."[17]

The growing throng of followers did not necessarily need a white person to confirm their own worth to them, nor was Christianity the only idiom that affirmed it. But the evangelical love preached by Martin offered a way to claim that message and express it in a sanctioned—and sanctified—forum. One early pupil, Mingo, "asserted on the authority of his teacher that black men were no less creatures of God and beneficiaries of the promise of eternal salvation, bought by the blood of Jesus Christ, than were the Whites." But the preachers also had to consider what to do with the combustible anger among pupils that their teachings were stoking. With a frankness that revealed how quickly Martin had gained the students' trust, as well as the emotions they were seeking to sort through, another student admitted that the line between asserting self-worth and fighting for it could blur. He was Emanuel, the young man whom Martin had met on his second day on St. Thomas, and who was now wrestling with the implications of Christian doctrine. "In the afternoon we read Christ's Sermon on the Mount in Matthew 5, 6 and 7th chapters, how one should endure the blows," noted Spangenberg. "One, named Emanuel, answered that he could not do that well, that it would offend his honor if he could not resist. We explained to him that the Lord wishes it, and that he should consider not only his honor but also the Lord's honor. He said he would pray to God to help him avoid conflict." It is true that the missionaries were not the ones absorbing the rain of blows, so their advice might have seemed cheap to the slaves. Still, all of them knew what happened to those who fought back, and it is likely that the missionaries' counsel was not offered, or taken, lightly.[18]

Thus the Bible classes, much more than rote doctrinal exercises, became searching discussions about slavery, violence, resistance, and the role of religion in helping people make sense of conflicting pressures. Through such conversations, students crafted an understanding that Christianity could be a radical vocabulary, if not of insurgency, then of spiritual opposition to oppression. In the case of someone like Emanuel, that awareness required him to redefine his own masculinity and transfer his sense of honor away from retaliation to a nonviolent notion of divine honor. The payoff was not simply a promise of some eternal reward—though that was part of the offer—but a belief in the slaves' own moral superiority over their tormenters in this world.

As the discussion with Emanuel revealed, a key Scripture was the

Sermon on the Mount, Jesus' meditation on the problem of evil. Here, in the quest for righteousness grounded in love, black students could find the essence of Christian ethics distilled by a sermon loaded with famous phrases and maxims so fundamental to the faith—"blessed are the meek," "salt of the earth," "judge not, lest ye be judged," "do unto others," "love your enemies," "turn the other cheek," and dozens more. Anticipating the Last Judgment, many of these statements pose an Old Testament lesson against the radical authority of Jesus, and of these the retaliation antithesis in Matthew 5:38–39 ("Ye have heard it said, An eye for an eye, a tooth for a tooth, but I say unto you, That ye resist not evil") could be, and historically has often been, interpreted as an obvious prop for the system of slavery. But by setting up a grander antithesis between belief and unbelief, the sermon in other ways deeply subverts the authority of slaveowners because in that contest they are no match for the moral power of the enslaved. Showering blessings on the meek, the merciful, the peacemakers, and the persecuted, the sermon bestows its soaring triple parable (salt of the earth, light of the world, city on a hill) on people loved by Jesus precisely because they are reviled and abused. The redeemed outcasts must "live against the world for the world." For the enslaved in a place like St. Thomas, the irony had obvious appeal: in their violent ungodliness, masters who barred Christianity from the slaves were themselves pariahs from the kingdom. Scorn for hypocrites (Matthew 6:1–8) was easily transferred to the slaveowners; their false claims to power were undermined by the warning that believers cannot serve two masters (6:24). In this inversion lay the power of the slaves' sense of moral exclusiveness, for "insofar as you have done it to the least of these my brethren, you have done it to me" (Matthew 25:40). Thus the Bible became not a primer for passive resignation in the face of evil, but, in the words of one scholar, "a magical formulary for African Americans; a book of ritual prescription for reenvisioning and transforming history and culture."[19]

Despite mixed motivations and reservations, a core of disciples began to emerge from the teaching and reading sessions on St. Thomas. "Liefde Heere, geeft my en syver Harte, en laat alles gnaad achter blyven, en geeft my gnade, dat ick alles mag leeren wat u behagt," Martin overheard one man pray ("Dear Lord, give me a light heart and let all pain remain behind me, and give me grace, that I may teach what pleases you"). The level of sincerity behind such devotions is of course difficult to penetrate—the supplicant might simply have been uttering in Martin's presence what the missionary wanted to hear. On the other hand, the fact that such supplicants sought him out at all suggests that they were hunting for something, whether the spiritual appeal of Christianity, the material advantage of literacy, Martin's advocacy on their behalf, a sense of communal fellowship, or all of these. Some were finding answers. During this period one man named Clas, a laborer on the Company plantation, built the first small wooden church for black worshippers, where he himself conducted prayer services, sometimes reading from the Bible. Martin described how on a visit to the plantation "we came to the house that our Brother Clas built and dedicated to the Lord, and there we prayed together." On September 30, 1736, before a small gathering, Spangenberg baptized three men: Clas, Emanuel, and Jost, who were christened Petrus, Andreas, and Nathanael. "Several verses were sung to them and they were consecrated with the kiss of peace," noted Martin. "Two Brethren led the baptized home and celebrated a love feast with water and wine." The three inductees became the first members of a new black congregation—the earliest such church in the Americas.[20]

From the beginning, women also reached out to the Brethren with urgency and bravery. Spangenberg described how several women repeatedly "implored" the missionaries for instruction, even after being turned away several times as a test. "We have thought much about it and would like to help them," he wrote. "I spoke with them at length and assured them that the Lord loves Negroes as much as the whites and that he would forgive their sins, which they previously committed through ignorance. There were women there who belong to a man so resistant to the Brethren that he has threatened all his people with whipping if they go to seek learning from them. I thought, how is it that now these Negro women come to us? If he has not allowed it, it is a great sign of faith that they ignore his threats." Some women risked peril in pursuit of biblical knowledge; others needed persistent coaxing. One was a manumitted African woman "of the Papaa nation" named Marotta, who, from one description, may have been Muslim. "Before she eats anything at all in the morning, she falls on her knees, lowers her face to the earth, and prays," according to Spangenberg. "Before she goes to sleep, she does the same thing, manifesting a great and extraordinary respect before God." She even had some knowledge of the Christian trinity, which the Brethren took as an indication that missionaries had visited her region of the Gold Coast. "She said that there was only one God, the Father, who is called Pao. His son Masu is the only door, through which it is possible to come to the Father." Marotta ridiculed what she considered the planters' lax godliness, saying that Christianity seemed to be mostly an exercise in "paying Him compliments." Respecting her devotion, the missionaries sought to channel it into Christianity, and when they convinced her of their seriousness, she put aside her scruples and was baptized, receiving the name Magdalena.[21]

It was because of women like these that Martin and the other Brethren were particularly interested in meeting Rebecca just as black interest in their lessons was intensifying. From their first encounter with her, they liked her quiet self-assurance, her inclination to teach, her managerial experience, and her ability to seek knowledge for herself. When she expressed doubts to them about her own spiritual state, Spangenberg urged her to think them through on her own. Referring to her baptism by the Catholic priest in her youth, the missionary wrote that Rebecca "has a *Scrupel* whether her baptism was proper, and whether she needs a new one." She had been told by others that the ceremony was invalid because no godfather had been present, and the bishop advised her to consult the Bible. "The next time she came to see me, she testified that all her *Scrupels* had vanished, because she had found in the Scriptures that the chamberlain baptized by Philip [Acts 8:26–39] also had no godfather. She researches diligently in the Scriptures, loves the Savior, and does much good for other Negro women because she does not simply walk alone with her good ways but instructs them in the Scriptures as well."[22]

We learn some revealing things about Rebecca from her brief exchange with the missionary. It suggests that she considered religious knowledge to be fluid rather than static and was not afraid to ask questions. She had the skills and initiative to go to the source for answers, and the one she came up with is telling. As recounted in the book of Acts, on a preaching trip to Gaza the apostle who would become known as Philip the Evangelist encountered a eunuch who was a prominent official at the court of Queen Candace of Ethiopia. The eunuch was reading about the prophet Isaiah, but after hearing Philip talk of Jesus, he asked to be baptized. "And they went down both into the water, both Philip and the eunuch; and he baptized him," without a godparent present (Acts 8:39). The Ethiopian was the first African to be baptized into the Christian church, and the episode was celebrated in medieval and early modern European iconography as a symbol of Christianity's universalism. The Brethren themselves may have pointed out the story to Rebecca, for they were well aware of its symbolism, having read the relevant passages aloud as they baptized the first congregants. Regardless of whether Rebecca came upon the story herself or someone pointed it out to her, she drew upon it for inspiration and guidance, which suggests that she saw something of herself in the Ethiopian convert and likewise embraced Christianity as a religion of inclusion for herself and others of African origin.[23]

Early in 1737, the Brethren began working with their new recruits to draft letters of personal testimony that were collected and sent back to the church headquarters in Herrnhut. The letters were intended partly as evidence of the missionaries' good work, but even more vitally, they were declarations of faith that reaffirmed the believers' active, continuous engagement with their own spirituality, which was so fundamental to the life of the church. Since reading and writing lessons had progressed for several months by that time, some black pupils wrote letters themselves, while other letters appear to be have been dictated or written on behalf of witnesses by a white or black scribe. Most of the earliest letters were written in Dutch, with occasional elements of Dutch Creole added, while later letters tended more toward Creole. Most were fairly formulaic, offering little personal information and reworking familiar themes of spiritual wandering and regeneration. One slave brother, Abraham, for example, wrote:

> I thank the Lord for letting us see that which we could not have hoped for, to allow us to become a community of Jesus Christ. Before that, we had been as cattle, and thus we did not think that there might be mercy for heathens. We thank the Lord that Baas Martin has come to St. Thomas so that we have learned that there is mercy for the heathens and that we can now tell that which is good from that which is evil. We express our heartfelt adoration for the Lord Jesus and hope for his mercy.

The missionaries may have coached the writers on what to say, or they may have written parts of letters in some cases. Still, flawed or incomplete as the letters may be as authentic historical documents, they give a voice to black religious expression at a seminal moment of shifting awareness. The practice continued among the Brethren for at least thirty more years, resulting in a collection of nearly two hundred testimonials that constitutes a composite spiritual autobiography of eighteenth-century black Christians.[24]

One such letter written by Rebecca—or, at least, a letter in her name—described her own religious convictions. The letter was written in Dutch, in a hand evidently not her own, judging by several letters written later that can be positively identified as her work. The letter addressed the unmarried women, or Single Sisters, of the Moravian congregation in Herrnhut, Germany. "My dear Sisters," she wrote,

> After the Lord has been so merciful and has let me know about you, my dear Sisters, I want to be with the Lord and reveal my puny form to you. My dear Sisters in the Lord, I never knew there was such a thing as a spiritual life. Although I have always longed to follow the ways of the Lord, I never had the right foundation and have always yearned for more instruction. I never knew there was both the worldly and the spiritual. Oh, how good is the Lord. My heart melts when I think of it. His name is wonderful. Oh! Help me to praise him, who has pulled me out of the darkness. I will take up his cross with all my heart and follow the example of his poor life. But how miserable do I find myself, my dear Sisters. And the dear Lord! If we cannot be together in person, let us be together in the spirit. Remember in your prayers that the Lord blesses all. Greetings to all the Sisters in the Lord. I remain a dutiful Sister, even if I am not taken in [i.e., confirmed] as a Sister. I hope you will remember me. I pray that you will try to write me. I am a housemaid in Adrian van Beverhout's house.
>
> *Rebecca*
> May 28, 1737[25]

Identifying the letter's authorship is a problem. The words written in Rebecca's name might have been framed entirely, partly, or not at all by her, and thus might have expressed either what she felt or what she was expected to feel. Perhaps the most we can say is that the letter was designed to express certain sentiments for a particular audience. With direct, emotional honesty, the letter—whoever its author or authors may have been—renounced Rebecca's doubt-filled, rootless life of searching, admitted the misery of her longing, and entrusted her to the mercy of Christ—all prescribed steps in the convention of early modern spiritual autobiography. In contrast to narratives from more Calvinist traditions, there was no debased confession of original sin, depravity, and corruption, nor did she describe an anguished crisis of faith culminating in a burst of revelation. Instead, the language was gentle, entreating Christ for a map out of the darkness but forgiving herself for not knowing the way. Her appeals to a group of women she did not even know sought to forge a bond of the spirit in mutual searching and candor. Even the homely device, almost an afterthought, of announcing herself as a house servant—a rare personal detail in a genre given almost entirely to spiritual confession—anchored her as a striving human being with whom the Sisters could empathize.[26]

The rhetoric pointed above all toward an active, reciprocal relationship with Christ that was intended to project the speaker into the world. The letter grounded Rebecca and any claim she might have to speak about matters of the heart in his inspiration, and here the question of authorship recedes. As Jesus had intervened in her life, she would emulate him and "take up his cross with all my heart." Even if she did not write the words herself, they expressed what she had already begun to do. In recounting Rebecca's spiritual journey, the letter proclaimed her broader vision—to preach among enslaved plantation workers and form a new black Christian community in America.[27]

This declaration is the closest we may get to glimpsing Rebecca's inspiration to teach. Why would a teenage girl claim the authority to witness in a society that encouraged neither women nor people of color, and especially not those who were both, to speak out? She had been testifying on her own plantation for several years by the time she met the Brethren and did not need their validation to do so; we can only speculate about the intellectual and spiritual sources that fueled her sense of calling. The conservative Dutch Reformed church in which she was raised had no tradition of women preaching or testifying publicly, although it is possible, if she learned to read and write from the van Beverhout women, that she emulated their example of women teaching each other in private. She would have had to look no further than the slave community around her to find examples of African women teaching and leading in various capacities, but there was no precedent for black exhorters of Christianity in the world Rebecca knew. Essentially, in her self-appointed role as Christian apostle, she appears to have simply invented herself.

From her reading of the Scriptures, Rebecca might have wondered about the seemingly contradictory Pauline pronouncements—the subject of endless commentary and debate among European theologians—that both denied and affirmed women's right to proclaim the Gospel. One passage from 1 Corinthians 14:34, for example, counsels men: "Let your women keep silence in the churches; for it is not permitted unto them to speak." Yet 1 Corinthians 11:5 seems to recognize women's teaching abilities by suggesting that women could pray or prophesy, as long as they covered their heads while doing it. There is no way to know whether Rebecca was familiar with these admonitions. Perhaps she had read Joel 2:28: "And it shall come to pass that I will pour out my spirit upon all flesh; and your sons and daughters shall prophesy." She might have drawn inspiration from any number of unquiet women in the Bible, including some in those same letters of Paul, such as Phoebe in Romans 16:1–2 ("Phoebe our sister, a servant of the church, a succorer of many, and of myself also"), and Tryphaena, Tryphosa, and Persis "who labor in the Lord" (Romans 16:12).[28]

And what of her namesake Rebekah, daughter-in-law of Abraham, wife of Isaac, who in Genesis finagled the patriarchal blessing for the favorite of her twin sons, Jacob, future father of the Israelites? She was, according to a modern scholar, "the most clever and authoritative of the matriarchs, and yet she epitomizes womanly beauty and virtue, in her conduct, in her energetic speech, in her thoughtful courtesy, and in her self-assurance." And in Romans

Rebecca (detail of Protten family portrait) by Johann Valentin Haidt, c. 1751. Courtesy of Unity Archives, Herrnhut, Germany.

9:10–11, "Paul refers to Rebekah to demonstrate God's divine elective purpose and grace, mercy, and compassion." As one so closely attuned to the power of scriptural antecedents, Rebecca might readily have sought to emulate such a model.[29]

Most important, the evidence suggests that Rebecca felt Christ had revealed his word to her, and the visionary force of that inspiration was the only authority she needed. That revelation can only have transformed her life as it did by saying something fundamental about her experience as a formerly enslaved woman in a culture that degraded black women. As later generations of African-American and West Indian evangelical women would show, the search for eternal truths of saving power welled out of the experience of oppression, and Jesus was the ally who would sanction and fortify their struggle for dignity. Nowhere was this spelled out more clearly than in Luke 4:18: "He hath anointed me to preach the gospel to the poor; he hath sent me to heal the broken-hearted, to preach deliverance to the captives, . . . to set at liberty them that are bruised." Rebecca never explicitly articulated that connection in any of her few surviving writings, but it is difficult to conceive of any motivation for the call she thought she had received that was not refracted through the lens of her own life circumstances. The spirit within was the bedrock upon which a new conception of the world rested.[30]

For the Moravian Brethren, these were key ideas that help to explain why they embraced Rebecca's interest and talents. They envisioned a role for her as a "worker" (the German *Arbeiterin*), or assistant in their mission. "She is well versed in the Holy Scriptures and could be a worker," wrote August Spangenberg, who came to know her well during his visit in 1736. "She is free, behaves like a White, and avoids all [bad] company. The Negro and Mulatto women have great trust in her, and she makes a special effort to instruct them. But she has much work to do, because she is in service to a master and carries the keys of the entire [household]. She is a trustworthy person." She had already made a role for herself as a teacher, but the Brethren's encouragement helped her widen that vision.[31]

Therein lay the great allure of this new life, the transformation of the very idea of work in a society driven by forced labor. This kind of work was joyous, purposeful, life-giving. One undertook the immense responsibility willingly, because it served the highest possible calling. Rebecca, a free woman with authority in her former master's household, could have found it easy to take cautious refuge in her status, but she was transfixed by the thought of working for Jesus. For the black women and men of this new fellowship, the idea was risky since it threatened the slaveholders' social order. On one occasion, the slave brother Petrus was accused of saying that "he was no longer obliged to work for his master, since he was no less a baptized Christian than they were," although the charge was eventually dropped. An enslaved woman who attended evening meetings with the Brethren was whipped because she wasn't available to take off her mistress's shoes.[32]

But those inside the circle of fellowship found their lives turned upside down by the new meaning of work, and among them was Rebecca. The former kidnap victim and slave, not yet twenty years old, found a regenerate life among these soldiers of the spirit. During the last few months of 1736 and the early months of 1737, she expanded her teaching among the women who came to meetings at night and on Sundays. She assisted Martin during lessons and filled in for him when he was absent. "Rebecca has taken upon herself [instruction of] the Negro women during my illness and proves herself to be true," Martin wrote in 1737. "It gives me joy to hear such good reports about her." In his history of the mission, Christian Oldendorp later wrote that she "sought to become useful among members of her own sex with her experience and thorough understanding of the saving truths. She had gained the confidence of the Negro and Mulatto women and thus provided the motivation for many of them to seek the grace of God and Jesus Christ." If it seemed to Martin that she had been tapped by God, it was because she needed no prodding to speak on his behalf.[33]

Just three years after the defeat of the St. John slave rebellion, people of African origin began to embrace a different kind of political and spiritual expression in evangelical Christianity. By no means did it promise freedom from slavery, but by using the son of the white masters' own God to condemn them, the slaves robbed their owners of spiritual power and redirected it toward themselves. Patiently counseling the curious, exhorting them to find spiritual liberty in the soul of Christ, winning converts one by one, Rebecca put herself on the front lines of this movement. Among this gathering of brothers and sisters in the spirit, the young, free woman of color with aspirations to testify and lead found safe harbor, an outlet for her calling. It must have been exhilarating to realize her words could upend the lives of others. Once an eager pupil herself, she had become a priestly woman.

CHAPTER FOUR

The Path

For the black women and men of St. Thomas, Christianity became a religion in motion, a church on foot. Curfews and work kept many away from the popular nightly meetings at the missionaries' house in town, so Rebecca and other black messengers of the Gospel fanned out along the rugged roads to bring their teachings to the people, like the Apostles in Acts 8:4, "everywhere preaching the word." The word was verbal energy and movement, revealed to workers in the sugar and cotton fields. Teams of African preachers called "fishermen" walked barefoot from plantation to plantation, trawling for souls in slave quarters across the distant reaches of the island. Convincing people that Christianity could be a faith for black folk was dusty, unglamorous, and dangerous work. Being a teacher in this traveling school required a sturdy pair of legs and a glib tongue, and more than one itinerant messenger was beaten up on the road by angry whites.

These exhorters were the foot soldiers of a spiritual revolution. Without them, white preachers knew their own ability to reach the kamina folk would be minimal. "In the missionary efforts to extend the work of God among the Negroes, the major contribution came from the Negroes themselves," one preacher acknowledged. "It was they who spread the good news throughout the island about Jesus Christ. One light kindled another, and he who had tasted of the divine love of Jesus Christ sought to help those around him enjoy it also." Many neophytes were drawn to the mission by the lure of reading and writing, and literacy continued to exert a powerful appeal. But the grappling hook of the movement was the spoken word. It moved quickly over the mountains into the fields and slave huts where people clustered to debate Christian doctrine. The electricity of speech jolted words on the page to life. In a church so grounded in emotion and depth of religious experience rather than formal learning, even biblical authority ceded ground to the democratic immediacy of talk. Thus, by taking face-to-face discussion directly to the people, Rebecca and other carriers of the word claimed practical control of the mission for themselves. Mobilizing conversion from within the slave community, making Christianity a religion of and for people of African origin, they were the spokeswomen and men of the emerging black church in America.[1]

When black preachers took the word into the countryside, they invariably traveled at least part of the way along the main road through the island, which was known as "the Path." Shaped like a skinny lozenge, St. Thomas is twelve miles long, four miles across at the broadest point, less than a mile across at the narrowest, and only about thirty miles square. A chain of mountains along the spine, almost unnaturally tall for such a small place—the highest, Crown Mountain, is 1,500 feet—effectively separates the northern and southern sides of the island. From Red Hook point at the east end of St. Thomas, the Path snaked around and over the mountains, here and there tracing the southern coastline, crossed a few narrow plains, and headed uphill again to peter out near the western tip of the island. A second major route, the King's Road, dipped and curled among the mountains through the heart of the island.

Along these arteries the life and traffic of St. Thomas flowed, but to a different rhythm for black and white travelers. Black islanders walked everywhere. They trudged shoeless for miles up steep hills while whites rode by horse or carriage. If they were enslaved, the only time they didn't walk was when they were forced to run alongside their master's horse. They carried heavy loads or hauled them by wagon to plantations high in the mountains. A trip of a few miles to visit a spouse at a distant plantation might take hours; both bond and free blacks could be stopped at any time and asked for identification. Slaves who failed to stand aside for whites would be flogged, and they were generally forbidden on the roads after dark. Ordinarily, the Path meant hard work and danger for black folk. Now, to the itinerant teachers of the Gospel, it was a conduit for a higher calling.[2]

In the eastern third of the island, the highway crossed through something resembling a valley, or at least a broad, fertile, and less hilly stretch (nowhere was it flat), past the large plantations of Creoles like Adrian van Beverhout, Jan de Wind, and Johannes Uytendahl, where some of the most intensive mission work would take place. Passersby could see terraced cane fields hugging the hills, the conical stone boiler houses for sugar, and rows of slave huts lining the rim of the fields, some fifty or sixty on the largest plantations. With a low door and a thatched roof of sugarcane leaves, these wattle-and-daub huts held three or four people, who spread kavannes, or reed mats, on the dirt floor to sleep. Nearby, in their provision grounds, or garden plots, slaves spent hours in the evenings and on weekends, raising enough food, particularly root crops like cassava, potatoes, and yams, to feed themselves and have enough left over to sell, thereby enjoying "a kind of freedom" on their little patch. Slaveowners liked the system because, in farming out to the slaves the duty of feeding themselves, they rendered them "all the more bound to the plantation insofar as [they had] a stake in the master's holding."[3]

Further west of these holdings, the Path plunged down a steep hill to the harbor, passing the Company plantation with its slave village and sugar works, and led into the town of Charlotte Amalie.

"The village," as it was known by white colonists, was called Tappus by blacks, after a former tavern, or "taphuys," there. A weave of several long streets bisected by a warren of lanes and alleys, Tappus was small by the standards of some Caribbean colonial capitals but still large enough to contain a busy urban port. With its fort, official buildings, and solid homes, the town's built environment was overwhelmingly European, but in public places the human presence was mostly African. Black dock workers loaded cargoes and bustled through the streets on errands. Skilled slave craftsmen such as carpenters, masons, coopers, smiths, and tailors were hired out by their masters for jobs in town, and planters brought fleets of female cooks, washerwomen, and nursemaids along when they came in from the country. Plantation workers brought produce from their plots to sell in town. "Before and after the sermon on Sundays, all the Negroes from all over the island bring all variety of the island's products and hold an open market under th[e] silk cotton trees," noted an observer. "And on other days, the free slaves sit there selling bread, fresh and fried fish, sugar cakes, pork, meat by the pound, fresh and salted butter, and all kinds of kitchen spices and herbs." A forum to buy, sell, barter, bring in cash, and mingle, the markets became an important release of tension from slavery itself.[4]

Behind the town, strands of road left the Path and hairpinned into the mountains. Throughout much of the island, the tree cover had been cleared for plantations, firewood, and shipbuilding, replaced by exotic import species of palm, banana, and fruit trees, but thick stands of native mahogany, cedar, and silk cotton woods still carpeted the mountain tops. The forest was dense enough in places to harbor small communities of maroons, who were described by a Dane as "slaves who knavishly run away from their masters or lords and assemble together," living in "the tops of mountains as well as below in the mountains' caves," eluding periodic attempts to root them out. From time to time they ventured out to raid plantations and Danish defense works, as they did in 1738 when they torched a fort. From high up, maroons and still-enslaved men and women could gaze far out to sea to other islands and hope of escape. Occasionally someone would make off with a boat and head to freedom forty miles west in Puerto Rico, which remained a tantalizing destination throughout the slavery period.[5]

The Path led through the mysteries of black St. Thomas, and a small core of spiritual "workers" emerged in late 1736 to guide the white preachers, Friedrich Martin—whom the slaves called *Baas,* the Dutch Creole word for overseer—and his new assistant Matthäus Freundlich, along the road in an aggressive recruitment drive for souls. Many of these volunteers were enslaved men, many of them Creoles, some with previous knowledge of Christianity, a few favored with positions of authority on their plantations, and skilled in the diplomacy of maneuvering between masters, slaves, and missionaries.

An important participant in the effort was Domingo Gesu, or Mingo, the Caribbean-born son of African parents Marotta, or Magdalena, and Joseph, both from Popo on the Slave Coast, and both early converts to the mission on St. Thomas. Mingo was an overseer at Mosquito Bay, the estate of Johann Lorentz Carstens, a planter who supported the mission and wanted to expose his workers to Christianity. Through the offices of Carstens, Mingo had already been baptized in the Reformed Church on the Dutch colony of St. Eustatius. Though enslaved, he was literate, spoke Dutch and German, played the violin, and "entertained the people with his music." Mingo had used these talents to forge a close relationship with Carstens, earning himself a great deal of independence and freedom of movement. When he met the Moravian Brethren, they saw an anger in his character which they warned him he "would regret, perhaps too late." Unsettled by the admonition, he eventually became "thoroughly converted" and agreed to help the missionaries. This savvy operator "maintained his own household and trade in Tappus," held prayer meetings for blacks at his house, even loaned the missionaries money, and later arranged the purchase of some land in town for them. In the 1740s he also bought his own piece of land in Tappus, built a house, and used it as a church. At a time when slaves needed permission just to leave their plantation, Mingo traveled to Denmark at least once on business for the Carstens family, and with his high profile in the island's slave community, he proved a valuable ally and envoy for the mission.[6]

Two other assistants, Andreas and Petrus, also made themselves indispensable partners in the project, accompanying Martin or Freundlich on long preaching trips into the countryside and helping them at nightly meetings in town. They were guarantors for the missionaries' trustworthiness, and Martin deemed their powers of persuasion "particularly useful and important, insofar as his message to the Negroes could be confirmed by a believer from their own nation." In one typical diary report from 1738, Martin wrote of visiting a plantation: "The entire house was full of people. I had three of our brothers with me, who taught them." Preaching that "whoever believed in the crucified Savior obtained forgiveness of sins, life everlasting, and eternal salvation, [Martin's] words made a lively impression on their hearts when Andreas or Petrus joyfully confirmed [them]." That authentication opened all sorts of doors. "On almost every plantation, there was a hunger among the slaves for the grace of God in Jesus Christ, with the result that Martin had attentive listeners wherever he went." This indigenous corps of leaders—people who knew the island, understood the nuances of black and white communities, had experience in getting things done—ensured that religious teachings were not simply imposed from the outside on an uncomprehending and sullen audience.[7]

Black evangelists used their credibility to take the message where Martin could not go and say things he could not say. One of them, Abraham, "had the advantage over his white co-workers of completely understanding the language of the Negroes, an ability in which his white brethren were still lagging behind. In addition, he was also more intimately acquainted than they with the superstitions, customs, and practices of his fellow Blacks." Putting knowledge of his audience to good effect, he was said to have "extraordinary gifts as a preacher" who gave public exhortations that mesmerized his audiences—sometimes including white listeners.[8]

An insider's imprimatur made the teams of black traveling preachers known as the fishermen powerfully effective as well. Eight pairs of men spent their free time on Saturday afternoons and Sundays walking over the mountains to spread the word throughout St. Thomas. Penetrating all corners of the island, translating the Gospels into terms their audiences could follow, they were credited with preaching on every plantation and drawing many recruits into the burgeoning congregation. This black ministry even gained a seaborne outreach. A few years later, when Martin extended his preaching to the third Danish colony of St. Croix, forty miles south of St. Thomas, he took a baptized slave brother, Stephanus, with him as an assistant. As the mission gained hold, he appointed Stephanus and three other men as fishermen for the island. Thus, both islands had a core of black assistants upon whom Martin depended to carry on the work during his long absences.[9]

There apparently were no teams of itinerant fisherwomen. Perhaps women could not free themselves from their weekend marketing duties, or Martin might have considered it unsafe or somehow inappropriate for slave women to venture out on speaking tours. Still, women were just as quick to recognize the possibilities opened by preaching in different venues. For some, speech became a lever of self-defense. One woman ended her abuse from a hostile overseer by reading Scriptures to him, causing him to relent and become more "indulgent" with plantation workers. Another, Mariana, a slave on Adrian van Beverhout's plantation, used her knowledge of the Bible to intimidate whites into silence. "She speaks to some *Blanken* with such authority about what she has read in the Bible that they can not open their mouths against her." She was particularly inspired by

Colossians 1, perhaps by this passage from 1:27–29: "To whom God would make known what is the riches of the glory of this mystery among the heathen, which is Christ in you, the hope of glory: Whom we preach, warning every man, and teaching every man in all wisdom; that we may present every man perfect in Christ Jesus: Whereunto I also labor, striving according to his working, which worketh in me mightily." In any other situation, Mariana might have had her tongue cut out for contradicting a white. Now, under the protection of the masters' own sacred text, she and others boldly talked back. Moreover, the slaves pointed out, the book of Revelation proved the slaveholders' wickedness for all the world but themselves to see. One woman who met Martin on the Path in 1737 told him that "the Christians do not serve their God," and that, although she was a slave, she could see that the world would end with the masters ignorant of the punishment they would face.[10]

Women taught and led each other as well. "Among the Negro women are at least six who are already beginning to teach on occasion," Martin wrote to church leaders in Germany. "Those who cannot yet read apply themselves diligently and will spell something many times until they can comprehend it. In the evenings they ask me to read to them what they have spelled during their daily work when they have a brief moment to look in their books." He singled out Rebecca, "a Mulatto woman whom I have appointed to be a worker among them. If there is ever any problem with one of the Sisters she will write a letter of admonition to her. It is a great joy to me, and a great inclination for this work has been stirred in her. I assure you she can quite properly be called a Sister, and she is quite eager to serve the Savior." The absence of black female itinerant recruiters like the fishermen meant that most of those duties fell to Rebecca, and no mission assistant stayed busier.[11]

Freedom gave her greater mobility than enslaved brothers and sisters enjoyed, and she was asked—or she offered—to walk farther, stay later, and teach longer. "Rebecca is a very diligent worker," wrote Martin in early 1737. "When I am out in the countryside, she takes my place so that the Brethren don't have to look after the Negro women, which they do not want to do. The Lord is with her and grounds her heart in faith. It is a serious duty for her to spread his word." Male missionaries believed that men should minister to each other, and women likewise. As the mission's foremost woman, therefore, Rebecca gradually took charge of the entire female half of the movement during the early months of 1737. From the time she began attending meetings, to the moment she became a worker, to her confirmation and admission to Communion in October 1737, the demands on her time and physical stamina increased steadily. She still discharged her daily domestic duties for the van Beverhouts, but on Sundays and after work every evening she walked back and forth several miles to hold class on plantations or at the Brethren's house in Tappus, joining the scores of black men and women—as many as two hundred, by one estimate—who at nightfall streamed across the island into town after an exhausting day in the fields. It was no light undertaking; on some days, no doubt, they passed a severed head or a pair of hands impaled on a pole by the roadside, reminders of the penalty for disobedience—which some planters suspected the mission was breeding.[12]

Meetings began with instruction in reading and writing, the part that many pupils anticipated most eagerly, followed by lessons in Christian principles, hymn singing, a sermon, and a prayer. Afterward, the teachers held private conferences with students, often until as late as midnight, allowing those with the longest walk home to leave first. It was in these sessions that Rebecca's role as instructor emerged most distinctly. "Rebecca helps teach the Negro women," Martin wrote in March 1737. "In the evenings when the Negro women come to school, she teaches them. She is true in her understanding, and the women love her." Another description by Martin gives us an idea of how these intimate scenes of instruction and nurture must have looked: "It is like this every evening with us. The women sit at the table, Rebecca speaks with them about whether they have understood or remembered things, and I work with the Negro men."[13]

Martin's reports and letters—the main source of information about Rebecca during these years—repeatedly refer to the sense of trust and confidence she instilled in followers. In the same way that a former slave in the antebellum United States, Isabella, renamed herself Sojourner Truth as a signifier of the righteousness of her religious evangelicalism and antislavery activism, Rebecca must have reached the battered and forgotten black women of St. Thomas with words they took for truth. Rather than begrudge her success, white preachers gladly acknowledged her ability to break through when they could not. She took under her wing the enslaved woman Anna, the original inspiration for the mission in early 1733 who, after initially welcoming the missionaries, had quickly cooled toward them and kept her distance. "I have great hopes that Rebecca will win over Anna," wrote Martin. "Anna shows her love, would rather go to her than to us, and is more candid with her. Rebecca has taken special interest in her and makes [lessons] comprehensible to her." In another instance, she recruited a woman who had "heard terrible things" about the Brethren that hinted of heathenish practices; Rebecca persuaded her to drop her misgivings and join the congregation.[14]

Rebecca's own words as well as Martin's diaries describe a disciple motivated by absolute conviction and the will, as she expressed it, to "follow the example of His poor life" with tenacious work. She was a conscience of the mission, exhorting fellow preachers and the uninitiated alike. When Martin and Freundlich became despondent in 1737 over their inability to pay the lease on their house in Tappus, "Mingo and Rebecca shamed us with their admonition to faith." Her best tools were persistence and the gift of reaching people with quiet but firm eloquence. Although she had a teacher's readiness to testify or give a lesson at any time, she apparently favored gentle persuasion over fervent elocution. Indeed, there is no record of her making a public address or preaching to the congregation as a whole, probably because the missionaries, abiding by the letter of the Scriptures, frowned on women's oration. Instead, Rebecca hewed to the spirit of the Bible by convincing women to convert through the less visible but equally important—and even clandestine—work of tutoring behind the scenes. It was there, in the subdued moments and unrecorded exchanges where teaching and learning took place, where insights were traded and the desire for knowledge quickened, that the hidden revolution in African-American consciousness emerged.[15]

Rebecca's vigor and enthusiasm made her the essential female itinerant, the one to plod long miles taking the word out on the Path. This was work for only the most dogged evangelist. She walked till her feet ached; she trudged out even when exhausted and sick. At one point in 1738 she was felled by a fever and a subsequent blood-letting, but she pressed on. "The Negro men and women have great love for her, she works with blessing wherever she goes, and she preaches of the Savior with joy," wrote Martin. "She is still so weak in her body that she can not go out very often, or very far." She seemed to be driven by the urgency of the work, the sense that her divine purpose could not wait for a fever. Perhaps she fed on the adulation she inspired among people who needed her assurance.[16]

She did not, however, always enjoy an uncomplicated relationship with her followers. Neither the miles she walked nor the passion of her voice could disguise the fact that Rebecca was free while almost all of them were not. As a former slave, she undoubtedly gained much of her effectiveness from her empathy for enslaved people, but her station in life was in fact quite different. She could go where they could not, and she endured none of the physical and sexual abuse that many of them suffered. Her increasing authority began to stir resentment, as Martin learned when a delegation of women came to see him in early 1738. "Many asked that Rebecca

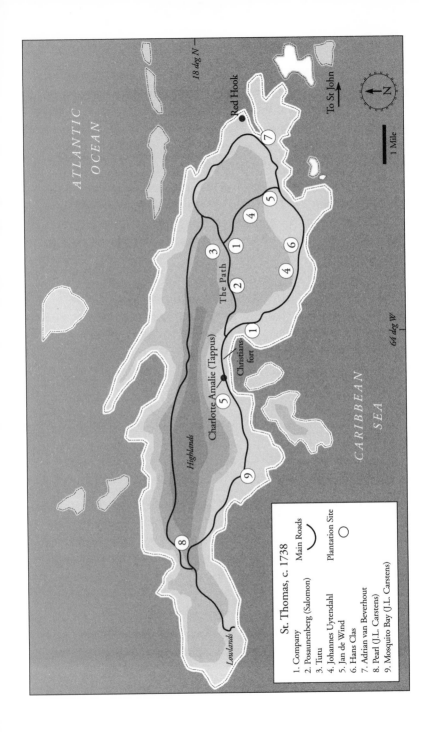

St. Thomas, c. 1738

Main Roads

Plantation Site ◯

1. Company
2. Posaunenberg (Salomon)
3. Turu
4. Johannes Uytendahl
5. Jan de Wind
6. Hans Clas
7. Adrian van Beverhout
8. Pearl (J.L. Carstens)
9. Mosquito Bay (J.L. Carstens)

ATLANTIC OCEAN

CARIBBEAN SEA

Red Hook

To St. John

N

1 Mile

18 deg N

64 deg W

Highlands

Lowlands

The Path

Charlotte Amalie (Tappus)

Christians fort

not come to us any more," he wrote. "Though they previously loved her, now they are beginning to envy her, and they lament her position." Maybe it seemed to these women that she was putting on airs with her new power; perhaps they felt her exalted status was widening the social distance between slave and free in a religious order that claimed to break down those distinctions. If Martin spoke to Rebecca about their concerns, or if she and the women resolved them, he did not say. They may have reached an agreement, for she seemed as popular as ever a few months later when he wrote: "Jesus gave our poor Rebecca faith and self-confidence. They follow her around where they can and are openhearted toward her. She is needed in the village as well as in the field. She is still weak, and has to sit down to rest while out on the Path." But the dispute underscored the importance of trust in a partnership based on personal revelation of the spirit.[17]

Rebecca and the other workers gained a foothold in the eastern part of the island, a central valley somewhat more accessible by foot, particularly to Rebecca from her nearby home with the van Beverhouts. Several planters granted access to their slaves after Martin convinced them that the mission would not make the workforce unruly, so recruiters focused on those adjacent or nearby plantations which formed a kind of chain along the main roads. From Tappus, with its core of urban converts, and the Company plantation just outside town, the Path created a kind of "geography of faith" as it wound east through the hills past the holdings of Governor Friedrich Moth, Pierre Pannet, Jan de Wind, Hans Clas, and Johannes Uytendahl, and past another large plantation called Tutu, on all of which lived cadres of black Christians.[18]

Following a careful strategy, mission workers strove to gain one or two converts on a plantation who, in turn, would win over another handful of recruits, and so on. The effort gained steady momentum as dozens of prospects entered the fold. The seminal figure on the plantation of Jan de Wind, for example, was an African named Matamba, from Loango. In 1737, according to the missionaries, he had "become possessed by the notion that God was to send some white men who were supposed to take care of him and instruct him. He had never before heard of the Brethren's efforts toward the salvation of the Negroes, but he was greatly concerned about his own condition." He confided his dream to a "Karibeer," a fellow African shipmate on the transatlantic Middle Passage, who expressed skepticism. Several weeks later, hearing of Martin's lessons, Matamba hastened to him, and the preacher gave him a book in which "he could find God's word, which he should obey." He began attending prayer meetings in town, taught himself to read, and started preaching to others on the plantation.

> Once, as he returned home from instruction, the overseer asked him where he had come from. From Tappus, he replied, because there the Negroes could learn of God's word, a fact with which the overseer would certainly be acquainted. Well, replied the latter, how could the Blacks keep the word of God if the Whites themselves are not able to do so? Matamba replied by saying that he himself had no doubt that those who did not believe the word of God but preferred to serve sin instead, could not abide by it. However, he also felt that whoever believes it is taught by the spirit of God and can therefore keep His word. Annoyed by the slave's candid response, the overseer called him a great pietist who was leading astray all the other slaves on the plantation . . . a troublemaker who had induced the other slaves to spend their rest period sitting in their huts and studying. He confiscated his booklet and assigned him fieldwork, though to that point he had served as the plantation's fisherman.

Another overseer was even harsher, administering daily beatings that caused a "thick, dangerous swelling" on the African teacher. Matamba was reprieved, however, by the planter de Wind, who "found nothing objectionable in the behavior of his slaves [and] even felt it desirable that all of his slaves might go to hear Martin preach"; he permitted Matamba to resume his lessons and to be christened Thomas in 1738. He was probably joined in his teaching by a woman named Elisabeth, also from de Wind's plantation, who was baptized in 1738. Within two years fourteen more people from the plantation, all women, converted, followed the next year by twenty-two more women and ten men.[19]

It was the same on other estates—forty from the Company plantation were baptized, thirty at Johannes Uytendahl's, and more on the estates of van Beverhout, Hans Clas, Peter de Wind, and others. Sometimes the congregation staged the spectacle of mass baptisms. Early on, many candidates were "plunged into the river beside Brother Mingo's house in the village"; other times, initiates clad in white robes trooped to the front of the prayer hall to be sprinkled with water and kissed on the cheek by missionaries and workers. On one occasion Martin baptized ninety people, including fifty-six women and thirty-four men. Many of the women must have been recruited or taught by Rebecca, including Anna, who finally succumbed to Rebecca's ministrations and joined the church eight years after the Brethren first approached her.[20]

Still, despite these dramatic results, and even with the best efforts of the black preachers, reaching out to the unfree was a formidable task. Many masters and overseers remained hostile to the mission and had their slaves beaten and harassed for trying to pray or read. One planter chained a slave to the ground "until he promised that he would learn nothing more from the brethren about Christianity." Even white missionaries were attacked and beaten on occasion. For a people who patterned themselves so closely on the book of Acts, the violence was expected and, in an odd way, almost welcome, for it confirmed the missionaries' sense of persecution and struggle in a righteous cause. They saw themselves as replicating the narrative of sacrifice and even martyrdom that would culminate in Christian triumph. As for the slaves who endured beatings, Oldendorp, echoing the New Testament, claimed their suffering "only strengthened their resolve to be converted." If the statement is true, their bravery suggests that scriptural teachings touched them in some deep way or offered a new source of spiritual power that was worth the risk.[21]

Many bondmen and women on St. Thomas, however, remained indifferent to the Gospel; others showed contempt and hostility toward what they considered the corrupt religion of their enslavers. The Akkran people, who lived near and traded with the Danish in West Africa, believed that Christianity "may be good for the Whites, but that it is not appropriate for the Negroes." Some slaves ridiculed and even attacked those who professed Christianity. One woman suffered knife lacerations at the hands of another. A black arsonist set fire to the missionaries' house, which was quickly put out, but someone else torched the house of the assistant Petrus and seven other slave cabins on the plantation. Violent opposition was only the most visceral sign of intense debates running through slave quarters across the island about the theological and practical value of the Scriptures and their political meaning in everyday life.[22]

It was not enough, then, for white and black teachers simply to assert that Christianity was a religion of spiritual freedom and expect recruits to embrace them uncritically. Their message had to be made attractive and intelligible to an extraordinarily diverse group of people, from West Indian Creoles to captives from a wide swath of West Africa who represented dozens of cultures, languages, and religions. An early church register identifying the origins of the new congregants gives a vivid glimpse of this diversity. Of 501 people baptized or accepted into the Christian fellowship between 1737 and 1750, 314, or a little more than 60 percent, were Caribbean natives, while 187 had been born in Africa. Of the latter, more than half came from a few nations or regions: 39 from Amina, 32 from Watje, 31 from Loango, 11 from Popo, and 9 each from Kongo and

Kazangtee. The rest represented 29 other points of African origin, mostly along the Gold and Slave Coasts.[23]

In later years the missionaries would gain a more nuanced understanding of the differences among these many peoples, but in this early stage, as novices themselves, they were too busy laying the groundwork to make advanced ethnographic distinctions. To entice their audience into forsaking African beliefs for the Bible, they sought to find ways of translating the lexicon of Christian myths, symbols, and rituals into approximate terms that would be broadly familiar to African and Afro-Caribbean students. Catholic priests had used that approach successfully in winning converts among Africans in Kongo and in American colonies such as Brazil and Mexico, where they equated African spirit gods with Catholic saints, African rituals and icons with Christian counterparts.[24]

The Moravian Brethren were probably only dimly aware of those strategies, and they could not put saints and statues to work on their behalf. But they found ways to make the same points by identifying cognates between Christianity and African religions. The Papaa woman Marotta, for example, had customarily offered an annual sacrifice of a goat or lamb to produce a "fine-smelling smoke-offering" that would "placate the divinity and ensure her own well-being." The Brethren got her to stop what they regarded as a heathenish practice by convincing her that Jesus had sacrificed himself for mankind. Now, after being baptized and christened Magdalena, "she comes to the Lord's Supper and preaches of Jesus in her own language." Some years later, when the missionary Johann Boehner prepared a Dutch Creole translation of the Bible published in 1761, he translated the phrase "white as snow" in Isaiah 1:18 as "Your sins shall be as white as linen" to convey its meaning to Africans who had no notion of snow. When Oldendorp visited the Danish islands in 1767, he was able, in contrast to his predecessors in the 1730s, to develop more sophisticated distinctions among African cultures. Still, he labored to explain the meaning of Christ's martyrdom to Africans who "did not seem to have an equivalent for the word 'sin' in their respective languages." Substituting the terms "uncleanliness," "evil," or "bad things," he asked people from twenty-six African ethnic or national groups to translate the phrase "Christ has loved us and has washed away our sins with His blood." In the Tembu language, for instance, it came out as "Christus ullunama, owaschumaa negu naschuma," which the missionary retranslated as "Christ loves us, has washed us of uncleanliness with His blood."[25]

Oldendorp's own example suggests another likely element of the missionaries' success: their emphasis on the blood sacrifice of Jesus. Building on medieval and Reformation theology, the Brethren celebrated the blood and wounds of Christ to a degree unusual in the eighteenth-century Protestant world, and all of their mission teachings paid homage to Jesus' blood. A Dutch catechism they developed in 1739, for example, posed a long series of simple questions about Christianity, concluding: "Why must I then be baptized with water?" "The blood shed for you by the Lord Jesus through his death comes unseen with it and washes all of your sins and punishments away." West African catechumens might well have recognized and absorbed such ideas easily, since many incorporated some form of human or animal sacrifice into their rituals, and blood was often seen as a propitiatory or purifying agent. Either because they accepted the Christian version of the sacrifice or because they recognized what was expected of them, black initiates quickly learned the vocabulary of supplication, as one missionary noted: "The blood of Jesus flows over them, softens their hearts, and makes them see how great his love is. . . . Many of them who were as dead as stone have been moved by Jesus' death, the constant subject of our preaching, and they now cry for mercy. Jesus' death and His blood have penetrated their hearts, making them cry out and search for their bloodied Redeemer."[26]

It also helped the missionaries that some Africans already knew about Christianity or related ideas from other sources. A few had received instruction in the Dutch Reformed Church or, like Rebecca, had been baptized by visiting priests from Puerto Rico; others, natives of west central Africa, had brought their Catholic faith across the ocean. Friedrich Martin reported having a conversation with "a Portuguese Negro who was baptized there [in Kongo], quite a respectable Negro." Records suggest that at least twenty-five black Catholics, or inductees previously baptized by Catholic priests, became members of the new congregation by 1759—enough that "believing Negroes who had been baptized by a Catholic Father and who chose to follow the brethren's guidance and teaching were accepted into the congregation with a kiss of peace" and a prayer. Mission workers also encountered Muslims from parts of West Africa where Islam had held sway for centuries; they held to their faith tenaciously in America and did not necessarily make good candidates for Christian conversion. Still, the Muslims were people of the book, and the missionaries approvingly noted their commitment to religious instruction, baptism, marriage, and holy writings, aspects they sometimes overzealously attributed to the influence of Christianity in Africa.[27]

Some Africans found their way to Christianity through dreams and visions. Revelation of the divine word was a source of mystical power common to both traditional African religions and Christianity that could reconcile the different belief systems. In several cases, the missionaries themselves figured in dreams as agents of black spiritual salvation. Matamba, the black teacher on Jan de Wind's plantation, sought out Christianity after dreaming that God would send him white men to provide spiritual guidance. By learning to read and becoming a teacher himself, Matamba fulfilled the prophecy. After a prayer meeting on St. Thomas in 1736, another man restlessly stayed up all night thinking about it and came to a missionary's door early the next morning to explain. "I had appeared in his dream, standing before him. He remembered what I had said and in his dream he prayed to God." To the missionaries, steeped in scriptural revelation, as in Joel 2:28 ("Your sons and daughters will prophesy, your old men will dream dreams, your young men will see visions"), such testimony was perfectly natural evidence of divine inspiration.[28]

Though they looked for points of convergence between Christianity and African religions, preachers expected converts to embrace a new life through rebirth in Christ, their "heathen" selves washed pure by the waters of baptism. The christening caught the spirit of this transformation. "The name given them at baptism is of great value to the baptized Negroes, and they refuse to respond to their old names. Once when a baptized Negro was addressed by his former name, November, his response was: 'November is dead.'" The baptismal ritual itself had spiritual reverberations for many inductees, since water often held a sacred place in West African cultures and was similarly used in religious ceremonies to connect initiates to the ancestral world. Among the Tembu, according to Oldendorp, "some families have their daughters undergo something resembling a baptism prior to their marriage. During these foolish ceremonies, she is thrown into the water and pulled out again only after she is half-drowned. After that, she is taken back home to the accompaniment of music, and afterward, eight days are spent in revelry." Baptism into the Christian church did not entail a simple exchange of one faith for another, however. In many converts, African religions and Christianity coexisted side by side, overlapped, and merged in complex ways that allowed congregants to acknowledge Jesus and worship the Christian God, yet seek additional power from traditional African spirits and deities.[29]

Constantly vigilant for signs of persistent African beliefs, the Brethren banished one woman for practicing witchcraft with "silly instruments of magic" she had inherited from a relative, consisting of "calabashes decorated with ribbons, bird feathers, sea shells, and the like," which conveyed strong refrains of Kongolese religion.

New shiploads of captives from the slave trade through the end of the eighteenth century continually reinvigorated African customs, so that missionaries were never able to stamp them out. One congregant, Cornelius, participated in African dances even while serving as a prominent elder. During the waning days of slavery in the 1840s (the institution ended in the Danish West Indies in 1848), thousands of black islanders still celebrated holidays with African music, dancing, parties, and the election of royalty—Kings, Queens, Princes, and Princesses—to preside over plantation festivities.[30]

Rebecca herself joined the effort to suppress lingering African religious practices. Friedrich Martin described one such instance: "I was present when some of the baptized were led astray and began singing in a heathenish manner. When Rebecca heard it, she hurried there and reprimanded them for their idolatry. They grew so afraid, they scarcely dared to return home." Though giving voice to songs from their homeland might have seemed harmless to the singers, the missionaries pressed the point. That evening a dozen offenders were summoned before the congregation to be asked by Martin "whether they did not believe they had done wrong in listening to the devil?" and whether their actions merited expulsion from the congregation. Such pressure tactics were intimidating and confusing, since the converts probably did not understand their offense. After apologizing and promising never to repeat the mistake, they were forgiven, having no doubt learned to keep future communion with African spirits private.[31]

In our own time Rebecca's support of such methods might be called intolerant; she might even be labeled complicit in a campaign of cultural eradication. After all, the missionaries had praised her for "acting like a white," which presumably meant she shunned African or Afro-Caribbean music, festivities, devotions, and other forms of cultural expression. It is true that, having shared a household for many years with white Creoles, she probably identified more with European practices than with African ones (though of course the

Caribbean milieu saw much mixing of the two) and was not disposed to admire African music or worship. She also appears to have had both a sense of her own authority and a forceful personality to go with it. However gentle and nurturing she might have been as a teacher, her dressing down of the singers revealed a stern and decisive side as well. Rebecca held what she thought were the best interests of Africans at heart. Judging from the limited clues she left about her own motivation, she believed that Christianity promised spiritual freedom for people of color; any deviation revealed lingering heathenism and might jeopardize the mission itself. In that time and place, and in her own mind, insensitivity to African values was not the issue—these values had to be subordinated to the survival of a divine project. Rebecca's insistence might well have contributed to the resentment black women sometimes felt toward her.

One practice the Brethren denounced vigorously was polygamy. Oldendorp described the custom as nearly universal in West Africa, and it continued among enslaved workers in the Caribbean. Another missionary blamed the planters for allowing, and even promoting, multiple partners by both men and women to boost slave reproduction rates. In April 1738 Friedrich Martin put a new policy in place stating that congregants would be limited to one partner. Their unions would be acknowledged in a public ceremony in the church, and though they would have no formal standing in the law, they would have sacred recognition. Transgressors would be barred from worship. This major intervention in black domestic life was an essential feature of the missionaries' campaign. "Unfortunately," wrote Oldendorp, "many Whites did not respect the married state of their slaves and continued their practice of separating married couples to suit their own convenience." Partly because of that hindrance, and in part because of African resistance to the anti-polygamy rules, the missionaries made a partial concession in 1749. Although no baptized male convert was allowed to marry more than one wife, converts with more than one wife before baptism were allowed to retain them. The result was a blend of traditional African and Christian practice that leaned toward practicality.[32]

In general, however, African converts faced the prospect of surrendering or hiding important parts of their culture. Many refused to do so, but why would others agree to that difficult bargain? An obvious reason was the sense that Jesus was their friend; his word refuted the brutal degradation they endured daily. "Those slaves who enjoyed the greatest freedom and had to face the fewest obstacles were also the least likely to become converts," observed Oldendorp. Christian worship furnished a refuge for the oppressed. The congregation offered a bond of unison, moreover, that attracted recruits and was usually powerful enough to hold them. Using practices imported from the Brethren's church in Germany and patterned after the example of the first Christians, black congregants developed a heavily ritualized theater of fellowship through a succession of elaborate ceremonies. Baptisms, confirmations, foot-washings, and the laying on of hands all contributed to the feeling of warmth, inclusion, and mutual purpose. The *agape* or lovefeast promoted "the spirit of love and fellowship among members of their congregation, which included representatives from a variety of African nations, dispersed among a number of plantations." Worshippers donated what they could to the ceremony. On one occasion "a Negro brought as his contribution to the feast a big fish that he had caught." In the midst of the plantation system's repressive machinery, fellowship offered an element of democracy. A congregational assembly even voted on policy measures.[33]

These rituals generated a compact of fellowship so tight that it was a wrenching punishment to exclude someone for singing African songs or defying a plantation overseer. That threat "usually turned out to be much more effective than punishment imposed by the whip of the bomba, for the culprits soon found their deprivation of the blessed instruction so intolerable that they often begged tearfully to be readmitted to services." The great paradox was that

Christianity was becoming the handmaiden of the plantation order even as the black church itself opposed everything the plantation represented.[34]

Although African deities and worship styles were discouraged, the congregation rested on two basic building blocks that were readily familiar to Africans: mentorship and kinship. In West Africa, people belonged to "overlapping networks of association and exchange," including extended kin groups and secret religious societies that were guided by corresponding groups of leaders and patrons. Divided by sex, the secret cults were supervised by male and female spiritual elders who absorbed new members into the band at adolescence by ceremonies of initiation. All of these groups defined a person's identity and place in the family, the village, the cosmos. During the Atlantic slave trade these ties of incorporation were largely ruptured, so enslaved Africans sought to forge new associations with a variety of people—fellow captives on slave ships, other plantation workers, countrymen and women, and new spouses. In the Danish islands, recently arrived Africans were taken under the wing of more experienced veterans who cared for them "just as a parent looks after his child," introducing them to the harsh new life ahead. Similarly, Kongolese slaves performed a baptismal ritual for new arrivals, evidently reflecting Catholic practice, which involved "pouring water over the head of the baptized, placing some salt in his mouth, and praying over him in the Congo language." The ritual provided "some kind of foster parents for the poor Bussals who find themselves in the West Indies as total aliens, without father, mother, or other relatives. Negroes of some means of both sexes often adopt those whom they have baptized in this way as children." Everyone called these mentors "baptismal fathers and mothers," and they were the sinews that bound the slave community together.[35]

Mission workers simply adapted many of these customs to fit their own message. They created a lattice of spiritual mentors and fictive kin who helped incorporate Africans into the evangelical family, then continued to teach and nurture them. In Catholic colonies throughout Latin America, black confraternities and other lay organizations served that purpose by drawing enslaved members into church networks that celebrated the faith in unison. Nothing comparable existed among Africans in Protestant America until black and white preachers put a similar system in place on St. Thomas, cobbling it together from a blend of Moravian and African practices. The church appealed to people whose intricate tendrils of kinship had been ripped apart by the slave trade. As one African told a missionary: "We have come here such a long way across the sea from Guinea and have lost both father and mother. That is why we want to get to know the Father above and partake of His grace. Otherwise, we will remain miserable creatures." Appealing to captives' desire to rebuild kin connections proved revolutionary, for those principles would come to form the marrow of black Christian fellowship in the Protestant Atlantic world.[36]

First, one or more black congregants would "adopt" prospective recruits and try to steer them into the fold. Sometimes they came from the same African ethnic group or could speak the languages of their adoptees. After arriving on St. Thomas, for example, one African (later christened Martinus) "quickly made the acquaintance of some Negro brethren who understood his native language," whom he "begged to help him find a good master." His mentors found a radical solution—they convinced the white missionaries to buy him; in time, he converted and became a preacher himself. Another mentor, Jonathan, "was viewed as a father among his people on account of his loving, beneficent attitude. He also sought carefully to introduce newly arrived Bussals into the company of awakened Negroes. His reports on the condition of those believing Negroes placed under his supervision were always both thorough and reliable." When a new convert was baptized, black elders served as witnesses or godparents who supervised the inductee's spiritual status, much as African elders guided novices through ritual initiation into secret cults. As the traveling preachers kept bringing recruits into the fold, new layers of advisers took on counseling duties. On the plantation of Jan de Wind, where by 1739 some eighty people had joined the church, Martin put in place a kind of buddy system that paired off two women and two men together "to converse with one another openheartedly about the state of their souls." The technique spread to other plantations, of which more than fifty claimed a core of converts, and on each plantation their progress was monitored by at least one spiritual elder.[37]

So effective were black men and women in ministering to each other that Martin organized them into a cadre of leaders called helpers, an adaptation of the Moravian helper system in Germany. As with everything the Brethren did, they followed the Bible for guidance, and in this case the notion of "helping" came from Paul's extolling of believers' diversity of gifts as apostles, prophets, and teachers, and their gifts of "helps" (1 Corinthians 12:28), as well as his references to Priscilla, Aquila, and Urbane, "helpers in Jesus Christ" (Romans 16:3, 9). Like deacons or elders, helpers were men and women who undertook all sorts of tasks to nurture worshippers and ensure order. "The black helpers Abraham and Cornelius were employed as teachers," noted Oldendorp. "They often addressed the catechumens and candidates for baptism. They also spoke at the evening meetings on weekdays and at funerals. Their candid testimonies had a considerable impact on their audiences, to such an extent that their listeners sometimes broke into loud crying."[38]

Helpers were to get to know others around them and understand their spiritual condition. "They were advised to light the way for the other Negroes by means of an exemplary conduct, thereby providing themselves with greater access to their people. They were warned that nothing would be more contrary to the purpose of their orders than if they were to imagine that they enjoyed an advantage over their fellows. Through humility and heartfelt love, their labor with others would be blessed." According to a Dutch document from St. Thomas titled "Plicht van Een helper Broeder en Suster" ("Duties of a helper Brother and Sister"), helpers were to "visit the sick, and be there for them to comfort them with the grace of our Lord and Savior" and to ensure that "every member of our community lives lovingly with each other." They were to report sins or offenses committed by their charges ("Brothers and sisters can be free, but they are obliged to tell us these things"), but they would be shamed if they gossiped or lied. "Dear Brothers and Sisters, let us be sincere with each other and with other people as we are with God. You are called out to love and to treat each other with love and respect." Helpers followed a careful list of instructions for church duty:

> The brothers have opened the church and the windows. They cut the candles and when a baptism takes place in church, they cut the bread for the Lovefeast and drink the water. At a baptism service or an induction service one brother will always sit next to the one who will be baptized or converted, so that he can make that person fall on his knees and stand up again at the right time. The sisters must do the same. Every Sunday the church has to be swept and the candlesticks and the lantern cleaned. At the holy supper the white tablecloth must be used. The same should be done for a Lovefeast or baptism when children who are breastfed by their mothers are brought into church.[39]

Helpers, or national helpers, as they were called, in effect selected themselves by their leadership in the slave community. Some were well-known figures on the island, while others came from the ranks of secular authority figures like plantation drivers. The first five helpers appointed by Martin in February 1738 were two sets of brothers—Andreas and Johannes, and Petrus and Christoph—plus one woman, Anna Maria. Except for Petrus, from the Company plantation, all lived on the small plantation of a widow Salomon just off the Path near the east-central valley. "Although they had no particular charge to do so, these persons had already been busy among their people. . . . They were loved and respected by their fellow slaves."[40]

Helpers took charge of small groups, called bands, of between five and ten people, divided by sex, who gathered weekly for discussion and prayer. The bands brought together worshippers of similar life circumstances, such as age and gender, who shared bonds of empathy, spiritual discovery, and friendship. "Through the bands, not a single person in the entire congregation is neglected or forgotten," said the Moravian bishop August Spangenberg. Though the bands were another innovation adapted from church practice in Europe, they were effective in the West Indies because, as the system grew, they could absorb initiates of all backgrounds. It is possible that some bands were organized by African ethnicity, whereby, for example, male and female Akan helpers led groups of countrymen and women, further mimicking the role of African cult leaders. Christoph and Anna Maria, two Creole helpers, "maintained their contacts with individual workers, who represented the various nationalities, in order to discuss with them the conditions under which the work of God among their people was progressing."[41]

Surviving lists of band assignments suggest, however, that Caribbean-born members and those of various African origins might be mingled together as well, often because they lived on the same plantation. Such a system incorporated converts from sometimes-rival African nations into a common system that may have provided a forum to resolve lingering tensions. The bands absorbed many Aminas, for example, the group that had fomented the St. John revolt in 1733 and that was so disliked by other Africans, although there is no record of their relationship to other congregants. In any case, spiritual kinship helped translate African religious beliefs into Christianity. Bands and helpers diffused authority through the congregation, giving followers more guidance, more chance to voice concerns, and greater access to spiritual power.[42]

"Baptism of the Negroes," St. Thomas, by Johann Jakob Bossart, 1757. Courtesy of
Unity Archives, Herrnhut, Germany.

These concepts emerge vividly in an engraving from 1757 titled
"Baptism of the Negroes" by the Moravian artist Johann Jakob
Bossart, depicting an induction ceremony in a prayer hall on St.
Thomas. In the scene, the congregation looks on—men on the
right, women on the left, all clad in white—as nine new members
are welcomed. A tub of baptismal water sits at the front of the room,
while the candidates either prostrate themselves or rise to their feet.
Assisting them are the black helpers, who lift the inductees up, then
embrace and kiss them. The helpers dominate the scene: they conduct the ceremony, they bestow the welcome of inclusion, they are
the brokers of grace. Black people create the visual vortex of the image and the sacred space of the divine transaction. They control the
moment. The three white pastors observing from the right side seem

superfluous, although they do represent an element of white supervision as a proxy for the planters, and therefore a reminder of the tensions inherent in the enterprise.

Women benefited the most from this system. In a plantation system designed to exploit and silence them, here was a verbal oasis where they could speak, teach, and lead. Female helpers were influential people, the liaisons between hundreds of worshippers and leaders like Rebecca or Martin. Women shared confidences with them, and since all believers were urged to bring doubts and questions forward, the surge of discussion and revelation in these therapy groups—to use modern parlance—represented the popular voice. Knowledge of the Savior and of oneself was supposed to evolve through prayer, self-scrutiny, and frank talk with peers and counselors. Each stage of life offered its own questions, and nobody ever arrived at a finished spiritual awareness. The letters to Germany that many congregants wrote or dictated were another outlet for this soul-baring. "This poor and miserable little worm would like to learn the proper way to love the Savior," confessed Maria, a black eldress from the Uytendahl plantation. "Why? He has forgiven my many sins. I was so lacking in faith that I could not image that the Savior could make something out of me. But I feel the greatness of His mercy over me. I thank Him for the blood He has shed for me and for letting it flow of my corrupt heart, thus washing it free of sins. . . . I will bear testimony to it to my people for as long as I live."[43]

In the bands, catechumens talked through each other's problems. Women, for example, probably talked about the sexual exploitation by planters that some of them were beginning to resist. The missionaries had long insisted that such behavior was ungodly and that the planters were wicked for forcing it, though they could not in good conscience order women to disobey their masters. But the rhetoric evidently emboldened a number of "Negro women who no longer wished to allow themselves to be abused for sinful purposes" not to submit. When many indeed suffered harsh retribution, their faith helped them endure, claimed Oldendorp, and the violence only drove them deeper into the arms of the church. "If I had previously been ready to suffer for bad causes, why should I not now be willing to suffer a bit for a good cause?" he quoted one woman as saying. If the portrayal is accurate, religion thus helped inspire and fortify black women against one of their greatest vulnerabilities under slavery—their sexuality.[44]

Rebecca was immersed in the heart of this system. Everyone—Martin, helpers, novitiates—turned to her for advice and guidance, but at the same time, she depended on them as well. As a mission assistant—a higher rank in authority—she worked with the helper Anna Maria to oversee female groups. Martin returned from a trip one day to find "many students who had been refreshed by Rebecca and Anna Maria." Not being of African birth herself, Rebecca could draw insight from helpers with a closer cultural connection to the women they instructed.[45]

Her own responsibilities were expanding, as a church membership list from a few years later shows. It contains a taxonomy of "the redeemed," listed by plantation of residence and neatly separated into bands. Sometimes all the members of a band came from the same plantation, but in other cases band mates might be culled from four or five plantations, organized perhaps by African ethnicity, age, marital status, or other factors. Of 300 congregants, 123 were men, divided into 23 bands supervised by Martin and two white assistants, Matthäus Freundlich and Valentin Löhans. The women's side was larger, with 177 members divided into 28 bands supervised by Rebecca and Löhans's wife, Veronica. Those figures alone are striking—women, outnumbered by men in the island's slave population, made up 60 percent of the congregation. Perhaps these numbers testify to the skill of Rebecca and others as recruiters, but perhaps they say something as well about the lure of Jesus' message for enslaved women, and about the power of fellowship to give refuge and comfort to the powerless. For Rebecca and her fellow assistant, Veronica, that appeal meant that each oversaw 14 bands comprising about 90 members, met regularly with the helpers, counseled worshippers, and foraged for souls in the countryside, all the while declaring that the church was a sanctuary of hope in a wasteland.[46]

Christianity would have been boring and inconsequential to people of African descent if it did not tell them something they wanted to hear. For all its compromises and trade-offs, for all those who rejected its mixed doctrines, it would have failed if others had not felt the desire to claim its prophetic revelation, preach it, take it on the roads. Though Rebecca was hardly responsible alone for this transfiguration, she was a leader in what was becoming a massive popular movement. Despite her own complex relations with her followers, a young woman with limited life options had found a message she believed was important, a way to deliver it, and someone to listen. In the years since she had begun her most sustained teaching, hundreds of people had adopted new ways of thinking, speaking, and organizing. The Path connected them all.

CHAPTER FIVE

Witness

$\mathcal{L}$ike all European colonizers around the Atlantic rim, the Danes had a habit of building forts wherever they settled. On St. Thomas, at the eastern edge of Tappus, they built a big stone fortress in 1689 as a forbidding symbol of their imperial power. To the elite *Blancken,* Christiansfort, as they called it, stood for stability and protection. From thick stone bastions at the corners, cannon glowered over the bay to ward off invaders from the sea, and the fort had something for the colony's internal enemies, the slaves, as well. Rebels, runaways, and the merely disobedient were jailed inside, then tied to a "justice pillar" by the fort's entrance and whipped. Those sentenced to execution died in a hedged square just outside the walls. To the slaves—that is, to most people on the island— Christiansfort represented fear and violence.[1]

In 1738, the fort became the comfortless new home of one very young female preacher of the Gospel. The colony's leaders, alarmed at the numbers of African men and women hastening up and down the roads to religious meetings, deemed the missionaries subversive, threw them in jail, and sought to stamp out the black congregation. At the heart of the controversy was Rebecca herself, and in her mind, God had summoned her to his blessed prison.

Outside of her duties in the van Beverhout household, Rebecca's life belonged almost entirely to the faith by early 1738. Religion defined her ideas, prescribed her actions, chose her companions. The bands were her family; the hours spent in lessons and worship her only social life. Perhaps it is not surprising, then, that the young white men who taught, prayed, and broke bread beside her day after day should regard her as a potential marriage partner. She was twenty years old in 1738, energetic and devoted to the cause—the perfect combination, as they saw it, for a life partner in God's work. If her mixed-race ancestry raised any doubt, they said nothing in their diaries and letters. The prospect of marrying, in fact, probably reaffirmed their belief that physical differences among believers meant nothing in the eyes of the Lord.

Whether any of them were physically attracted to her, or in love with her, is another matter. There were three white missionaries in St. Thomas at the time: Friedrich Martin, Matthäus Freundlich, and Timothy Fiedler. In theory, their faith required them to spurn romantic love, not because they were ascetics who bottled themselves up in monkish isolation but because marriage served a higher purpose. For the Brethren, wedlock meant *Streiterehe*, "militant marriage," a union born not of romance but of the common struggle to internalize and spread the word of God's love. Marriage between a man and a woman was a sacred institution, the earthly mirror of "the heavenly marriage between Christ and the Church," with the husband representing the former and the wife the latter. Sexual intercourse was a natural act blessed by God, not only for the sake of procreation, but as a symbol of Christ's embrace of the church. During sex, the husband served as a "Vicar of Jesus Christ," fulfilling the "Office of a Vice-God," as a wife was expected to acknowledge. Erotic pleasure and lustful thoughts, however, derived from sin and impurity and needed to be continually cleansed by Christ's grace. Of course, the young men in St. Thomas were not automatons, and while they might have regarded marriage with Rebecca in spiritually utilitarian terms alone, it is also possible that at least one of them, Fiedler, struggled to quell or reconcile romantic feelings toward her.[2]

Never undertaken lightly, marriage involved a complex set of match-making negotiations. Church elders arranged marriages, sometimes after determining that two people should be joined. In other cases, a Brother approached the elders and asked permission to marry a certain woman, or he asked them to find him a wife. Usually they drew lots to pick a name and determine whether the Lord endorsed the match. When the Lord agreed through a positive lot, the elders then approached the Sister and asked her consent. She was free to decline the offer, an option that gave women some voice in the selection of their marriage partners, although they could never initiate the process themselves. In the case of Rebecca, it appears that Timothy Fiedler asked Martin to arrange a marriage with her. Fiedler was not on a secure enough footing to have much chance. He had come to St. Croix as a missionary in 1735 before joining the group on St. Thomas, but he had gotten more interested in making money and had become "estranged from the society of his brethren." Martin still kept in touch with him, but Fiedler's errant ways made it unlikely that Martin would have proposed a match with Rebecca. Nonetheless, Martin approached her in early 1738 to inquire on Fiedler's behalf. "I asked Rebecca whether she would like to marry Brother Timothy," he reported. "She said she sees him as a worldly man, who spends his time playing the violin and is very confused. But she said she would abide by the will of the Lord." Martin pursued the issue no further—Rebecca's lack of enthusiasm effectively vetoed a marriage she had no appetite for.[3]

But Martin decided that, for the sake of the mission, Rebecca should be married. Church doctrine held that people developed spiritual empathy in large measure out of similar life circumstances, so he reasoned that her "work among the Negro women, the majority of whom were married, would be even more effective if she were married herself." Perhaps he thought marriage would improve her relations with the African women with whom she worked. The missionary "also thought that any misgivings concerning the propriety of her close association with the Brethren could be removed if she were married." Martin might have been trying to shield the mission from further controversy. So he asked Matthäus Freundlich to consider the proposition. "I asked my Brother Freundlich whether he wished to change his [marital] status, should the good Lord suggest someone? He answered: Yes. I then explained my mind to him." Martin wrote to the congregation in Germany proposing the match, and "since Rebecca was known to be in the grace of God, as well as a devoted worker and also a free person, the congregation had no objection against such a proposed marriage, which would serve as a means for furthering God's work among the Negroes."[4]

Ever the ambassador, Martin then discussed the proposal with Rebecca herself, but she still found it difficult to agree. "I asked Rebecca whether she wanted to change her status. I asked her several times, but she still gave me no answer, in part from bashfulness and in part because she felt herself too lowly." He applied gentle pressure, as pastors sometimes did when they wished to seal a match. "I explained to her the rules that come from God's word, and how he arranged this order of things. Finally she said: 'God guides our hearts according to his will. Not my own, but my Savior's will should be done.'" Whether Rebecca was concealing deeper reasons for her reluctance behind an outward show of modesty is difficult to know. There is no sign of any personal tension between her and Freundlich, but perhaps she had doubts about their compatibility. Or she might have wondered about the wisdom of an interracial marriage, albeit between two free people, in a society predicated on black social inferiority. In any case, by surrendering her hesitation and submerging personal desire in divine will, she reaffirmed a sense of herself as the instrument of a greater cause.[5]

As the final stage in this elaborate diplomatic dance, Martin took the news to Adrian van Beverhout, who endorsed it, although a few days later he told the preacher that "his wife and Rebecca cried together because she will leave her." Martin then announced the impending marriage to the congregation. "I asked if anyone had any objections? They answered in loud voices they had no objections but were very pleased." A few days later, Rebecca and Matthäus were married on May 4, 1738, in the missionaries' house in Tappus. Matthäus had been battling a fever all day, but no one wanted to postpone the service, so they held the ceremony at ten o'clock after the evening lessons were done. Present were several black brothers and sisters, including Mingo, Flora, and Anna Maria, as well as a few unbaptized worshippers. Despite the sanctity of the moment, Martin noted an uneasiness in the room because of the late hour: "Those that were afraid left, because no Negro should be found on the street after nine o'clock." Nonetheless, after prayers and hymns, Martin asked the couple "whether they would live in the sight of God as married people, and whether they would walk with cheer and courage in their youthful way with the heathen? They answered everything with a heartfelt, Yes, yes." Martin read from the book of Moses, then joined their hands as he quoted from Matthew 19, "What therefore God hath joined together, let no man put asunder." The Lord's spirit, he added, "confirmed itself in our hearts, so that I can truthfully declare that this wedding has taken place in God's true order." For Martin, as with all his journal-keeping in those years, writing about the ceremony was itself a sacred act, and in his mind the marriage was a divine signal. When news came the next day that soldiers had arrested the helper Johannes after the service and taken him off to jail, it reinforced the missionaries' sense of the dangers attending God's work.[6]

Rebecca moved into the Brethren's house, bringing along a load of housekeeping items from the van Beverhouts, "everything that could be of use to her," a gesture they wanted to make "from the heart," according to Martin. The three housemates now constituted the core of mission workers. Matthäus, a shoemaker by trade, brought in most of their income with that craft, which supported a growing family of black children they had adopted—as many as nine by mid-1738. Who these children were, and how they ended up with the mission, is unclear; perhaps they were orphans or free black children whose parents were unable to care for them. Rebecca, whom the Brethren praised as a "faithful house-mother," largely assumed responsibility for their care and education, duties that filled many of the hours she had previously spent managing the van Beverhouts' household. Sometimes she and Matthäus stayed home and taught the children or knitted and sewed with them. "Matthäus and Rebecca are both poor and childlike, and what they are not yet, they seek to become," Martin reported. "In a word, they belong to each other, and not to themselves." Rebecca's main work flourished as never before during the summer of 1738. Brief notations in Martin's journal give a sense of the rhythm of her many activities. On one typical day, "Rebecca was busy with spiritual and practical matters." On others, "Rebecca is very weak but went out visiting anyway"; "Rebecca went to meet with the bands on the plantation which have children who cannot come to town"; "Matthäus and Rebecca have many students among the children at home." Experimenting with new ways to inspire students, the three came up with a "Musique," or musical play, to capitalize on the acting abilities of several congregants.[7]

In July, Martin made what seems like a startling decision—he bought a plantation and slaves. He had not the least moral hesitation or embarrassment about doing so, for he considered it part of the Lord's work. Since the spring, he had been dissatisfied that worldly circumstances had hindered the mission workers. Their house in town was too small to hold the growing throngs of worshippers, and van Beverhout was often harassed by angry planters for allowing the missionaries to hold meetings there. The nine o'clock curfew deterred many slaves from attending class except on Sundays, and they continued to be roughed up on the way to and from meetings. Moreover, Freundlich's work as a shoemaker could scarcely support three adults, nine children, rent, and other expenses from the mission, so Martin considered buying several slaves to help bring in extra income. He must have mentioned that wish to the Brethren's main benefactor on St. Thomas, the Danish planter Johann Lorentz Carstens, who saw a chance to act on it. When a widow, Dorothea Salomon, was banished from the island after having an affair with her sister's husband, her plantation and slaves were confiscated and put up for public auction. Among the widow's sixteen slaves were two baptized congregants, the helpers Anna Maria and Christoph, whom Carstens bought for the mission. Shrewdly, Rebecca urged Martin to try to capitalize further on the planter's largesse. "Listen, since we're forced to go everywhere, ask Mr. Carstens to buy that piece of land for us," she told Martin. "They're asking 300 Reichstaler for it, without the people." Martin put the case to the planter, who responded by buying the plantation and seven additional slaves, which he deeded over to the Brethren. A bill of sale lists the nine slaves as Pieter, the bomba or driver, Jefferi (Christoph), Claes, Sezar (Caesar), Jantje, Anna Maria, Magdalena, Mariana, and "een Meydt," or girl, May.[8]

Just off the Path near the estates of van Beverhout, Hans Clas, and Johannes Uytendahl, the plantation was in the heart of the eastern district known intimately to Rebecca and the other mission workers. The plot, 3,000 feet long and 600 feet wide, was less than ideal as a lucrative holding, packed as it was into a series of steep slopes and narrow valleys that had supported mainly cotton and food crops. But its deficiencies as a plantation were offset by its proximity to hundreds of black Christians who now lived within an easy walk of a mile or less. The missionaries envisioned the place as a kind of sanctified retreat, "incorporating us in His image," where meetings and lessons could take place almost continually, free of harassment. On July 10, 1738, the evening of the purchase, some forty worshippers gathered at the house in Tappus for a thanksgiving prayer; then the next morning Martin and Christoph went out to the site. "They all called out, 'The Lord has done this!' when they saw us, and fell to their knees," Martin wrote. One of the slave brothers could play the trumpet, making it possible to call together worshippers "who respond to the sound of these instruments" from a dozen surrounding plantations. Martin named the place Posaunenberg, or Trumpet Hill, and he, Matthäus, and Rebecca moved there in early August.[9]

The three empathized deeply with the slaves; they regarded them as brothers and sisters in the spirit. How, then, could they even think about buying and holding them as chattel? Here was a fundamental paradox of eighteenth-century Christianity, although the mission workers probably didn't see it in those terms. Europeans like Martin believed that slavery had divine approval, and thus they regarded their ownership of slaves as consistent with God's law. Even Rebecca's views on slavery are hard to determine. Unlike Martin, she knew quite well what it was to be a slave, but like him, she never, as far as is known, spoke against slavery either in public or in private. Nor should we expect her to have done so. Anyone denouncing slavery was immediately subject to arrest and punishment. Rebecca might have opposed the institution in principle but realized she had no platform to speak against it; just as possible is that her religious views led her to endorse a justification of slavery on biblical grounds. Judging by their actions, it appears the three missionaries believed it was more important to fuse slave ownership with spiritual fellowship, thus humanizing slavery. It is also possible they wanted to signal to the planting class on St. Thomas that, by holding bondpeople themselves, they posed no threat to slavery. As for the congregants who cried out "The Lord has done this!"—those who now found themselves owned by the very church to which they belonged—they might have had mixed reactions as well. Some might have wondered how the mission workers could have approved of slaveholding, while others perhaps saw no contradiction at all; many were probably pleased that they at least knew the mission workers well and would find Martin an easy master.[10]

Posaunenberg thus became an odd hybrid of working plantation and spiritual refuge, whose enslaved labor force also doubled as part of a congregation. Worshippers from all parts of St. Thomas immediately made the new Moravian plantation their destination after hours. But the sight of hundreds of black men and women trekking to meetings raised new fears among planters and officials that the mission was a cover for slave insurrection. Rebecca's marriage to Matthäus Freundlich compounded their suspicions. Interracial marriages between free people were not illegal in the Danish colonies, but they must have been extremely rare, if they took place at all; indeed, lawmakers, perhaps spurred by the Freundlichs' example, barred such unions later in the eighteenth century. In the case of Rebecca and Matthäus, black and white social equality undergirded a marriage between two people who preached spiritual equality to the slaves. Though no one ever said publicly that the biracial aspect of the union was a threat to public order, it had all become too much for the planters. They began a campaign to crush the mission through legal means.[11]

On August 27, 1738, Pastor Borm of the Dutch Reformed Church filed a petition with the governor challenging Martin's right to baptize, administer communion, and perform weddings on the ground that his ordination was not recognized by the Danish crown. The charges, if upheld, would mean not only that Martin would be barred from performing essential duties but also that Rebecca and Matthäus's marriage would be ruled invalid and all three could be prosecuted—Martin for unlawfully administering the sacraments, and the Freundlichs for fornication. Martin had been ordained by the Moravian bishop David Nitschmann, one of the original missionaries to St. Thomas, who had since risen in the church hierarchy in Germany; he had mailed a notice of ordination to Martin in early 1737, notifying Danish officials in Copenhagen and St. Thomas as well. Martin began administering the sacraments only after the notice arrived in late 1737. Pastor Borm, however, claimed that the king had never endorsed the ordination, meaning that Martin had no authority to perform church functions. Appealing to the governor, Martin said he had understood such approval to be implied in the king's 1733 decree permitting the missionaries to work in St. Thomas. Until the court clarified its position, the governor allowed him to continue preaching but forbade him to baptize or hold communion. Martin hastily wrote for help to Carl Adolph von Pless, a royal official in Copenhagen who had supported the Brethren's mission, and then began the long wait for letters to travel to Denmark and back.[12]

The missionaries' troubles were only just beginning, as they learned a few days later when they were implicated in criminal charges against their former comrade, the erstwhile missionary Timothy Fiedler. Before finding employment as an overseer on the estate of Hans Clas near Posaunenberg in August, Fiedler had worked on a plantation in St. Croix, whose manager now accused him of stealing valuables from a chest and named Martin, Rebecca, and Matthäus as accomplices. It is not clear whether the accusation was legitimate or merely a trumped-up reason to haul the missionaries into court. Fiedler was arrested and imprisoned in the fort on St. Thomas, and the other three were summoned to testify in lower court, setting up a conflict with their religious beliefs that overshadowed the particulars of the case. Witnesses in Danish court proceedings were required by law to take an oath, but the Brethren, patterning themselves on the New Testament, considered the swearing of oaths to be ungodly.

On the stand, Fiedler testified that none of the goods found in his belongings had come from the plantation, but when the missionaries were asked to verify his statements, they repeatedly refused to take the oath, saying it was a violation of conscience. When Martin was called to testify on September 30, the prosecutor, Jens Aquilin, assured him that taking the oath did not violate the law of either God or the king, and that, in fact, both demanded it. Martin still refused, as did Matthäus Freundlich. What religion do you follow? Aquilin asked. The religion of the New Testament, they responded, offering to supply written testimony as long as they did not have to take the oath. Though the court denied the request, the three nonetheless testified in writing on October 20 "with full awareness of Jesus Christ our Savior" that, to the best of their knowledge, Fiedler's trunk contained only some tools and a few other commonplace items. The court refused to accept the testimony as valid.[13]

Over the next four months, Martin and the Freundlichs were in and out of court at least half a dozen times on different charges, shifting from witnesses to defendants themselves. Three versions of those proceedings and the events surrounding them have survived to give valuable clues about their motivations. Rebecca's testimony is particularly important, for it helps to reveal sources of her belief that other documents do not. One version is contained in Friedrich Martin's journal and in a long diary-like letter he wrote to church leaders in Germany on October 30 describing their ordeal. This account describes the missionaries' actions, and some of their conversations in court, shortly after they occurred. A second Moravian account of the events was published nearly forty years later by the missionary and historian Christian Oldendorp, who used and followed Martin's descriptions closely while supplementing them with other documents. Like any history, Oldendorp's contains certain biases—in this case, he believed the protagonists were agents of God forced to transcend unjust roadblocks. And a third account, a vital addition to these Moravian versions, is provided by a collection of extracts from Danish court transcripts. These records contain several important exchanges between the missionaries and the prosecutor not reported in the other descriptions. Though they reflect a different point of view, the Danish extracts do not contradict the Moravian accounts; they depict a version of the defendants' view of themselves that is remarkably consistent with their own writings. Each of the three versions, then, contains segments of significant testimony not included in the others that, when pieced together, yield a composite portrait of who Rebecca, Matthäus, and Martin considered themselves to be.[14]

Rebecca's statement before the court on October 6 reflects the value of these complementary—and occasionally countervailing—accounts. Neither Martin nor Oldendorp described her testimony, perhaps because they believed she simply echoed what Martin himself had said a week earlier. But the court extracts report her words in enough detail that it can be seen that she articulated the missionaries' rationale clearly. When the judge attempted to swear her in, she, too, declined to take the oath, saying: "Christ had commanded in the 5th chapter of the book of Matthew that they were not allowed to swear, but that their speech should be Yes, Yes and No, No." The text from which she drew was Matthew 5:34–37, the Sermon on the Mount again: "I say unto you, swear not at all; neither by heaven; for it is God's throne: . . . but let your communication be, Yea, yea; Nay, nay: for whatsoever is more than these cometh of evil." Prosecutor Aquilin tried again, repeating that it was no violation of God's law to take the oath. The judge reminded Rebecca of her duty to the laws of God and the King, warning that she would be prosecuted for refusing. Still she would not back down, insisting that the court accept her testimony as "Yes, yes, and No, no" without an oath. The judge rejected the appeal but allowed her and the others to leave the courtroom and return home for the time being.[15]

Martin sympathized with the court officers, who, he believed, were honest men baffled by the dilemma the witnesses posed, groping for answers without proper guidance. "They have great anxiety about our case, so that one would like to console them," he wrote. "Jesus, help them through and let them arrive at a breakthrough. We are preparing only to suffer." The mission workers thus set up the dispute as one between God's law and mere legalism that needed only a flash of divine light to be resolved.[16] Though Martin wanted to believe that the officers were well-intentioned on their behalf, his own letter reveals the judge's mounting frustration and hostility. Again in court on October 21, their exchange with him went like this:

> The judge said, "Will you swear?"
>
> I answered: "We remain with Jesus and his word, we wish to tell the truth from our hearts."
>
> "Will you swear?" he asked Matthäus.
>
> "We can do nothing else but stay true to the Savior's words."
>
> "Rebecca, will you swear?" She gave the same answer.
>
> Then he spoke to me: "Do you have 10 Reichstaler [imperial dollars] to pay?"
>
> "I cannot collect that much money."
>
> "Do you have any security?"
>
> "No."
>
> "Who owns the plantation?"
>
> "Mr. Carstens."
>
> Then the bailiff asked: "Have you read of the false prophet?"
>
> "Yes, his works are clearly described."
>
> "Then you must pay 30 gold Reichstaler in three days, or we will confiscate everything you have."

The judge seems to have concluded that the Brethren were charlatans, and the reference to the "false prophet" suggests his own desire to show he knew something about religion too. Outside court, Martin went to Governor Friedrich Moth to appeal for help, but was told that legal decisions were out of his hands. Unable to pay the fine, the missionaries went back to Posaunenberg and awaited their fate.[17]

For Martin, it was important to record their attempts to fortify themselves and the congregation spiritually for their coming arrest. On the night of October 24, they held a lovefeast on the plantation.

Two hundred black brothers and sisters left their quarters to attend, giving a huge show of support for the besieged trio. Secretly defying the governor's orders, Martin baptized ten people in anticipation that he might not have another chance to do so: "These ten were baptized because we will soon be under arrest, and the governor has forbidden me to baptize any more. I thought, though, that as long as our feet are unbound, I cannot let this chance go." The candidates were led forward to the baptismal water by the workers, who served as witnesses. "We went to the baptism with Psalms and hymns, pointing out the sorrow they should expect, because some of them are with hard masters." Regardless of their own punishment, Martin's account suggested, the church's survival was assured.[18]

The next day, at four in the afternoon, the bailiff, prosecutor, and several soldiers came out to the plantation. The missionaries greeted them "as friends," welcomed them to the house, and even served coffee. Agitated, the bailiff tried to reason with them by quoting from the book of Isaiah, finally saying that he wanted to help them if they would let him, to which Martin enjoined him to be "true to his own conscience." With no options left, the soldiers arrested them—almost apologetically, Martin thought—and the group marched off to jail, with the three prisoners singing hymns. Spectators gathered to watch as the procession moved along the Path into Tappus, and children, noted Martin, asked, "Why are they arresting them, what have they done?" At the end of their march, they entered the gates of Christiansfort.[19]

Inside, slaves were held in a "foul detention hole" under the fort, but other tiny jail cells built into the thick walls looked out on a central courtyard on the main level, and it was in one of those that Rebecca, Matthäus, and Martin were probably confined. As word of their incarceration spread, the fort became an even greater symbol of persecution to Africans, who gathered outside the iron bars to listen as the prisoners inside sang and prayed. "They all came to our window, Negroes and *Blancken,* soldiers and others, to hear us preach,"

"Fort Christian, St. Thomas" (Christiansfort), by Camille Pissarro, 1852. Courtesy of the Ashmolean Museum, Oxford.

wrote Martin in a letter from jail. "The Negroes were chased away but came back again; those Negroes who previously hated us now grieved for us, and their hearts were deeply moved." Carstens visited to give support and bring a bottle of wine, while Fiedler, whose case had begun their trials, was released from jail and came to their window to apologize (the charges against him were later dropped).[20]

It was as though the three were following a script written by the apostles. Each element of the ordeal confirmed their sense of destiny: the self-perception as a New Testament people on God's errand, the refusal to compromise their faith, Rebecca's insistence on the literal command of Jesus, their arrest and imprisonment, the strengthening of followers and the winning over of enemies through their own persecution. Enduring the test would demonstrate their own worthiness to serve God's cause. "Since we are here to spread

Jesus' words, we can do so only as he preached them, and if necessary we will bear witness with our blood," Martin explained in a petition to the fort commandant asking that their case be resolved quickly. "We need make no other *Scrupel* than that we believe the words of Jesus and the Apostles as he preached them. . . . Body and soul belong to Jesus, because they cost his blood. We remain willing to explain the truth before God and his deliverer, Jesus Christ." They had read the Acts of the Apostles. When, during one hearing soon after their imprisonment, the judge asked about their identity papers, Matthäus said they carried such documents but reminded him that the apostles did not. They knew that Paul, accused of being a "pestilential fellow and a mover of sedition" who did "exceedingly trouble our city" and "teach customs which are not lawful for us to receive," was arrested, beaten, and imprisoned in Philippi (Acts 24:5, 16:20–24).[21]

As for Rebecca, the lessons from her childhood came into sharper focus under duress. She had always liked stories of the martyrs, possibly because she admired their courage on trial; now she had been given a divine chance to emulate them. "Let us seek no one," she said. "Jesus is our intercessor, and that is enough for us." Standing up to authorities who could take away freedom was not something one did on a whim, and it was the clearest illustration yet that she considered herself a tool in God's hand, ready to serve and, if necessary, to sacrifice for his purpose.[22]

Their case got worse, however. When nothing changed in several more court appearances, the judge doubled their fine to sixty imperial dollars, then tripled it; their ability to pay did not rise correspondingly. They languished in jail. During the day, their cell was close and hot in the tropical autumn, but at night it got so cold they could see their breath, and Martin became sick. The commandant at least allowed them out to walk about the courtyard. The two men made buttons and wrote letters, while Rebecca sewed. As they waited, they prayed constantly, sang hymns, and taught slaves through their window. In all of these actions they again emulated their models, the apostles, as in Acts 16:25: "And at midnight Paul and Silas prayed, and sang praises unto God; and the prisoners heard them."[23]

Outside the bars, they learned in November, plantation owners were using increasingly sadistic violence in an attempt to keep black worshippers away from the missionaries, and from Christianity altogether. One master, Lucas Uytendahl, made a practice of setting the slaves' Bibles on fire, and then "his wife and children laughed as he hit them on the mouth until the burning books were extinguished." The planters, wrote Martin, "admitted that the Negroes had gotten such good teaching from no one else, and the *Blancken* could not get it for big money. [Uytendahl] asked a Negro whether he was still going to the Pietists. He answered: 'Yes, master, we can't help it, the word we hear is too sweet. We have never heard from your sects the kind of words we are hearing now.' Uytendahl was quiet and went away." Planters and slaves alike understood that the missionaries' struggle involved larger stakes, and enslaved Christians were willing to endure considerable ferocity to continue their devotions.[24]

The vigil went on. In late November, after the missionaries had spent a month in jail, Martin's illness deepened and he grew weak with fever and diarrhea, even fainting several times, so Carstens petitioned the governor to let the preacher come home with him to recover. The governor agreed, and Rebecca and Matthäus were left alone in the fort. When Martin regained some strength after a week, he went to see his friends back in jail, and his description of the visit reveals not only the sense of forbearance undergirding the couple, but several more surprising layers of Rebecca's persona as well. One was a practical skill. "I was still weak and had an earache and a bad headache when I got to the fort," Martin wrote. "When they heard that I was coming, they both met me at the door and led me inside. Rebecca warmed up my head with her hands and warm towels, then she put cooked onions in my ear until midday. I went home, lay down, and felt better." On top of everything else, it appears, Rebecca was a healer. The medicinal properties of onions were a well-known feature of colonial folk cultures, and presumably she would have known something about the mix of African and European remedies that employed the plentiful array of indigenous plants on St. Thomas. In American slave societies, healers held status and spiritual power. There is no way to tell whether Rebecca practiced her healing arts often enough to be known widely as a folk doctor; her prowess might have been only ordinary. It is also possible that her knowledge gave her additional clout in the slave community as a kind of Christian *obeah* practitioner, a manipulator of the spirit world. Either way, medical knowledge simply added to the arsenal of abilities that made her the versatile doer and fixer upon whom people depended.[25]

Martin also described how a sailor had been imprisoned at the fort for a long time with nothing to eat, so Rebecca gave him some money. Giving charity was part of her ethics, not despite, but especially during, her own ordeal. Did someone require a translator in yet another language? While his ear was stuffed with onions at the jail, Martin observed this exchange: "Soon an Englishman from another land came to us and asked from where we came. Rebecca answered him in English, and I recognized [her response] from the Testament. He was greatly astonished and went away." English was once her primary language, and she had not lost it even after many years of speaking Dutch and Creole, retaining the ability to quote conversationally from the Bible in English at a moment's notice. Perhaps, in fact, she had gained her first exposure to the Scriptures long ago while still a child in Antigua. In any case, the exchange again underscored her ability as a mediator in this multilingual environment, even while in prison.[26]

She and Matthäus waited with little inkling of the direction their case would take. In late November the authorities switched tactics, renewing the legal assault, as court papers described it, against

"Matthias Freundlich and Rebecca, a mulatto, and their scandalous life as a married couple without lawful marriage." While Martin's ordination remained in limbo, Rebecca's former employer, Adrian van Beverhout, along with Jan de Wind, anticipating this ploy, urged the two to spare themselves another long battle over principles by remarrying in the Lutheran Church, but they declined. To marry again would be to admit that Martin was unqualified, undercutting the entire mission.[27]

On December 15, Aquilin, the prosecutor, questioned them intently about the wedding—when it occurred, who witnessed it, what Martin had said. It had taken place in Tappus at ten o'clock in the evening after class, they said, and it had been witnessed by "our Brethren the Negroes," including Mingo, Flora, and Anna Maria, as well as several others whose names they could not remember.

"What sort of ceremony did you have?" the prosecutor asked.

"Brother Martin put us together and asked if we would live in the sight of God as married people, then we gave each other our hands and he read from the Bible," they answered.

"Do you know how marriages are consecrated in the Lutheran Church?"

"Yes, but we are not of the Lutheran Church, but of a small congregation by ourselves."

"Do you not know that you need permission from the religious authorities to get married, and that the banns must be published?"

"Yes, but it is enough that we were betrothed to each other and married before God," said Matthäus. "We are a congregation instituted by God, even though we are still only three souls, who find in ourselves the spirit and awe of God."

"Do you not have the same religion as the Lutherans, since it is the same word of God?"

"Anyone converted to God, any black person, Jew, Greek or heathen, may unite with us and God and be of our congregation," Matthäus said, "but God's commands have been obscured since we are now told that we may not observe them, even though everything is possible for God." Such testimony contained a significant twist on the famous passage from I Corinthians 12:13: "For in one Spirit were we all baptized into one body, whether Jews or Greeks, whether bond or free; and were all made to drink of one Spirit." By including blacks in the list, he tailored the ancient text to the situation on St. Thomas.

Is it not true, the prosecutor asked, that everyone should observe the law of the authorities? They wanted to do so, Matthäus and Rebecca answered.

"Why are you not willing to be married by the Reformed minister?"

"We have already been married by Brother Martin."[28]

Tired of their stubbornness, the prosecutor ended the interrogation and summed up his case:

Matthias Freundlich should be considered an unemployed person who is to pay his fines and be deported because of his deliberate violation of the law. In the same manner, the mulatto Rebecca, as a person brought up on this island in the Reformed religion, shall be punished according to the law and submit to the discipline of the church. Furthermore, because of her disobedience against the law of the King and warnings of the authorities she is to forfeit everything she owns, or else be arrested and put on bread and water until she makes amends and the congregation helps undo the scandal.[29]

In attacking their "scandalous life . . . without lawful marriage," prosecutors seem to have sought a pretext for assailing the far more significant issue of interracial marriage. But why, then, were the authorities willing to let the pair remarry? The offer was probably a bluff, since court officials knew the couple had to decline, or else admit that Martin was a fraud. If so, the court's strategy was to corner the Freundlichs with their own principles. The escalating legal challenges against the couple signaled the authorities' desire to break their defiance, ultimately undermining their dangerous appeal to the slaves.

Back to jail went Rebecca and Matthäus to await the judge's verdict. Even then, the two could have submitted, agreed to swear the oath, and taken vows administered by Borm, the Reformed pastor. But another week behind bars changed nothing. Siding with the prosecutor, the judge ruled that the teachings of the Brethren were "contrary to the commands of God and the King," and that Rebecca had been "seduced by the heretical religion of these people, which is in conflict with what she was previously, namely Reformed." The marriage was to be considered illegal, and if they would not consent to be remarried they would be banished "since their unchristian and scandalous living on this small island causes great disturbances." Matthäus would be expelled from St. Thomas, barred from the other Danish islands, and fined one hundred dollars. If he could not pay he would be sentenced to life behind bars at Bremerholm, the imperial prison in Denmark.

Rebecca was sentenced to be excommunicated from the Reformed congregation and fined her entire fortune. Since she had none, however, she would lose her freedom and return as a slave to Adrian van Beverhout. Her value was put at two hundred dollars. The couple went back to prison to contemplate their fate. Like Martin, they, too, were growing weak from their ordeal, and they were about to serve life sentences.[30]

The verdict may seem harsh, even shocking. But Rebecca might not have judged her sentence in those terms. She knew, as all freed people did, that liberty in a slave society was ephemeral, easily and legally retracted by the authorities. The sentence was entirely to be expected, and her own stance helped create the circumstance that jeopardized her freedom. She knew exactly what she was doing. She had refused to bow to the court twice—to take an oath or to deny the validity of her own marriage. Her words and actions suggest that Rebecca did not see herself as a victim. From our vantage point, she was forced into a terrible choice, but standing before the judge, perhaps she believed there was no choice to make. Given one chance after another to back down, she declined, understanding full well the punishment that awaited. Compromise would have meant betrayal, and now she would become a slave again. By refusing to remarry, she doomed her earthly marriage but fulfilled the vows to her heavenly union with Christ. That was the obligation of a "militant marriage." And if, earlier in life, she had connected Christianity to emancipation from slavery, now she was saying the opposite: freedom of the spirit was more important even than that of the body. Here was the essential idea behind her voice, the force driving her to walk over the mountains and hold meetings till late at night. She embraced martyrdom. Claiming the radical ethics of the Sermon on the Mount as her guide, she saw herself as making a stand for her religion, for black Christianity, for all time.

Or did she? Perhaps it is more accurate to say that Rebecca simply did what she believed God required her to do, without any self-conscious fanfare about grand issues at stake. There is no hint in the transcripts or diaries of her wavering. But martyrs can have doubts, too. Did she ever consider accepting the court's offer of a deal? Was she afraid? Did she think herself courageous? Or was that emotion a luxury she could not afford? The records do not say. It is improbable that she saw herself in heroic terms, since she had been schooled to believe that pride and self-gratification were sinful. And even though self-sacrifice had its logic and its rewards, it is at least as likely that she and the Brethren preferred not to offer themselves up if it could be helped, given the important work they believed was yet to be done.

Rebecca and the others might also have thought that obeying the command of Jesus would inspire black worshippers through a demonstration of principle. The slaves had followed the missionaries' ordeal closely, watching to see who would give way first. The debate, theologically and legally, was ultimately about them, and their own stake in Christianity depended on the outcome. Whatever their understanding may have been of the doctrinal issues involved, it was pretty plain to enslaved brothers and sisters that the harassment of the three defendants was an attempt to suppress their teachings and, perhaps, drive the mission out for good. Had Rebecca and the two men given in to the pressure, they might well have been seen as weak and their teachings exposed as fraudulent, which the missionaries well understood. How much confidence could the sight of Matthäus and Rebecca renewing their vows under pressure inspire? It was as though she was sending a message to black Brethren that, although they might not always like her or her style, she was willing to be a slave again too. She held them to a high standard, but it was no higher than the one she set for herself.

The defendants' willingness to bear punishment earned them huge credit in the slave quarters, where, according to Oldendorp, "the love and respect of the Negroes for their teachers intensified as a result of their mutual suffering." Now the worshippers mobilized their own elaborate leadership network to keep the congregation afloat. Anticipating trouble even before the imprisonment of Martin, Rebecca, and Matthäus, congregants had elected two elders, Zacharias and Abraham, to serve as "general ministers," while the helper Christoph and seven others were elected as "special ministers"; all were consecrated by Martin. The difference between the two offices is not clear, but no matter: as a democratically chosen council, they represented the popular will to continue with meetings. The sense of persecution ignited a whole new awakening in the quarters. As the missionaries sat in jail, the helpers Christoph and Anna Maria at Posaunenberg, reported Martin, "held school with the workers from the congregation. . . . They remain true to their work." Brother Mingo held class and supervised worshippers in town. Under these leaders, operating virtually autonomously, church membership increased from 450 to 650 during the winter of 1738 and early 1739.[31]

This surge of activism became the new focus of the court, revealing the authorities' ultimate intention of wiping out the mission. As Rebecca awaited re-enslavement and Matthäus imprisonment, prosecutors began a court inquiry into their teachings. This time, the investigation involved a different set of respondents: black Christians themselves. On January 25, 1739, planters were asked to bring to the fort all their slaves who had been baptized by Martin to submit to an examination by court officials, Pastor Borm of the Reformed Church, and the pastor's council. Martin was summoned, and presumably Rebecca and Matthäus looked on as well. As planters and ordinary citizens gathered to watch, the inquisition became a public spectacle that must have been terrifying to the slaves, who were asked by Borm, individually and in groups of two, what they had learned from the missionaries.

The minister focused first on the sacraments. As recorded by the planter Carstens, who observed the interrogation, the exchanges went like this:

Question: "In what were you baptized?"

Answer: "In Christianity."

Question: "In any other name?"

Answer: "In the name of the Father, the Son, and the Holy Spirit, that is the name of the triune God, we were baptized."

Question: "What is baptism?"

Answer: "The washing away of sins by means of not only water but also the Holy Spirit."

Question: "Where does evil come from?"

Answer: "We have inherited it from our first parents, Adam and Eve; but in the new life, God's spirit prevails."

Asked to explain the meaning of communion, respondents "declared that it was bread and wine and that, if one believes, one receives the body and blood of Christ through it."[32]

Thus far, their instruction had prepared the witnesses well for Borm's inquiry. When the pastor began asking more involved questions about Christian doctrine, however, they faltered. Martin interjected that "the poor slaves could not be expected to answer such questions on the spur of the moment," and in an attempt to protect them, he "started to examine the Negroes in a more comprehensible manner. However, he was soon deprived of that option and was ordered not to utter a single word during that investigation." Borm's questions became increasingly aggressive, revealing why he and the planters held the Brethren in such suspicion:

> The Negroes were asked if Friedrich Martin had ever implied that his own faith was better than that of the Lutheran or Reformed persuasion; whether he had complained about the suffering and persecution to which he had been exposed; whether he had told them that come resurrection day Blacks will be ruling the Whites. They were also asked if he had given them anything other than bread and wine during communion and if he had asked them to pay him or serve him as compensation for the instruction he had offered them. Such questions were either not answered or answered very briefly by the Negroes.

The slaves denied that Martin had said his teachings were superior, or that he had complained of persecution, or that they had paid him anything for lessons. As for the "alleged rule of Black over White come resurrection day," one unnamed woman answered simply: "After death, we will be with God, and there we will all be equal."[33]

When the court adjourned after a day of testimony, Matthäus and Rebecca returned to their cell. But those parting words from an enslaved sister framed this woman's understanding of the trial. Any promise of equality with whites, even if only in the afterlife, was a risky statement before a hostile court. Yes, yes, no, no; after death we will be equal. Like Rebecca, another Afro-Caribbean woman invoked the Scriptures to proclaim her truth. Called as witnesses in a court of law, they used the opportunity to testify in God's court as witnesses to his word.

The belligerent waters of the north Atlantic in winter seldom filled eighteenth-century voyagers with a sense of comfort. Those brave enough to embark at that time of year were usually prodded by necessity or desperation to face a transatlantic journey of two months or longer. Freezing winds slashed at passengers and crew; giant waves could smash a ship to splinters. None of this mattered to an energetic 38-year-old man who boarded a vessel in the Netherlands in late December, 1738, bound for the Caribbean. He was Count Nikolaus Ludwig von Zinzendorf, the leader of the Moravian Church, and though he had little experience with sea travel, he was determined to inspect the progress of the mission in St. Thomas, which he had closely followed for years through the letters of Friedrich Martin and others. After an unusually short voyage, his ship entered the harbor at Tappus on January 29, 1739, and he came ashore to the utter surprise of the Brethren there, for he had told no one of his plan to visit. If the beleaguered prisoners needed any further validation of their place in a divine plan, it had arrived, a dark-frocked *deus ex machina* come to save them.

The Count had left Europe before Martin's letters had arrived telling of the missionaries' desperation, so he had no idea of their predicament. Accompanied by two mission couples who had traveled with him, Georg and Maria Elisabeth Weber and Valentin and Veronia Löhans, Zinzendorf arrived on St. Thomas just four days after the slaves' testimony. He made his way to Carstens's plantation, astonishing the planter and Martin, whose "joy was indescribable," according to Oldendorp's history. They quickly brought him up to date on their ordeal. Zinzendorf himself recounted his own version of the arrival on St. Thomas in a story he told some years later:

I left the others on board ship and took Weber with me on land, and there my first question was: "Where are our Brethren?" Domingo from Poppo answered: "They are all in prison, Friedrich Martin was lying deathly ill in Karstens' house, and the others were in the fort." I asked further, "What are the Negroes doing?" Answer: "They have stayed together and there are five or six among them who have taken on [leadership of] the others." I proceeded on to see Friedrich Martin the same day, and the following day I went to see Rebecca and her husband, who looked *miserabel,* just like carcasses. They had sat in the hole for fifteen weeks, and their fate would have been to perish there.

The next day the Danish governor of the island, Friedrich Moth, visited the Count, who pleaded for the temporary release of Rebecca and Matthäus. As an aristocrat with connections at the court in Copenhagen, Zinzendorf had the kind of clout the missionaries lacked—the governor came calling on *him.* He persuaded Moth that the jailed Brethren were harmless and should be freed. Eager not to make martyrs of the prisoners, the governor saw the Count as an authority with whom he could negotiate a solution. He agreed to the request and ordered a furlough for the couple, claiming he had never sought their incarceration in the first place. Their release was intended to last only a few days while the governor and Zinzendorf further discussed their fate, and that of the mission in general.[34]

Miraculously, it seemed to the Freundlichs and other Brethren, God's intervention had given them a temporary reprieve. After four months in jail, a string of court hearings, and receiving life sentences that would separate them forever, they were free, if only for a short time. More important, they now had a powerful defender on the island, whom Rebecca and Matthäus went to visit upon their release, escorted by a government officer. The Count and the former slave were well known to each other by reputation: he, the guiding light of the Unity, and she, the mulatto sister mentioned so often in Martin's letters, the tireless worker on the Lord's frontier. Zinzendorf "kissed these two prisoners of the Lord on the hand, in the presence of the officer who brought them with compliments from the Governor. They were, especially Freundlich, more dead than alive after fourteen weeks in captivity. Their hearts were filled with inexpressible joy and astonishment at how wonderfully the Savior had arranged things, and their hearts were filled with praise and gratitude for the help accorded them in their desperate need."[35]

Remarkably, in the aftermath of their release, it was reported that Rebecca had actually foretold the event exactly as it happened. The story was told by Zinzendorf at a church synod in Germany later in 1739, where a scribe recorded it: "The Brethren in St. Thomas had languished for three months. Two days before Zinzendorf's arrival, Freundlich said to Rebecca, 'I would dearly love to leave this prison.' Rebecca said: 'If we are to leave, the Saviour will send us a key, perhaps Count Zinzendorf.' In two days came Zinzendorf, and two days later they were given permission to leave the prison." Whether Rebecca had actually made such a forecast is impossible to verify. It would seem to have been an astonishing display of telepathy. Perhaps divine inspiration or semi-delirium indeed caused her to make the remark. Or did she or Matthäus spread the story to highlight the miraculous nature of the deliverance and enhance her image as some kind of oracle? Did the Count himself concoct the tale to dramatize further his mythic role as God's rescuing angel, whose spirit was so implacable that an imprisoned martyr could sense its onrushing force? Whatever the explanation, the story created a powerful spiritual bond between Rebecca and the Count, and it did endow her with a prophetic mystique that underscored her leadership capabilities in the eyes of church leaders, and possibly of black congregants as well.[36]

When she had rested and regained a bit of strength, Rebecca herself reflected on her experience in prison a few days later in a letter written in Dutch to Anna Nitschmann, the leader of the Single Sisters group in the Herrnhaag congregation in Germany and one of the most powerful female leaders of the church in Europe. Whether it was Rebecca's idea to write, or whether she was encouraged to write by the Count or someone else to demonstrate her thanks, is not clear. Either way, the letter was intended as heartfelt testimony to God's inscrutable power by one woman reaching across the ocean to another. The letter is also valuable because it is one of only four written by Rebecca known to have survived, and one of the two in her own hand. Her writing is a rough scrawl, and the right corner of the letter is smudged and illegible. But her meaning is clear:

S Tomas, 16 feb
anna [illeg.]
My dear Sister [illeg.] if I his voice [illeg.] but oh, how I must be ashamed because of my disobedience and unfaithfulness that I again [illeg.] daily I have spent 15 weeks in prison and I have enjoyed sweetness in prison we were brought 7 times before the court and if I was brought before the justices it was sublime to me that the dear Savior used me poor worm to testify the 30 January we came out of prison through his miracles. The count is the key that he used to get us out of the prison the 30 the dear Sisters arrived on Son Tomas we have received each other with great joy my dear Sister, time is short and I am a bad writer so that I can't express in words as I would like remember me in your prayers I have here among souls in great [illeg.] that he decides I kiss your foot and hand and [illeg.] I greet you affectionately from our dear sister marilies and my husband and from martin and greet all brothers and sisters kiss the sisters' hands the savior be with you amen I greet you very affectionately your poor slight sister Rebecca[37]

Returning to the motif of the Count as divine key, she praised him as the instrument of a higher will. But she also saw herself as such a vehicle. Voicing not a word of complaint about her ordeal, Rebecca chastised herself instead for disobedience and unfaithfulness. Prison was foreshortened to a sweet experience; the harsher her trials, the more sublime was the knowledge that God was working through her miserable form. As with the ancient martyrs, blessedness was earned in proportion to suffering. Her letter was a survivor's testament, but it was also a gentle shout that something greater had happened. It is possible, of course, that Zinzendorf or Martin coached her on what to write. Referring to oneself as a poor worm

Rebecca's letter to
Anna Nitschmann,
1739. Courtesy of
Unity Archives,
Herrnhut, Germany.

beneath the Lord's awesome majesty was a standard rhetorical technique of Pietist thought generally and Moravian expression specifically, and Rebecca probably learned the device from the Brethren rather than in her Dutch Reformed upbringing. But perhaps she had simply grown accustomed to thinking of herself in those terms and needed no further instructions on writing the letter, putting her thoughts down as they came. In any event, the sentiments she expressed were consistent with her words and deeds in court and prison. The letter contained no hint of artifice, no ideal she had not already lived.

This sense is reinforced when the letter is compared with a second one, dated the same day, in her name, but written in a different, more elegant hand. Someone must have thought her letter needed more polishing and elaboration if it was to be presented, perhaps even read aloud, as suitable testimony of God's marvelous grace. The second letter is a rewrite of her original, kneading many of her ideas into a smoother flow. The doctored version is for the most part properly punctuated and capitalized, and full of florid phrases. "Dear Sister Nitschmann," wrote "Rebecca":

The Savior has shown me his eternal love so I may rise mute and see for myself that I was not worthy but to be cast off from his holy countenance and to cry with the bad spirits, oh, for ever, so that I could do nothing else but fall down and cry out: o lamb; o lamb, give mercy to me, poor worm. And he has shown me how full of mercy he is. So I will no longer love myself, but give myself willingly to him, with body and soul, to do his will. I have prayed to him that if there was a drop of blood in me that did not want to be obedient to him, for him to reveal it to me and take it away and I have a great hunger after the souls. And the dear Savior has put me in the midst of the souls, as I wished, I am a child of mercy, so I pray that you do not forget me in your prayers. There are 600 and 60 here, who come to us to learn there are many among them who are very [illeg.] we were in prison for 15 weeks and 7 times before the court. But I tasted true sweetness there, and while I was brought before the court so many times, it was very sublime that the sweet Savior wanted to use me for that purpose. On the 29th the merciful Count arrived on St. Thomas, and he is the key the Savior sent to open the door, the 30th we got out and the dear long-awaited Sisters have received each other with great joy, the Savior be praised above all. We are very well-contented with each other. I have no time to give you more details, and I can't express myself as I would like. I greet you all affectionately and kiss your hand and foot, and pray you kiss the hands of the dear Sisters, and greet all the dear Brothers the Savior be in you and with you, amen. I remain your poor slight but faithful sister Rebecca Freundlich[38]

Whether the second letter, also in Dutch, was written by a church official or by a missionary in St. Thomas is unclear; the handwriting is neither Martin's, Zinzendorf's, nor Matthäus's. Someone in Germany might have written the letter months later after Rebecca's original arrived, but the scribe would have had to have access to other documents to be able to add such knowing phrases as "there are 600 and 60 here who come to us to learn." In any event, the rhythmic cadences of this version give the feel of having been used before. Only a practiced narrator could deliver such flourishes as "I was not worthy but to be cast off from his holy countenance" and "o lamb; o lamb, give mercy to me, poor worm." By contrast, Rebecca's unpolished original sounds as though it was written by someone just out of prison, a person convinced she was a worm, but who did not, or could not, embellish her own wormhood with fine language. In evangelical fashion, writing was an extension of her sensation. She wrote as she felt, not as someone else wanted her to feel. She admitted being a "bad writer," but writing well did not automatically put anyone closer to God.

Rebecca's stand in the courtroom clarified to herself what her life had been about. Her letter was the exhilarated testimony of someone who had just realized what she had done. She had passed God's test and proved to be his worthy servant. Her trial and that of Matthäus and Martin, moreover, had become a fulcrum for a larger struggle over the meaning, and the fate, of black religious fellowship on the island. The three had stood firm, joined by hundreds of enslaved men and women determined to preserve their fragile spiritual domain. That struggle, however, was far from finished.

The Devil's Bargain

Count Nikolaus Ludwig von Zinzendorf hit St. Thomas like the hurricanes that batter the Caribbean each autumn. Exuding self-assurance and unlimited vigor, he came across to his many enemies as arrogant and imperious at best, a heretical charlatan at worst. To some, his militantly Christ-centered religious ideas gave off the whiff of derangement. His words often had immense appeal to ordinary people, particularly the oppressed and downtrodden, but his aristocratic worldview alienated others. Stumbling into the volatile controversy over the mission among the slaves on St. Thomas, he immediately polarized everyone—as he did everywhere else he went—in this case, along the fault lines of race and freedom. By rescuing the missionaries, the Saxon Count became an instant celebrity in the slave quarters and an anti-hero to most of the planters. "The Negroes have received him as an angel, but the citizens look upon him as a devil," wrote the Danish governor, Friedrich Moth. Zinzendorf's charismatic presence energized black worshippers and provoked a violent reaction from whites. Soon after Zinzendorf's arrival, armed horsemen, determined to drive the mission out for good, crashed into prayer meetings, raining blows on the slaves, who defended themselves with Bibles and hymns. By the time the Count left the island just a few weeks later, his short visit had created far-reaching repercussions for black Christianity, which had been articulated as never before by Rebecca's stand in the court-room.[1]

The great irony was that the man who played such a crucial role in eighteenth-century Afro-Protestantism knew almost nothing about Africans, empathized not at all with their bondage, and was interested in them only as potential souls for Christ. Born in Saxony in 1700, the Count had already established himself as one of the most controversial figures in the religious reform movement known as Pietism, which sought to introduce greater emotion and spiritual-ity into worship in the Lutheran Church. Educated at the Pietist academy in the eastern German town of Halle, he began develop-ing in early life his view of Christ as the lodestar of the spirit—Christ the divinity, more important even than God himself. In his early twenties, Zinzendorf rejected his family's wishes that he enter government service, dedicating himself instead to the church. The Moravian refugees who sought sanctuary on his estate in 1722 be-came the new focus of his attention, especially after they reorganized in 1727 as the Renewed Unity of Brethren—not a separate church but a branch of the Lutheran Church loosely affiliated with Pietism. When, in Copenhagen in 1729, the Count heard the Afro-Carib-bean servant Anton Ulrich's tale of plantation life in St. Thomas, he eagerly seized on the possibility of the Brethren becoming Christ's agents in overseas missions. His interest was entirely spiritual. Al-though Zinzendorf almost certainly had seen Africans in European courts and universities, none of his training or outlook reflected any interest in worldly concerns such as African slavery in the Americas. He was a feudal lord who believed in a conservative social order and whose tenants on his Saxon estate helped support the mission work through their labor.[2]

The Count's position in Europe was precarious, however. He was disavowed by former allies in the Pietist movement who viewed his patronage of the religious settlement and charities at Herrnhut as a threat to their own institutions. When a neighboring baron com-

Nikolaus Ludwig von Zinzendorf, by Balthasar Denner, 1731. Courtesy of Unity Archives, Herrnhut, Germany.

plained that too many tenants had left his land to seek refuge on Zinzendorf's estate, the Saxon court banished the Count from his lands in March 1736. For the next two years he traveled constantly across Europe, setting up new Moravian settlements and gaining ordination as a Lutheran bishop, which was intended to give the Brethren greater respectability and clout. It was during this exile that Zinzendorf decided in the fall of 1738 to visit St. Thomas, leaving before word arrived of the missionaries' ordeal.[3]

The Count's first steps on the island in late January, 1739, were his first anywhere outside of Europe. Whatever his reaction may have been to the sight of African workers unloading cargoes or sweating in the fields, he did not write it down. Instead, he charged into action as if he were a veteran of the West Indian scene. After obtaining Rebecca's and Matthäus's release, he continued lobbying the governor to guarantee the missionaries' freedom from harassment, which was still uncertain since no letter had yet arrived from the Danish king confirming permission to preach. He wrote an affidavit asserting the validity of the Freundlichs' marriage "in accordance with the customs of their church, and that this action was well justified on the basis of the privileges accorded to the Moravian Brethren, who, belonging to Christ's community, practice the principles of religious freedom; further, that they owe no one an explanation, but they have been married without offense to the Holy Name." These measures proved effective. What was to have been a temporary release from jail was extended by the governor, and the couple did not return to prison.[4]

Zinzendorf also met with influential men to try to convince them the mission was harmless, but they remained unpersuaded. In one interview, when the Count told Jacob Schonneman, a planter and vice-commandant, that the apostles had died for their beliefs, the official brushed him off, replying that the missionaries had no business baptizing slaves, that planters didn't want their workers tired after late-night worship, and that slaves probably just used the meetings as a pretext for planning rebellion.[5]

This last complaint remained the heart of the matter: the planters were terrified of slave insurrection. Willemsen, the court bailiff, who had been so active in the prosecution of the missionaries and was bitter about their release, spelled out the case further. "A man so dangerous as Martin should not be free," he wrote in protest to the governor. The bailiff accused the Brethren of sneaking into the country without permission and "seducing" the slaves. He criticized the planter Johann Lorentz Carstens for abetting the missionaries "against his oath of allegiance as a citizen" by holding religious meetings with hundreds of slaves on his plantation without their masters' knowledge, even acting as doorkeeper. By buying a plantation for the Brethren, Carstens allowed them to hold nightly meetings where "they act ungodly and careless with the sacraments." The planter, charged Willemsen, "even allows his two Negroes Mingo and Andreas to act as teachers, to teach (though they mostly seduce) other inhabitants as well as Negroes. Sometimes they go to other plantations and sometimes the Negroes go to the Salomon plantation [Posaunenberg] at night to learn this religion that Mingo and Andreas themselves do not know, and that is not approved at any college, academy, or faculty, or by the king. They do not teach according to Luther and the catechism but bring dangerous books to the country and thereby harm the absolute power of the king." Here was a potent mix of threats—dangerous missionaries in stealthy collusion with a renegade planter to fuel the popular enthusiasm of slave teachers and worshippers.[6]

The memory of the St. John revolt, just five years past, was still uppermost in the planters' minds. They were also aware that the St. John incident was part of a determined, and extensive, effort during the 1730s by enslaved Africans throughout the Americas to throw off their shackles. When, in 1735, authorities uncovered a massive plot—partly inspired by a veteran of the St. John affair—in Antigua, 200 miles to the east in the Leeward Islands, they executed dozens of suspects. A cycle of smaller, but still threatening, revolts broke out across Caribbean and North American plantation societies before being put down. "The contagion of rebellion is spread among these islands more than I apprehend is discovered," wrote a governor of the Leewards in 1737. The decade ended with a violent outburst in Stono, South Carolina, where Africans in the rice-growing colony killed about twenty whites in September 1739 before being subdued. The Dutch and Danish planters of St. Thomas, outnumbered as badly as the slave masters in all these other places, likewise saw themselves as imperiled, and Afro-Christianity intensified the threat. A Moravian preacher on his way to St. Thomas in

1739 was told in Copenhagen that some colonial officials believed "the surest way to have a Rebellion in St. Thomas in which all the *Blancken* would lose their lives is to continue tolerating the Herrnhuters."[7]

The struggle over evangelical slave religion was spreading elsewhere in the hemisphere at about the same time, partly as a result of Moravian influence. The Brethren planted a small settlement along the Savannah River in the new colony of Georgia in 1735; then in 1738 they began a mission among Africans across the river in Purrysburg, South Carolina, which lasted several years. Two of the founders of Methodism, John Wesley and George Whitefield, had been impressed by the Moravian sense of piety, which they emulated when they preached in South Carolina and Georgia in the 1730s. Like the Brethren, both men reached out to enslaved Africans, many of whom turned out to hear the charismatic Whitefield on his itinerant journeys through the South Carolina plantation country between 1738 and 1740.[8]

Followers of Whitefield began forming biracial Methodist fellowships. After experiencing a mystical vision, one planter, Hugh Bryan—something of a counterpart to Carstens on St. Thomas— even held evangelical meetings with his slaves and proclaimed "sundry enthusiastic Prophecies of the Destruction of Charles Town and Deliverance of the Negroes from servitude." One observer in 1741 overheard "a Moorish slave woman on a plantation singing a spiritual at the water's edge." Other reports complained that Bryan's slaves were learning "a Parcel of Cant-Phrases, Trances, Dreams, Visions and Revelations" and that they did "nothing but pray and sing and thereby neglect their work"—all of this cause for alarm by planters after the Stono revolt, and all familiar echoes of what whites on St. Thomas had long feared. The colonial legislature censured Bryan and he renounced his visions, but evangelical Christianity had already taken hold in low country slave quarters.[9]

Events on St. Thomas prefigured the conflict in South Carolina.

At a public meeting on February 11, 1739, more than thirty planters angrily criticized the Brethren and Zinzendorf, then signed a petition to the governor asking that they be barred from further teaching and kicked off the island. Planters who wanted their slaves to learn Christianity, they claimed, could hire their own preachers. Still waiting for the king's directive, Governor Moth took no action and reassured the Count that the missionaries could stay.[10]

Meanwhile, black worshippers gave Zinzendorf a different reception. Three days after arriving, he held a prayer service with the congregation, noting with pleasure "the heartfelt and forceful supplication to the Savior by the dear Brother Abraham, a Negro worker." Eight days later, on a Sunday at Posaunenberg, "about half the plantation Negroes, who have turned to the Savior and given their troubles to Him, visited me, and had hardly any room to stand in the great hall." He described the meeting as a success: "The Lord makes them willing; they came in multitudes, and . . . they gave me their word, they would turn to Him."[11]

The Count installed some new practices in the mission. To spare many congregants the long walk to Posaunenberg from other parts of the island, he created a new preaching post called Little Northside at Pearl, Carstens's plantation in the western central mountain district. He created a new fleet of leaders and recruiters, building on the core of helpers that Martin had installed in 1738. The slave brother Petrus was consecrated "dear elder" of the men, the free African sister Magdalena "venerated evangelical elder" of the women. Seven people were appointed as assistants to the congregation, including five European men and women, plus Rebecca and the slave brother Abraham. Rebecca, along with four slave men and women, also became a servant to the congregation, while four men were designated "admonishers" and another, Mingo, was appointed "keeper of the alms." Mingo, Andreas, and Abraham received the titles "blessed and accomplished teachers of the heathen," while the sister Anna Maria became a "faithful helper." Whatever the distinctions may have been among this confusing hydra of offices, they carried honor and prestige for their title-holders while reaffirming a sense that the congregation was guided largely by its own representatives.[12]

Zinzendorf also began a practice used in European Moravian congregations known as the *Stundengebet,* or hourly intercession. "Twenty-four persons were selected, including both white and black workers, who were to see to it that not a single hour of the day or the night should pass without prayer." Each person, including Zinzendorf himself, was assigned to pray during a specific hour. This precise use of clock management in religious devotions—a spiritual economy of time—was an extraordinary feat to attempt when many of the hourly watchers were plantation laborers on rigorous work schedules. "Since the discipline of fieldwork made such a practice impossible to maintain during the daytime, they used the night for that purpose. Even during fieldwork, they made arrangements by means of which they took turns in praying to God and asking for His intercession every hour of the day. In the absence of a clock, they determined the approximate hour by the stars and by the crowing of the cocks. In this way one slave awakened the next whose turn it was to pray during the next hour." If the planters knew about this arrangement—and it is not certain that they did—they would have seen it as one more infringement on their control over workers' time. And they could not have been pleased at the image of a German nobleman participating in rituals alongside African bondmen and women, further fueling the idea of racial equality.[13]

Having gained a reprieve for the mission workers, at least until the king's permission arrived as anticipated, the Count prepared to leave St. Thomas after only about two weeks. His last order of business was to meet with black congregants "at the express recommendation of the governor." On February 15, 1739, Carstens opened his house in Tappus for the meeting, and some three hundred African and Afro-Caribbean worshippers filled a large room. The Count delivered a speech in Dutch, which the helper Mingo translated into Creole. It soon became clear why the governor had urged him to make the address, for Zinzendorf delivered the strongest proslavery statement yet by the Brethren.[14]

He was gratified, he told the assembly, that so many had found their way to Christ, but he expressed fear that "the devil and the world will be paying you considerable attention. If you do not remain faithful and if any of you who have heard the gospel, and particularly those who have been baptized . . . should waver, the world will ridicule you, and the devil will denounce you before God, our Lord." He warned them to think only of their souls when they sought Jesus.

A heathen must have no other reason for conversion than to believe that Jesus, Son of God, his Lord, has died in order to pay for the sins of men and now lives again to enable them to live with Him. A heathen cannot be naturally inclined to do as much good as a man who has been taught to do good and to avoid evil since childhood. For a heathen is accustomed to evil since his youth and has not learned anything better. When, however, Lord Jesus grants him forgiveness for his sins and he is washed by His blood, he is empowered to forsake all evil and to do good. He now hates sinning as much as he used to like it.

He urged them to "deal honestly with Martin and the others who instruct you" and not to "pretend to be better than you are." All this prepared the way for his real message. "Remain faithful," he said, "to your masters and mistresses, your overseers and bombas, and . . . perform all your work with as much love and diligence as if you were working for yourselves. You must know that Christ himself puts each one of his children to work; for the Lord has made everything Himself—kings, masters, servants, and slaves. And as long as we live in this world, everyone must gladly endure the state into which God has placed him and be content with God's wise counsel."

Not only did God create slavery, said Zinzendorf, but he intended Africans to be enslaved as a divine curse which they must patiently bear. "God has punished the first Negroes with slavery. The blessed state of your souls does not make your bodies accordingly free, but it does remove all evil thoughts, deceit, laziness, faithlessness, and everything that makes your condition of slavery burdensome. For our Lord Jesus was himself a laborer for as long as he stayed in this world." Though he, the Count, had been born free, he now devoted his life to work as Jesus had done, and as they must do. With that, Zinzendorf blessed his audience and bade them farewell.[15]

To appease the planters, and as part of a quid pro quo for releasing the missionaries from jail, it appears that the governor wanted his august visitor to make explicit to the slaves that Christianity was no ticket to freedom. The Count obliged with gusto. With his aristocratic and Lutheran heritage resonating in every word, he invoked a standard set of ideas deeply embedded in Christian doctrine: the social order was ordained by God, and to disobey was to defy him. The idea that Africans were punished with the stain of slavery for the sins of Noah's son, Ham, had a somewhat different genealogy, but Europeans had used it since the fifteenth century to justify the African slave trade and the plantation system in the Americas. The heathen, who were inherently evil, could purify themselves with Christ's blood, but that cleansing freed only their spirits, not their bodies.[16]

Did Zinzendorf actually believe these notions, or was he simply telling the slaves what the governor and the planters wanted to hear? It appears that both were true. The governor had clearly urged him to emphasize to the slaves that Christianity would not bring them freedom—a position that the Count himself shared. In previous writings, he was firmly on record as endorsing a divine social hierarchy, in which he had no trouble including slavery, and he fully agreed that the enslaved had no business seeking liberation. He had not been so explicit in connecting Africans to what he saw as the divine rightness of slavery, but he gladly made that argument as well.

It was a pivotal moment in eighteenth-century Afro-Christianity. To save the mission, the Count articulated positions that would become the Brethren's party line on African slavery in the Americas, their trump to the planters' hostility. The Brethren, courageous advocates of the slaves in so many ways, now enslaved themselves to biblical and racialist defenses of bondage. The radical impulses that had driven them just a few years earlier—celebrating the slaves as God's chosen people, criticizing the planters as cruel and ungodly—would begin to drift away. Now they promised to become the planters' best friends. How the three hundred black listeners responded to the Count's speech is less certain. According to Oldendorp, they were "moved both by the content and the delivery of the count's speech, promised to remain faithful to their Savior until death and wished the count a thousand blessings on his return voyage." Listening as the Saxon landlord urged them to accept their enslavement, however, they concealed any other reactions they might have had, which must have been considerably more complex than the missionary allowed.[17]

Despite his best efforts, Zinzendorf's words won over few planters that day. After the Count finished speaking, the slaves left the plantation to follow him back to town. A gang of whites attacked the slaves with clubs and swords, beating them badly, and then rushed to Posaunenberg to assault the worshippers who had stayed behind, smashing furniture and glass in the meeting house. Taking their fury out on the slaves, the assailants little realized how far the Count was willing to go to placate them.[18]

In the face of this new violence, and still emboldened by the Count's protection, black leaders tried a tactic of unprecedented daring.

They drafted several letters to the king and queen of Denmark imploring them to intervene and stop the beatings, allow them to study the Scriptures in peace, and end the missionaries' persecution. Africans in the Americas did not ordinarily write petitions to European monarchs. Rare as it is to find any letters written by the enslaved, it is still rarer to uncover missives with the salutations "Merciful King!" and "Great Queen!" as these begin, going over the plantation masters' heads to request royal protection against those who had the power of life and death over them.

One letter, dated February 15, 1739, was written in Dutch Creole and signed by the helpers Petrus, Mingo, Andreas, Abraham, Magdalena, and Anna Maria, as well as Rebecca, "in the name of over six hundred and fifty black scholars of Jesus Christ taught by Baas Martin." The signers proclaimed their determination to continue worshipping "despite all the oppression by those who have come to beat and injure us when the *Baas* teaches us about the Savior, by those who burn our books, call our baptism the baptism of dogs, and call the Brethren beasts, declaring that Negroes must not be saved and that a baptized Negro is no more than kindling wood for the flames of hell." The imprisonment of Martin and the Freundlichs, complained the petitioners, was an attempt to drive out the mission. They emphasized the positive effects of Christianity on their own lives: "We want to remain obedient to our masters in all things. We used to steal from our masters, run off as maroons, run away to Porto Rico, indulge in laziness, and pilfer provisions from our masters. But now it is otherwise with us, as our masters themselves well know. Many a Negro has suffered the amputation of feet and hands as punishment for his pursuit of evil. As for ourselves, we would gladly place our heads under the axe in defense of our congregation and for the sake of Lord Jesus, if our masters have us killed, as they say. May the Lord bless our most merciful king a thousand times."[19]

A second letter, by Mingo's mother, the free African-born elder Magdalena, sounded a similar theme:

Great Queen!

At the time when I lived in Papaa [Popo], in Africa, I served the Lord Masu. Now I have come into the land of the Whites, and they will not allow me to serve the Lord Jesus. Previously, I did not have any reason to serve Him, but now I do. I am very sad in my heart that the Negro women on St. Thomas are not allowed to serve the Lord Jesus. The Whites do not want to obey Him. Let them do as they wish. But when the poor black Brethren and Sisters want to serve the Lord Jesus, they are looked upon as maroons. If the Queen thinks it fitting, please pray to the Lord Jesus for us and let her intercede with the King to allow *Baas Martinus* to preach the Lord's word, so that we can come to know the Lord and so that he can baptize us in the name of the Father, the Son, and the Holy Spirit.

Of these two remarkable letters, Magdalena's stands out in particular, because she wrote or dictated it in her native language from the Gold Coast, signing it with her African name, "Damma," perhaps to emphasize her Africanness. Someone then translated the letter into Creole, adding the phrase "in the name of over two hundred and fifty Negro women" above the names "Marotta or Madlena of Poppo in Africa." The original words and sentiments, however, could only have been Magdalena's own because they reflected her African experience. Appealing across the ocean to the bonds of female empathy with the Danish queen, the letter was born of an optimism that, if only the higher authorities knew how badly the slaves suffered for trying to be better Christians than their masters, surely they would intervene. Grounded in a belief that Christ was her protector and literacy her weapon, Damma/Magdalena's letter is ex-

XII.

Der Aelteſtin der Gemeine der
Negros in St. Thomas Schreiben an die
Königin von Dännemarck.
An. 1739.

Ne acadda.

CAbe my le ad ga Tome minge bruhu
mau , mi wago voltomé, Gewoma
dihé, na mangi Bruhu Ajuba malle na mado
wi tu ma gagni na mu , quaſſi nangi netto
dy a Wo Du Gowo maja powo Dn. Poppo
leoſi , Mia meyji diké bowo dn. mille dikbe
migeé Meacadda nadak be no vo Dn Mau
e na dak bena Anibà daſſi ſala Martinus na
doclio na mi naſſé na mi angé vo Dn. na
coſſi de tami , denikó Do Batrœ Mau lé
Mau mé agnisà ne a cadda.

*Minzu Gnonù en ho
ma poppo!*

Damma.

Uberſetzung ins Cariolische.

Groote Koninginne.

DIe tyd mi a wes na Poppo op Africa ,
doen mi a dint die Heer Mau , nu ko-
me na blanco land , mi no wilt gu din de
Heere. Mi no ha di grond vor tú dien die
Heere ; mi ben bedrœv na min herte , voor
dat Negrinne no kan dien die Heere Jeſus in
Thomas , die Blanke no wil dien die Heere.
Lat ſo as ſili wil , maar ſoo de povre ſwarte
Brœders en ſuſters wil dien de Heer Jeſus ,
ſo mœt zilli dœn , as ſi bin maron volk. As
Neacanda belyv , gy mœt bidde de Heere Jeſus voor ons , en bidd ook A Niba , voor la
ſtan Bas Martinus prek de Heere woord ,
voor ons mœ leer voor kenn de Heere , en
voor Doop ons Negers , op Naam des Va-
ders , Sons en Hilig Geeſt. Die Heer be-
waar ſinder , en ſeegene ſinder , ſon en doch-
terlen , heel Familie , en mi ſal bid den Heer
Jeſus voor ſinder.

Ob naam van over Tweehondert en
Vyſtig Negersſen Zrouwen , die
den Heere Jeſus beminnen , ge-
ſchreven door

Marotta
nú
Madlena
van Poppo uyt Africa.

Letter from Marotta/Magdalena, in a West African language (perhaps Fon) and Dutch Creole translation, *Büdingische Sammlung*, 1741.

traordinary as an act of self-assertion and as a documentary record of African language and thought in the Americas.[20]

Who hatched the idea for the petitions? It is not clear. Several manuscript copies of each survive, all written in unknown hands, making it difficult to tell who put pen to paper. Their rhetoric in places (assigning the blame for amputations on the slaves' "evil," for example) might indicate the heavy hand of a white author or editor, and it is possible the missionaries staged the whole thing themselves, appealing to Danish royalty behind an elaborate Afro-Christian smokescreen.

It is just as likely, however, that the helpers themselves devised the plan, or that it welled up from the hundreds inside the enslaved Christian community. Canny black authors trying to convince distant monarchs might well emphasize their own depravity as a ploy to gain sympathy while boldly pointing out the ungodliness of their white tormenters. Several literate helpers were capable of writing letters. One possibility, for example, is Mingo, or Domingo Gesu, the violin-playing overseer on Johann Lorentz Carstens's plantation, who had proved to be a crucial intermediary between missionaries, planters, and slaves, and who had translated Zinzendorf's words into Creole as the Count addressed the three hundred assembled black Christians. It is doubtful, moreover, that the missionaries would have used helpers' names in such a scheme without their consent, knowing the potential punishments that awaited. Whatever the collaboration may have been—if any—between missionaries and black Christians in conceiving and composing the letters, at the very least, African and Afro-Creole helpers were heavily involved in producing and signing them—an audacious act in the face of violent retaliation.

Promising to send the petitions on to the monarchs, Count Zinzendorf left St. Thomas on February 16 for the Dutch colony of St. Eustatius. From there he intended to proceed to the Moravians' new settlement in Georgia, but his plans changed and he returned to Europe in the spring carrying the letters. Their subsequent history transcended the struggle on St. Thomas that had spawned them. Presumably the Count sent the letters to Denmark, although the reaction of the king and queen is unknown. Aware of their Christian publicity value, however, Zinzendorf had them published in Germany two years later, in 1741, in the *Büdingische Sammlung*, a collection of tracts, letters, and diaries from diverse corners of the Moravian world. Mingo's letter was printed, in its original Dutch Creole, under the heading "The awakened *Negros* in St. Thomas write to His majesty the King of Denmark." Magdalena's original African text was published, along with a Creole translation, as "The

Eldress of the Congregation of *Negros* writes to the Queen of Denmark."[21]

From the *Büdingische Sammlung,* the letters were picked up and published, in 1744, in English translation by an evangelical journal printed in Edinburgh called *The Christian Monthly History: Or, an Account of the Revival and Progress of Religion, Abroad, and at Home.* The liberal translations varied considerably from the original texts. "Remember most Gracious Queen, the Sighs of the poor *Negroe* women, whose Souls I bind on your motherly Heart" was a sentence not included in Magdalena's own version, and the author was identified as "Anna Van Popo." Still, as missions to the "heathen" were becoming a subject of increasing interest to Europeans, this Afro-Christian testimony would inform many English-speaking readers for the first time of a thriving, though oppressed, congregation of Caribbean faithful. If the names Mingo, Anna Van Popo, Abraham, Rebecca, and others did not become household words, they at least humanized the abstract idea of African-American people striving for the cause of Christian worship. Within a few years, British evangelicals eager to convert slaves in the West Indies and North America would point to the example of St. Thomas as their blueprint for action.[22]

In the meantime, life on the island got rougher for the congregation after Zinzendorf's departure in early 1739. As punishment for having gone to see the Count, one slave brother, Gottlieb, was beaten by his master and sent to St. Croix for construction work. Planters pressured the governor to enforce a sundown curfew on slaves and to station patrols in each district; anyone caught off-plantation after hours would be taken to the fort and given thirty lashes. Believing that black Christians were included in the governor's temporary edict granting freedom to worship, the Brethren nonetheless continued holding services as usual, further enraging their opponents.[23]

On February 23, a Monday evening, a posse of six armed white men came to Posaunenberg during evening prayers. They had caught the helper Abraham and another man out on the Path, bound and beaten them, and now claimed they had orders from the governor to stop the meeting. Friedrich Martin asked to see the order, and when they could not produce it, he continued the service. "As we were praying, a drunk, Adrian Rondels, came through the door with his bare sword and pistol, shouting as we sang," he wrote.

> Two of them went and beat up the children until they all jumped out the window and wherever they could. The men stood by the door with swords and guns. No one was badly hurt, except Hans Clas's Elisabeth, who was hit on the head with a bare sword before our eyes, and on the first blow the blood poured through her bandana. He continued beating her, but she could not escape because of the baby on her back. Adrian Rondels stood before me with bare sword and pistol and said: "Hold your tongue." But I began to sing with all our members and said not a word. Then they beat the bound Negroes and shouted at me, "Brother Martin, come out and see!" Then they left, and we heard them shouting as we sang. The Negroes all came back and praised Jesus that they should be considered worthy to suffer for Him. Peter and Abraham prayed with tears for their attackers.

Abraham, perhaps in shock after the assault, or releasing nervous tension, "could not stop laughing that he had been so badly beaten and stabbed." Keeping a defiant sense of humor about the attack, however, he took the cords with which he had been bound and sent them back to the marauders "with apologies that he could not help that they were torn."[24]

Two nights later another group of whites came to the plantation, but finding few slaves there—the nightly meeting had been called off—they confiscated books and interrogated the mission workers about their teachings. Witnesses identified the men as Uytendahl, father and son, Rosenstang, Creutzer, and Molg, at least some from prominent planting families. "We remained quiet and gave short answers to their questions. Then Rebecca, who stood by herself, began to sing. They went up to her and Rosenstang asked, 'What are you singing?' 'Of the Savior,' she said. 'Of the devil, you mean,' he said to her, and threatened us with his bare sword and pistols. He asked her: 'In which grave have you found the Savior?' Finally Creutzer came into the room riding a white horse, and as he rode around the room they said, 'Here comes the devil.'" The men read aloud the governor's order that no slave was to be found on their plantation or on the Path after dusk upon penalty of thirty lashes. "They said that Rosenstang wants to give us double that amount and throw us in the black hole," wrote Martin. "They said: 'What have you to do with our Negroes? They are our capital, we can do what we like with them, we can chop their heads off, or whatever we wish.'" As they left, the missionary Valentin Löhans closed the door. "They said, 'You slam the door in our face?' Valentin said: 'This is our house.' They said: 'You have no house here.'"[25]

In the days following these threats, black and white Brethren kept a low profile. Perhaps thinking their work of intimidation done, the night riders stayed away. The helper Peter suggested that worshippers divide into small groups and meet in secret hiding places in the bush while a lookout kept watch. Walking on the Path, Martin met many men and women who admitted their timidity about returning to the school, but gradually they began trickling back as the threat of white violence eased. The workers rested. In Martin's description of one day's activities in early March, "Matthäus and Valentin made shoes. Veronica has much to do. Rebecca is sick and does as much as possible, with meals and whatever she can." Quietly, the helpers again sought out their band members. "Veronica and Rebecca went visiting in the village . . . On the 19th, they came back again to see Anna." Martin, Peter, and Abraham went to hold communion with Magdalena, who was ill and unable to leave home. Black congregants continued to worship on their own, in secrecy. "Their urge to know Jesus Christ and to experience His mercy was strongest whenever they were subject to pressure and suffering on account of it," wrote Oldendorp. "When they were forbidden to attend the regular meetings in which their teachers were to preach the gospel to them, they did not fail to take pains to visit them in private. They also compensated for the loss in instruction resulting from such a ban by getting together in small groups on their own plantations for purposes of mutual edification. By going into the wilderness of the bush, many of them found a safe retreat." The slaves' interest in Christianity remained high, not simply despite their persecution, but, perhaps, because of it.[26]

Rebecca's energy and ability with languages anchored her in the center of all this. Perhaps energized by a sense of destiny from her prison experience, she pushed herself harder than ever. Her new partner in the mission, Veronica Löhans, who along with her husband, Valentin, had accompanied Zinzendorf from Germany, was a little awed. "What can I tell you about Sister Rebecca?" she wrote to Anna Nitschmann in April 1739. "I have great love for her. She has the courage to work day and night bringing the word to the souls. Everything depends on her, because of the language. The Lord gives her a warm heart." Veronica's brief testimonial provides another glimpse of Rebecca in action. We can envision her in perpetual motion, walking the roads again, meeting privately with women, or shuttling between bands during a mass meeting, translating between German, Dutch, and Creole, at which most of the missionaries remained unskilled. If "everything depend[ed] on her," she must have felt an acute sense of personal fulfillment during these busy months. As a newcomer to St. Thomas, Veronica had much to learn from an experienced hand like Rebecca, and doubtless felt her own reliance on her mentor keenly.[27]

That dependence might have led to a sense of rivalry or jealousy on the part of either woman, or both, who were nominally coequals in directing the women's mission. Though she mentioned no specific incident, Veronica was noticeably less enthusiastic in another letter to Nitschmann written just a few months later: "What can I tell you about Rebecca? It would greatly please me if she would come to know the Savior more sincerely." Presumptuous it may have been for Veronica to snipe at someone who had nearly been re-enslaved for the sincerity of her belief. But Veronica, born in 1706, was twelve years older than Rebecca, and it is possible that she tried to assert a more senior place in the hierarchy. If Rebecca felt her authority threatened, words might well have been exchanged, for their shared devotion to the cause did not give them immunity from the human emotions that complicated the task. As she had shown, Rebecca was not known for backing down. Still, the stresses of the common task demanded coexistence. The Löhans, who had been staying at Carstens's house in town, moved to Posaunenberg in October 1740 to assume management of the plantation; this meant that Veronica and Rebecca had to share a house and would have had to find ways to live and work together.[28]

Count Zinzendorf himself, who read all the reports from the West Indies, might have obliquely addressed concerns such as Veronica's when he wrote to St. Thomas from London in September 1741: "To my Sister Rebecca I wish with all my heart that, as I was the key to her prison, so she should have the luck to find the key to the heart of the Lamb, and to let her see His wounds from inside and out." Though it seems puzzling that her spirituality would be questioned after all that had happened, no one in the church ever assumed that anyone's knowledge of the Savior was sufficient or secure. Constant exhortation of others to unlock Jesus's inner secrets was simply part of their daily litany. What the Count, like Veronica, seems to have regarded as Rebecca's unquiet spirit might simply have been the feisty personality of the congregation's most tenacious fighter.[29]

The church had a well-defined protocol for resolving differences. When congregants, including married couples, had a disagreement or personality clash, they were urged to solve the problem through prayer and rituals of reconciliation like the lovefeast. But in the case of a special ceremony like communion, quarreling parties or bickering couples, or even those filled with doubt—anyone with an impure heart—abstained. For one communion, it was reported, "Matthäus Freundlich and Rebecca stayed away, because there is something between them that they have not yet worked through."[30]

While the mission workers sorted out their private frictions, Governor Moth intervened to protect them by forbidding further attacks on their persons or property. A turning point came when the king's proclamation granting them license to preach finally arrived in June 1739, removing some of the pressure on them. Whether the king was responding in part to the black petitioners' letters is unknown. Nevertheless, for six months and more, Afro-Christian converts and their allies had to wage a fierce battle against hostile planters to keep their congregation alive. Fueled by the sense that they were engaged in a mighty struggle, they used whatever means they had at hand—letter-writing, secret meetings, self-organization, a vast capacity to endure suffering, and the willingness of advocates like Rebecca, Magdalena, and Abraham, as well as their white allies, to stand on principle. Had they not done so, the king's decree would ultimately have been meaningless, for there would have been no congregation to minister to. But the price of this new security was high: they would need to take extra care not to offend the authorities, and the mission workers officially committed themselves to a theology at peace with slavery.[31]

Rebecca, as Martin mentioned, was briefly sick in early March. She might have been showing signs of morning sickness, for some time in February, evidently, she became pregnant, after she and Matthäus were released from jail, perhaps during a spare moment when they were not fending off assailants. No mention was made in the mission records of Rebecca's pregnancy or the delivery itself, but she seems not to have slowed her daily activity before giving birth to a daughter, Anna Maria, on November 13, 1739. The child was baptized by Martin two days later. Probably of three-quarters European descent and one-quarter African, Anna Maria would likely have been considered a quadroon under the racial classification of most West Indian slave societies. Tellingly, however, Martin or some other Moravian record-keeper put her name first on a new list of "white" children born to mission workers in the West Indies.[32]

Rebecca had some experience with children, having been a foster mother to nine children adopted, or taken in, by the missionaries in 1738. What became of those children during the months she sat in jail is uncertain. In 1740, three children were reported as part of the church family at Posaunenberg—apparently given to them by free black families—and Rebecca was again appointed their caretaker. "I will be her helper, and the others will assist as well with advice and action," wrote Christian Israel, a new missionary on the scene. Even now, while caring for her own child and the others, Rebecca's pace did not slow. She resumed her long trips into town and through the countryside; she taught classes and oversaw band meetings at Posaunenberg. In West Indian fashion, she hauled her infant around in a sling on her back. "We all went out visiting," Martin noted. "Rebecca went with little Anna Maria." There is no mention at all of Matthäus's relationship to the child, but Martin took a liking to her. "Rebecca and little Anna Maria send their greetings, especially to the women and children," Martin wrote to the congregation in Germany in May 1740. "Anna Maria is a good child. She is six months and a few days [old]."[33]

Martin even found an opportunity to do some research into Rebecca's own family history. In June 1740 he traveled to New York to restore his health, which had suffered after years in the tropics, and to meet with Count Zinzendorf (although, unknown to Martin, the Count had already left for Europe and the meeting never took place). In August he returned by way of Antigua, Rebecca's birthplace, where he used the occasion to ask around about her, since all he really knew about her past was that she had been kidnapped there some fifteen years earlier. "He inquired about Rebecca Freundlich's mother but could find out nothing about either her or her family, except that an old free Negro woman knew that Rebecca had been missing." He tried evangelizing among the slaves there, "among some with no effect, but others appeared eager to seek the kingdom of God, and he was sorry to leave them." Though Martin's search proved inconclusive, his oral history project reflected an abiding respect for Rebecca as a person as well as a broader interest among Pietists in genealogy as a wellspring of Christian belief—a desire to connect believers' personal history with the divine plan. It also revealed that, in this slave society where people arrived and vanished all the time, part of Rebecca's history lived on in the mind of one woman, at least, recalling the child who had disappeared years earlier.[34]

After Martin's return to St. Thomas, the uneasy truce between planters and missionaries did not necessarily make things easier for the congregation. Many slaveowners, still resentful of the mission, settled into a campaign of retribution against the slaves by sending them to the "justice pillar," the whipping post at Christiansfort. "A Negro woman was whipped at the fort over her desire to convert," wrote Israel. Though forbidden to attack the missionaries, planters still threatened them sometimes. On the Path one day in 1741, Martin met a planter who said, "'Listen, I have something to say to you. Don't teach my Negroes to be Pietists, or you'll know what I will do.' I left him, and wished him good day. That evening the Negroes came to tell me how he was out for me, and how he was watching them. I urged them to be patient, that he would grow weary. He has already beaten them twice over it." Threats of violence continued for years. On nearby St. John, the missionary Jacob Tutweiler received permission to preach on a plantation in 1744, but when he finished, "the manager grabbed him by the arm and started to beat him in a most cruel manner . . . berat[ing] him with severe threats, indicating that he was not about to allow him to come again to lead his Negroes astray." Tutweiler eventually died from the thrashing.[35]

For the hundreds undeterred by the terror, worship became a much more elaborate and scripted enterprise. The early days of prayer meetings held on the fly, in a field or a house, gave way to a carefully orchestrated schedule of services and activities adopted by the missionaries in the summer of 1740. The roving ministry continued; male and female black helpers visited plantations with numerous converts once a week for private and group conferences. Prayer and study meetings were held at Posaunenberg each night, and on Tuesday, Saturday, and Sunday converts from particular plantations were summoned to worship and for band meetings. On Sunday morning, congregants gathered on the plantation for Bible study class; then in the early afternoon, baptized members and baptismal candidates attended a large meeting. At five o'clock the admonishers held a conference, followed by the visitors' conference at five-thirty, then a children's meeting, another general meeting at six-thirty, and finally prayer by those serving in the hourly intercession. Many of these changes were instituted by the new missionary, Christian Gottlieb Israel, who took over during Friedrich Martin's four-month absence in 1740. Israel sought to create a more systematic worship format from all the elements put in place by Martin and Zinzendorf during the previous four years.

Alarmed as planters were that hundreds of Afro-Caribbean men and women were plotting insurrection, the converts themselves came to regard Posaunenberg as their refuge for worship and social activity. Since the meeting house was too small to accommodate their growing numbers and many services were held outdoors, even in the rain, they began building a new hall in October 1739, which, by working on Saturdays and Sundays, they were able to complete in September 1741. Perched on the side of the hill overlooking the

Posaunenberg (Neu Herrnhut), St. Thomas, 1757. Courtesy of Unity Archives, Herrnhut, Germany.

Path, the meeting house reflected the builders' proprietary sense of spiritual investment in their sanctuary.[36]

But the mission workers also made concessions to new realities. Concerned that enslaved worshippers did not fully understand the Christian message and were backsliding into "heathenish" ways, they simplified their message, deciding to "preach among the Negroes on nothing other than the cross of Christ, that is to say, the Savior's suffering and death as a redemption for our sins." They did not spell out the implications of this theological stripping-down, but it likely meant the end of the radical criticism of the slaveholders that had infused their preaching five years earlier. In addition, suspicious that many worshippers were merely feigning interest in Christianity to gain literacy, they restricted the time-consuming lessons in reading to students they deemed sincere. "Meanwhile, there were many among the believing Negroes who could already read and who could themselves give instruction to the others," they reported, and eventually, the missionaries' "growing work load forced them to suspend such efforts altogether, thus relegating all future reading instruction to the Negroes themselves." Behind a literate cadre, black Christians—and perhaps those less interested in the religion—mobilized even more urgently than before to teach and lead each other.[37]

If mission reports are to be believed, never was enthusiasm for the Gospels higher among black men and women. Daily, Martin claimed, they came to him asking the way. "Whenever one goes out, one can hear someone here in a sugarcane field, someone there in the bush or from behind a house, praying and crying out to the Savior, asking Him to wash away his sins with His blood." Dissemblers who wanted only to learn to read were gone, leaving the sincere to grope with their own sinfulness. Perhaps Martin exaggerated, or perhaps the slaves had learned how to give a well-timed shout of praise as he rounded the corner. The spectrum of worshippers' motivations surely ranged from those who sought only the social and material advantages of literacy or fellowship, to those who embraced Christianity as a religion of deliverance, with many degrees in between. But something kept them trudging the Path by the hundreds to Posaunenberg.[38]

The physical and mental strain of the mission, the constant pressure and the opposition of powerful men, wore down even the most vigorous worker. Rebecca, Matthäus, and Martin were all exhausted by the summer of 1741. In September, when Martin planned to return to Germany to rest and seek medical treatment for an eye ailment, Rebecca and Matthäus, who "had also longed for some time for such a voyage," decided to come with him. As required by Danish law, they requested, and received, permission from the governor to leave, and on November 15 the three, along with the Freundlichs' daughter, a boy named Coffee, or perhaps Cuffee, who had been in Rebecca's care, and a convert from Posaunenberg named Hanna, boarded a ship. There was no record of an emotional farewell, no extended prayers the night before, since they expected to stay in Germany for only a few months before returning. As far as is known, Rebecca had not been on a ship since her voyage in captivity to St. Thomas as a child, and her thoughts as the wind carried them out of the harbor can only be imagined.[39]

Their first destination was St. Eustatius, a small Dutch colony about a hundred miles southeast of St. Thomas in the Leeward Islands. There they were grounded for two months, waiting for a ship to Amsterdam. In the meantime, they learned that Friedrich Mueller, the newly arrived missionary who took Martin's place at Posaunenberg, had died of fever, so Martin decided to return to St. Thomas. The others departed for Europe on February 23, 1742, joined by two Moravians, Johann Christian Erhardt and Conrad Kilian, arriving in Amsterdam on April 29. From there they continued on by coach toward Marienborn, a Moravian congregation town in the principality of Wetterau, twenty miles northeast of Frankfurt am Main. But in the Dutch town of Nimwegen, still far west of their destination, Matthäus became sick. His body was feverish, he began passing blood, and his stomach got stiff. He might have been suffering from an intestinal disease like cholera.[40]

Their wagon rattled on into the German countryside, with Matthäus in torment and the others helpless. "He said with broken words that we could hardly believe nor understand how weak he was," wrote Erhardt in an account of the journey, "at which his wife answered that he should not admit such thoughts, or doubt his belief in the Savior, who began this journey with us and would see it through, and that though his body was weak the Savior would give him strength." They stopped at an inn called the White Swan in Marienbaum, a day's travel further east, where Matthäus and Rebecca crawled into bed and slept. Erhardt mixed up some gruel and heated a bit of wine. Matthäus took a bit, then slept again. When Rebecca got up and left the room, Erhardt "asked him if he wanted to eat anything, to which he did not reply, so I took a spoonful of wine and held it to his mouth, which he took, then lay back down. I told him he should sleep a little more, for we had to leave again in an hour. He made no answer, but smiled at me. His wife came back into the room and stood with me by the bed, and his eyes rolled back in his head. He went to sleep, and we saw no more breath from him. Brother Conrad lay on top of him and sang: 'The soul of Christ blesses you.' But we were all quite miserable."[41]

They scrambled to find a coffin, have the body examined by a physician, and arrange a burial at the local church. A Lutheran preacher said a few words, and after haggling with the innkeeper who presented them with an expensive bill, the group traveled on to Cologne, where they took a two-day boat trip up the Rhine River to Mainz. From there they boarded another boat up the Main River to Frankfurt, where they took a coach for the last twenty-five miles to Marienborn. They must have been an odd sight, this interracial party of travelers from the West Indies rolling through the German territories. Tired and dispirited, they arrived on June 3, 1742. "Sister Rebecca Freundlich, with her daughter, the Negro woman Hanna, and the small Negro boy Peter, arrived from St. Thomas," a church diarist noted. "Our Brother Matthäus Freundlich and his Sister Rebecca, who have served the Lamb as witnesses and workers in the black congregation in St. Thomas, left from Holland, where they had journeyed from St. Thomas, but while underway Brother Matthäus . . . completed his witness. She, however, has arrived in Marienborn and will stay for a time in our congregation to receive further preparation for service in the Moors' congregation in St. Thomas."[42]

Rebecca's own witness had taken her across the Atlantic to the unlikeliest of places, four thousand miles from home. As her brothers and sisters in the Caribbean, nearly seven hundred strong, stood their ground at the justice pillar, their newly widowed apostle found herself and her daughter in a small village in Germany, almost alone among strangers.

CHAPTER SEVEN

A Pilgrim in Europe

*B*ack to Germany he came, back again after another failed mission overseas, chastened, perhaps, as some thought, by hardship and disappointment, but still confident in himself. Modesty was one trait of which he was seldom accused. "Christianus Jacob Protten Africanus," he styled himself with a jaunty Latinate flourish—Christian Jacob Protten the African. Still, proclaiming that identity was one thing; managing it was anything but easy. Born on the Gold Coast of West Africa to an African mother and a Danish father, Protten lived his first ten years in Africa but thereafter was raised and schooled in Denmark. Every facet of his life straddled the fault line between his lineages. He had been virtually stolen from his native land, or so he thought, yet he adapted well to his new home, becoming comfortably well-connected in educated and religious circles in northern Europe. When he met the widowed sister Rebecca Freundlich in 1745, three years after her arrival in Germany, the similarities between them were remarkable, even beyond their mixed racial parentage. Like Rebecca, Protten spoke at least five European and African languages, perhaps as many as eight or ten, was literate in several, and moved easily among an international mélange of people. Attracted to Christianity at an early age, he had found his calling as an evangelist, returning to West Africa to teach the faith, even spending time in jail for his trouble. The two moved among the same people, embraced a common cause, and sailed across oceans to get to the same places. Africa, Europe, and America intertwined in the lives of these cross-racial, transatlantic sojourners, who reflect the surprising, if at times complicated, prominence of black Pietists in some parts of northern Europe.[1]

Protten's early years are documented only slightly better than Rebecca's. Three years older, he was born in 1715, the son of a sailor stationed at the Danish fort, Christiansborg, and a woman from the Ga people in the village of Osu near the fort. They were said to have been married in the Christian church. Protten was another among thousands of mixed-race children born to black mothers in West African port towns after Europeans began trading there in the mid-fifteenth century. Entire "mulatto villages" peopled by these offspring grew near many of the slaving forts along a two-thousand-mile stretch of African coastline. Young Christian's upbringing reflected this bicultural parentage. His native language was Ga, and he also spoke a dialect of Akan called Fante. His mother was probably the daughter of Ofori, the king of Anecho, or Little Popo, a Ga outpost about a hundred miles east on the Bight of Benin, and Christian might have been in line to inherit, if not the throne, then the wealth of the kingdom. On the other hand, a significant part of his early upbringing reflected his father's European influence. Christian attended a school at the Danish fort run by Elias Svane, a Lutheran minister, from whom he learned to read and write Danish and gained his first exposure to the Gospel.[2]

When he was eleven, Christian was chosen to journey to Denmark to further his training. He left the Gold Coast in 1727, accompanied by a schoolmate named Frederik Pedersen Svane, also the son of a Danish father and an African mother, born in 1710, who had taken his teacher's name in his honor. In a kind of memoir and spiritual testimonial written in the Moravian town of Herrnhut in 1735, the twenty-year-old Protten described the circumstances of his departure:

My whole life to this point has been hidden. My parents did not think of Herrnhut when I came into the world in 1715. In the year 1720 a Danish preacher named Mr. Schwane came to Christiansborg on the Acra coast in Guinea, and I was sent to him because he had written to my father. He gathered together all the Danish mulattoes to instruct them in Christianity. In the year 1726 Rev. Schwane was called back to Denmark with orders to bring some of his students with him. He chose two, one of whom was already on board ship. The other was sick at first, and when he regained his health, his mother did not want him to leave. Since the ship was nearly ready to depart, Governeur Samm [Suhm] allowed two others to be taken out of school, one of whom would be chosen by him and given to the minister. He chose me, and handed me over to some seamen who were experienced swimmers and were to take me to the ship. They dared not take the risk, saying: the God of the sea would be angry, because there was a powerful storm at low tide, it was very dark, and the ship was more than a mile from land. The governor insisted that the same night I be taken in a small vessel to the ship, which finally happened so well, though with some peril, that I forgot both my fatherland and parents and, out of joy, did not think of the danger, because the minister had told me that I should learn to be a preacher. While we were stuck in this difficulty, my brothers, sisters and other relatives stood on the bank wishing that the boat would be broken to pieces, but they waited in vain. With trouble, we finally came to the ship, which soon sailed away. Thus was I torn away by force from Africa, about which some have wondered.[3]

War between his African and European selves framed Protten's recollection. As a storm threatened, the governor's insistence overrode the protests of the youth's African family and the seamen, whose reluctance to anger the god cast a sense of spiritual foreboding over the enterprise. Protten himself professed to have blocked out all else through joy at the thought of becoming a preacher, but in hindsight he saw his removal from Africa as an abduction. Intentionally or not, Protten's narrative set up his life as a working out of this tension.

"On the 14th of August in the year 1727," he continued, "we finally arrived in Copenhagen after various dangers through which the Lord prevailed with the power of his arm. On the 17th of November in the same year I was baptized with the other from Africa [Frederik Pedersen Svane], after which we were examined and given witness that we understood our Christianity well." Another report asserts that King Frederick IV and other dignitaries served as godparents for the youths, giving them the highest connections possible and indicating the symbolic importance the crown attached to the conversion of Afro-Danish mulattoes. Symbolic it was, however, for royal patronage did not necessarily confer upon the boys the chance to develop their spiritual capabilities in school as they had hoped. Instead, they learned with dismay, they were destined for the craftsman's life. "We were assigned to the blacksmith trade, because that was said to be very profitable in Africa, but we had no desire to do it and gave the preacher no peace until he permitted us to continue our studies, which we did for the next four years." An aversion to smithing might have motivated them as much as the desire to study, but Protten presents himself as the insistent agent in his own drive for religious knowledge, not satisfied to accept the station into which he was slotted by others.[4]

African-born figures like Protten and Svane were unusual but by no means unique in early eighteenth-century Europe. Since the mid-1400s, European merchants trading in West Africa and, later, the Americas had brought back hundreds of Africans as retainers for royal courts and aristocratic houses. These men and women might be held as slaves, or given their freedom; many lived in a kind of nebulous legal status somewhere in between. Valued more as exotic trophies and status symbols than for their labor, they often wore elegant clothes, sometimes of vaguely "Moorish" or "Turkish" design emphasizing their mysterious appeal. Some served as musicians in military bands, while a few gained an advanced education and found places in European universities and seminaries.[5]

Two prominent contemporaries of Protten, for example, were Anton Wilhelm Amo and Jacobus E. J. Capitein, both natives of the Gold Coast like him. Amo was brought by a Dutch trader to Amsterdam as a child in 1707 and placed with a noble German family. Gaining fluency in German, Latin, and Greek, he went on to earn advanced degrees in philosophy at the universities of Halle and Wittenberg in the 1730s before falling out with his patron and returning to the Gold Coast in the late 1740s, where he lived several more decades far removed from his previous academic life. Capitein, two years younger than Christian Protten, was brought to the Netherlands by his Dutch owner in 1728 and educated at the Latin School in the Hague. He completed his dissertation in divinity at Leiden University in 1742, which argued for the compatibility of slavery with Christianity—the perfect emblem of his cultural suspension between Africa and Europe. An engraving of Capitein accompanying his published dissertation carried the caption: "Observer, contemplate this African: his skin is black but his soul is white, since Jesus himself prays for him. He will teach the Africans faith, hope and charity; with him, the Africans, once whitened, will always honor the Lamb." The thesis made its author famous in Europe.[6]

Like these African theologians, Protten felt the call of Christianity, but spent several years frustrated by his inability to find a connection with Jesus. Recalling his sense of spiritual restlessness (though avoiding direct discussion of whether his cultural deracination in Europe contributed to it), he wrote:

I felt that the Lord wanted to help me in many ways. He shook and jolted me, he stirred me to the core. But I always crept away from him and wept: I was still too young to give myself up to the Cross. If I had been a student and had had a little freedom, I would have wanted to give myself over to the Lord. I became a student [at the University of Copenhagen] in 1732, and as I made my way further in the world the unfettered free life led me to be deceived by fleshly desires. I entered, in a word, into the greatest unhappiness and danger, so that I thought, not only do you fare badly among people, you have no peace with God. I can go on no longer in the world with my heart so restless. Indeed, I found little lasting peace either day or night for two or three years. Then the law constantly pressed me and unfulfilled duties made demands on me. I could not accept the Lord's grace because I did not know him yet.[7]

Protten studied at the university for three years but never finished a degree. He was still grasping for direction when, in 1735, according to his account, he and his countryman, Svane, were asked to return to Africa as missionaries by Carl Adolf von Pless, a councillor to the king and president of the directors of the Danish West India and Guinea Company, who had been an effective advocate for the Brethren's mission on St. Thomas. The pair agreed, and Pless arranged their travel. When the time came, Svane boarded the ship but Protten backed out. "There were greater splendors here for me yet to enjoy," he admitted. "I felt great distress that I had promised Pless. I felt my arrogance and that I was not prepared to go to Africa, and I feared I would cause offense." The councillor forgave him, and Protten found a way out of his unhappiness when the Moravian leader Nikolaus Ludwig von Zinzendorf visited Copenhagen soon thereafter. The young African had thought he would try his luck learning a trade in Holland, but upon hearing of the Brethren's community in Herrnhut, he "could not imagine a more

Christian Protten, date unknown. Courtesy of Unity Archives, Herrnhut, Germany.

comfortable place," and arranged with the Count to visit the town. It was there, in September 1735, that he wrote the short account explaining his life as a tormented prelude to the peace he finally claimed to have found with God:

Since I have been here, I have often felt disquiet and have perceived a provocation to leave. But the Lord wields power with his arm. I am a witness to his awesome majesty that can do anything it wants. Whoever is his friend is blessed, blessed. . . . Has someone been arrogant? I, too! Has someone been unclean? I, too! Has someone been unneeded and useless? I, too! Has someone sought the friendship of this world? I, too! In a word: The devil has had me in his power and service, and I had to obey him. I could not free myself from this slavery, though I tried in many ways over the years. I could not do so until I humbled myself and begged for the grace of Christ to open my eyes and drive out my self-love. Everything I have sought and yearned for, I have found in the reconciliation of the blood of Christ. I long for nothing from this world but to be obedient in all things to my Redeemer who loves me . . .

Herrnhut, 21 September 1735
Christianus Jacob Protten Africanus[8]

Protten stayed in Herrnhut for two years, where he learned German. He was attracted by the Moravians' evangelical devotion and simple life-style, but, as he hinted, he had reason not to feel entirely welcome there. For all their professions of spiritual equality among the godly, the white Brethren regarded him as different, not quite of them. They called him *africanisch wild*—an African savage—and *mohrisch*, Moorish. For centuries, Europeans had ambiguously applied the term "Moor" in all its linguistic variations—*maure* in French, *more* in Italian, *moro* in Spanish—to non-European, and usually non-Christian, people of darker complexion. It could mean Muslims, Saharan and sub-Saharan Africans, or all three. A Moor could be any non-white person from anywhere—a gypsy or a black American. The term set civilized Europeans apart from all these people, and it conveyed heavily weighted cultural messages, as when Count Zinzendorf remarked in 1750: "The Lord wishes to make slaves of the Moors first before they are blessed, because they are so proud."[9]

It was Protten's pride, in fact, that most irritated Zinzendorf. "It is a dangerous thing when Brethren are haughty and think they are really something," the Count remarked in 1740. "Protten has a high opinion of himself. Presumptiveness [Praesumtion] and a high opinion of oneself only prostitute a person and carry no weight with the Saviour, who has his ways of bending such people." Perhaps it was needling of this kind that prompted Protten himself to admit the weakness in his own narrative. Constant reminders of his Moorishness might also have fueled the inspiration to return to Africa, fulfilling his promise of two years earlier and reawakening his African identity. Zinzendorf approved the voyage, and together with another Moravian missionary, Heinrich Huckoff, Protten left for the Gold Coast in 1737. The Count's last instructions to him, outlined in a letter as the two waited in the Netherlands for departure, read in part: "Dear Christian: In order to convert the Moors, you must leave all your Moorish bad habits in Amsterdam."[10]

Thus, at almost exactly the moment when Rebecca took to the Path in St. Thomas, Protten embarked on the same errand half a world away. Along with his friend, Frederik Pedersen Svane, he was among the very first generation of African-born expatriates, educated in Europe, to return to Africa for the cause of evangelical Protestantism. Also in their number was Jacobus Capitein, who, inspired by the Moravian missions, served as a chaplain at the Dutch fort of Elmina on the Gold Coast between 1742 and his death in 1747. Of a later generation, Philip Quaque, a native of the Cape Coast, spent twelve years in England from 1754 to 1766, becoming the first African to be ordained in the Church of England before returning to Africa as a teacher. All these men were motivated by a love of Africa, but their primary desire was to save their land spiritually rather than protect it from the slave trade. Dependent on patrons and institutions in Europe and Africa that were heavily invested in the trade, they either defended slavery, as Capitein did, or declined to challenge it. It would take another generation before African evangelicals like Olaudah Equiano argued that Africa needed an end to the slave trade as much as it needed Christianity, and that the two causes were linked. In the meantime, the early evangelists, envisioning Africa through a new, international Afro-Protestant imagination, were motivated by their own form of antiracist belief. European condescension toward "Moors," they thought, should not exclude Africa from the possibility of Christian redemption.[11]

Protten's success did not match his ambitions. He and Huckoff arrived in Elmina in 1737, where Huckoff died a few months later. Protten pressed the Dutch governor for permission to start a mulatto school at Elmina, but the governor, busy waging war against the kingdom of Dahomey, wanted no part of it and imprisoned Protten for a few years on an island near Little Popo. Upon his release, he went to Christiansborg as a teacher at the Castle School between 1740 and 1741 before Count Zinzendorf called him back to Europe with virtually nothing to show for his four years on the Gold Coast. The next year, Protten traveled to St. Thomas to serve in the mission for two years. Rebecca had already left the island by then, but he worked with all the same people as she had, and undoubtedly he heard much about her there. Despite his familiarity with some of the African languages spoken in the Danish colonies, however, he had little success there; he stayed mostly in Tappus, inexplicably aloof from the other Brethren, and "to their distress remaining a long time on St. Thomas, where his change was not edifying."[12]

Traveling back to Germany in April 1745, Protten rejoined the community of Brethren in Marienborn. One church diarist interpreted his return after years of wandering as proof of a divine reclamation project: "The lost but found-again sheep Protten has returned to the sheepstall in Marienborn. He has spent the time during his absence in peculiar ways, but the Lamb has constantly held his hand over him and guided him with joy back to His herd."[13]

It was a melancholy group of travelers that arrived in Marienborn from the West Indies in June 1742, just days after burying Matthäus Freundlich. What was to have been a visit to Germany of spiritual refreshment, away from the exhausting work on St. Thomas, had made Rebecca a widow in a strange land with a young child to support. There is no record of her reaction to the place. Perhaps she was struck by the stark contrast with the violent, fear-driven society she had left. The young West Indian who had spent her life among sugar plantations worked by gangs of African slaves now could look out across undulating fields of rye and barley harvested by German peasants. But she no doubt wondered what future that pastoral landscape held for her. She was on a "pilgrimage to Europe," as one church diarist wrote, implying that her stay would be finite. How long that stay would last, and how it would be spent, were not clarified. In St. Thomas, an entire church culture blossomed and grew around her. She had power, and she believed God had chosen her for a special task. Now, the prison parolee and veteran of a brutal struggle seemingly had no divine appointment, no authority or audience, no outlet for her energy and organizing ability. What was to become of a voice that had helped galvanize a movement?[14]

She quickly found that, for anyone committed to the cause of the church, her new—albeit temporary—home could be an exciting place. Rebecca had long craved a personal relationship with Jesus, and her quest found ample encouragement in Marienborn, a spiritual center that was calibrated for intensity of emotional experience. Much Moravian activity shifted there after Count Zinzendorf's banishment from his home estate in Saxony in 1736, when he found refuge on the estate of another count in the principality of Wetterau, leasing the castle of Marienborn for his new headquarters. Marienborn, along with its nearby sister community of Herrnhaag, became the spiritual and emotional crossroads of the growing worldwide church. During the 1740s, Moravian congregations flourished in dozens of mission stations around the world and in Britain, Ireland, and the Netherlands, while a "diaspora" community of Moravian migrants built a new communal town in Bethlehem, Pennsylvania, which became an American headquarters for missions to the West Indies and to Indians in Pennsylvania and Ohio. Mis-

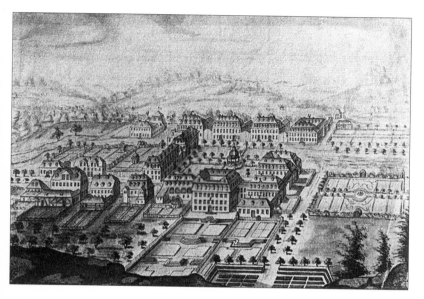

Herrnhaag, 1753. Courtesy of Unity Archives, Herrnhut, Germany.

sionaries and settlers continually passed through Marienborn on their way to and from these many outposts, bringing reports of successes and setbacks in faraway lands.

In 1738 a larger, more elaborate, planned communal town called Herrnhaag was built two miles east of Marienborn. Located on a ridge in the rolling countryside, this congregational town featured a central square with a fountain in the middle, around which some twenty spacious Baroque buildings were gathered, including a house for Zinzendorf that doubled as a prayer hall, houses for single men, women, and widows, an orphanage, and a mission house. As hundreds of migrants—mostly urban craftsmen, but many aristocrats as well—were drawn to this spiritual showpiece, Herrnhaag and Marienborn became, by the early 1740s, the scene of an intensely heightened—and controversial—religious enthusiasm.[15]

As Rebecca also discovered, she was not a complete stranger

there; in fact, she encountered a handful of very familiar faces. Since the late 1730s, a few black converts from St. Thomas had returned with white missionaries to Germany, where they were to receive further religious training before returning to the island. Some were free, while others had been purchased as slaves by the church and lived quasi-free in Europe. Some succumbed to the cold climate and unfamiliar disease environment after a short time; Anna Maria, Rebecca's co-worker and helper for the women's bands on St. Thomas, had come to Germany in late 1739 but died in March the next year. When Rebecca arrived in Germany, however, she saw two old friends: the helper Andreas, one of Friedrich Martin's first converts, and Maria, the eldress, who were now married and living in Herrnhaag. Both had been purchased by the Brethren and had left St. Thomas in the early 1740s for the church's new communal settlement in Bethlehem, Pennsylvania, where they married before traveling to Germany. The couple were emblematic of an emerging triangle of black Moravian communities in the West Indies, Bethlehem, and Germany, with St. Thomas the source of them all.[16]

The small band of Afro-Caribbean Brethren leaving the island represented a first wave of black Christians migrating back across the Atlantic from the Americas—a tiny current against the mighty tide of the slave trade—to intersect with the transnational vision of Afro-Europeans like Protten, Svane, and Capitein. For these men and women, religion provided a new and different sense of purpose as well as an opportunity for mobility across vast geographic spaces. Just as black sailors on merchant vessels circulated news and ideas to black communities throughout the Americas, Europe, and Africa, evangelicals were beginning to do the same thing. As the sea and the church became their escape routes from America, they began to plant the seeds of the black Protestant international movement.[17]

Rebecca herself was well known by reputation among the European Brethren, who held mission workers, especially "natives," in high esteem. Martin's letters through the years had documented her work on St. Thomas and her marriage to Matthäus. Her stand in the courtroom and redemption by Zinzendorf gave her a deep reservoir of respect in the Moravian imagination and a special connection to the Brethren's leader. Indeed, the fact that she had dreamed of Zinzendorf's arrival in St. Thomas two days before it actually happened—a divine signal played up by the Count himself—heightened her mystique and, within the limited circle of the Brethren, made her something of a star. For a short time after her arrival, documents referred to her as "Rebecca Freundlich," but soon everyone simply called her Rebecca, which appears to have been a gesture not of condescension, but of respect, since only a handful of prominent church women—such as the leader of the Single Sisters, Anna Nitschmann—were usually called by their first name. In the world of the Brethren, there was only one Rebecca.

The question was what to do with her. At a meeting of church leaders in September 1742, one minister said that "the aim should be to marry her to a Brother and send her back to St. Thomas," pending the approval of Zinzendorf, who was away on one of his many trips to other congregations on the continent, the British Isles, or America. In the meantime, Rebecca would begin to take part in church conferences and in the *Stundengebet,* the 24-hour prayer cycle in which participants took turns praying for an hour, waking each other up in succession through the night. Elaborate gender-divided schedules preserved from the period—indicative of the high degree of bureaucratic organization in the church—show Rebecca regularly filling an hourly time slot along with dozens of other women, including the two other West Indians, Maria and Hanna.[18]

Such rituals convey the degree to which non-European brothers and sisters were assimilated into this sacramental world. They prayed and sang with their white counterparts in the elaborate services and festivals that made up the Moravian devotional culture; they bunked with them in gender-separated residential halls; they spoke German, the community's lingua franca; they wore the distinctive clothing of the Brethren. Trading in her West Indian clothing, Rebecca now wore a dark dress laced at the breast and a *Haube,* or bonnet, fastened with a white bow to indicate she was a widow; married women wore blue bows and single women, pink. These markers designated each sister's membership in a church "choir," a group divided by age, gender, and marital status under the authority of a supervisor. At some point—exactly when is not clear— Rebecca appears to have taken up lodging in the widows' house in Herrnhaag, as did Maria, along with nearly two hundred women of the widows' choir.[19]

Choirs were the basic social units of the church, in which most of the teaching and worshipping took place. Single men were housed together, as were single women, married men, married women, infants, children, widows, and widowers, the theory being that congregants followed the divine light best if surrounded by comrades of similar personal circumstance. An expansion of the band system that had worked so effectively in St. Thomas, the choirs served as surrogate families in a church culture that de-emphasized and separated nuclear families. Believers were expected to submerge their own desires in the will of the group. Choir members ate and bunked together, often worked side by side, and met at least once a day, often more, to worship and discuss religious texts. Each congregant also met weekly with the choir leader in private conferences called *Sprechen,* or "speakings," to review his or her spiritual progress. With authority to punish backsliders and bar the wayward from worship, house leaders were the congregation's first line of defense in maintaining social order. Choirs enforced the community's sexual regulation by ensuring that single men and women would never meet until the elders arranged their marriage.[20]

But choirs were also important for women because they provided social and religious spaces apart from men, reflecting the church's reverential view of female spirituality. Women were ordained as acolytes and deaconesses, a rare conferral of status and recognition among eighteenth-century Christian churches of women's ability as teachers, leaders, and organizers. Anna Nitschmann, known to all congregants as "Mutter," or Mother, wielded immense authority in her own choir and in the inner circle of church elders; she even embarked on an itinerant preaching tour of Pennsylvania in the early 1740s along with two other women, including Benigna Zinzendorf, the Count's daughter. On one occasion Nitschmann preached to a Quaker meeting "[to] the greatest astonishment of those present."[21]

Rebecca had capitalized on many of these ideas in St. Thomas and, as far as the records indicate, appears to have been comfortable absorbing herself into this new family. At the same time, she might have been surprised by the arrangement made for her two-year-old daughter, Anna Maria. Moravian children were raised by the community, not by their parents. Count Zinzendorf believed that children should be inculcated as young as possible with church principles, a task better handled by trained foster parents than by birth parents. Children were taken away from parents and put in the nursery between the ages of one and two, and parents took little subsequent role in raising them. In 1743 a church board considered putting Anna Maria into the nursery, but, as they customarily did when determining congregants' living arrangements, they consulted the lot, which was considered the Lord's will. Posing the question, "Should Rebecca's child be received into the small children [choir]?" they drew from a bowl containing yes, no, and blank answers, and picked a negative lot, meaning Anna Maria could not be admitted. Instead, they placed her in the orphans' house across the square from the widows' quarters. Mothers socialized into the church from an early age generally accepted and even embraced such forced separations, but it is impossible to gauge Rebecca's reaction. Undoubtedly she accepted the arrangement outwardly as the expression of divine intent, but, accustomed to Anna Maria's constant presence with her, she might have privately found it unsettling. The daughter whom Rebecca had hoisted on her back to go tramp the hills of St. Thomas probably now saw her mother only occasionally.[22]

Rebecca and other brothers and sisters of color lived as spiritual and social equals among white congregants, but as Christian Protten had discovered earlier, their physique and culture also tagged them as *different*. Such distinctions applied not only to black West Indians, but to all the converts from the church's many mission fields who lived in Herrnhaag and Marienborn, which, despite the insular quality of the church, were remarkably international places. During the 1740s, at least thirty-one non-Europeans lived in the German congregation towns—a small percentage, to be sure, but visible enough reminders of the church's worldwide outreach. On one occasion, Rebecca participated in a *Mohren-Liebesmahl*, or "Moors' Lovefeast," in Herrnhaag along with three black *Mohren* from St. Thomas—Hanna and two youths, Peter and Andreas—as well as Felix, a Malabar from Ceylon, Benedict Weist, a gypsy, and Michael Samuel Jeremias, a Tartar, all lumped together as "Moors." Why such a gathering took place is unclear. Were the participants encouraged to meet by church leaders who believed that all non-Europeans, vaguely distinguished by their darker skin color or "heathen" origins, shared a spiritual and cultural affinity? Or did the converts call the meeting, believing themselves marked as different, and sensing an otherwise artificial spiritual kinship with one another? The records do not say, indicating only that "it gave the workers heartfelt joy to see them gathered all together." But the very ambiguity of the issue reflected the Brethren's insistence on defining people by outward appearance while denying that "race" existed in the eyes of Jesus.[23]

However they were perceived, these brothers and sisters from around the world were fundamental to the identity of the Brethren. They were among a group of seventy people—fifty men and twenty women—who climbed into carriages in Herrnhaag in July 1743 to ride to Hirschberg, in the province of Vogtland, a few days' travel to the east, to attend the annual synod, the church's most important decision-making meeting. The party included all the foremost leaders of the church as well as representatives from far-flung congregations in England, Estonia, Holland, Pennsylvania, Greenland, Ceylon, and elsewhere. Rebecca and Maria attended, representing St. Thomas, as did two "savage Indians," Ludwig and Anna, from America, and Andreas, speaking for "Moorish matters."[24]

Despite the diversity of attendees, discussion at synods was usually dominated by a small group of male leaders, especially Zinzendorf himself. Although extensive minutes of the meetings were kept, they reveal very little of what participants outside the inner clique might have said. One important item on the agenda, however, was to compile a list of all the workers and assistants in the church, and the group came up with a list of 1,031 people—606 brothers and 425 sisters worldwide. It is an extraordinary document, probably unique in the Protestant world at the time, for no other church had extended its mission reach so widely; the list includes not only Europeans but also the hundreds of indigenous workers who formed the core of the helper class abroad. Rebecca, "a leader herself who should go back into service," is listed among the women, along with Maria and Marotta from St. Thomas, Sara, "a Malabar eldress," Buhimega from Greenland, Sara from Checomeco in Pennsylvania, and many others—a multiethnic, global sisterhood of the spirit demonstrating that where Christianity took root around the world, it was spread largely by indigenous women and men themselves.[25]

There was another issue on the table at the synod of 1743, and it came from deep within the soul of the church itself. In Herrnhaag, Rebecca unwittingly found herself in what, to modern sensibilities, and to some contemporary critics as well, was becoming one of the most bizarre spiritual experiments in eighteenth-century Europe.

It had to do with blood. The Brethren had always celebrated the shedding of Christ's blood, and his mutilation, as the ultimate saving power of his sacrifice. There was precedent for this; the medieval church had long glorified the stigmata of Christ and the violence with which the martyrs died. Lutheran theology, upon which many Moravian beliefs were grounded, was steeped in "blood and wounds" as well. But among the Brethren in the early 1740s, these doctrines entered a new dimension altogether, and they were not for the faint-hearted. In their choir meetings and congregational gatherings, the Moravians chanted that they were "corpse bees" or "fishes" swimming in Christ's blood and drinking his sweat. They sang of their longing to crawl for haven inside the Savior's "moist and juicy side-wound," to sit in the "treasure hoard" of the "cavernous wounds of Jesus." They spoke of dining at the "Cross-Delicatessen" offered by the ritual eating of Christ's flesh and drinking of his blood at communion.[26]

Much of this heightened relish for gore had happened during Zinzendorf's prolonged absence, promoted by a group of young Brethren, including the Count's son, Christian Renatus Zinzendorf. Favoring a more enthusiastic approach to religion, they opposed a body called the "General Conference" of twelve men and women who ran the church while the Count was away. Some of these leaders wanted to separate from the Lutheran Church, with which the Brethren were still formally aligned, and return to the more austere forms of worship of the ancient Unity of Brethren, the Moravians' fifteenth-century predecessor. When Zinzendorf returned to Herrnhaag in the spring of 1743 he found the church rent by generational and theological divides, and he used the June synod to restore order. Rebecca witnessed the end of the power struggle as the Count, siding with the younger group, ousted the General Conference, reclaimed his own leadership, and launched the Brethren on a new exaltation of Christ's bloody gift.[27]

Through poetry and prayer, Zinzendorf and others set about constructing an elaborate linguistic shrine to the principal wound of

Christ—the *Seitenhölchen,* or little side-hole, the bleeding gash left in Jesus' side by a Roman spear. The side-hole, as one scholar has written, was "the narrow door, the portal to paradise, the means of entry into the body of Christ." It provided life, answered every question, comforted every trouble. Jesus gave birth to mankind through the opening: "Side-hole, side-hole, you are mine . . . the Mother-place of our spirit," went the incantation. The wound even became the subject of erotic imagery in Moravian art and verse, a kind of vagina that the faithful were enjoined to enter, to lick, to taste, and through which they sublimated sexual desire. During one service, "the whole congregation fell before its bloody husband and lay there trembling in the presence of the side hole." A series of hundreds of tiny watercolors, painted on small cards by an anonymous artist, depicted the side-hole in the form of female genitalia enclosing pleasant domestic scenes—a bedroom, a meal-laden dining table, a cottage and garden enclosed by a picket fence. The cards bore inscriptions such as "I enjoy strolling in the side-hole," or instructions on how married couples should have sex. The side-hole thus became a vehicle for an erotic relationship with Christ, the "bridegroom" of the church, with whom spiritual union was termed "sleeping in the arms of Christ."[28]

Zinzendorf himself penned some of the most vivid imagery of this gruesome theology, especially in his "Litany of the Wounds," a long recitation from 1744 in which two choirs, in call-and-response form, hailed the saving mysteries of the wounds:

Purple wounds of Jesus,	You are so succulent, whatever comes near you Becomes like wounds and flowing with blood.
Juicy wounds of Jesus,	Whoever sharpens the pen and with it pierces you just a little, and licks it, tastes it.
Near wounds of Jesus,	I want to be even a hair's-width from your hole.
Painful wounds of Jesus,	Sensitive to the Lamb, and even for that reason, so connected to the cure and so proven.

Soft wounds of Jesus,	I like lying calm, gently, and quiet and warm. What should I do? I crawl to you.
Hot wounds of Jesus,	Go on heating until you are able to cover the entire World with your warmth.
Treasure wounds of Jesus,	To you slaves, beggars and kings, farmers and counts make pilgrimages.
Eternal wounds of Jesus,	You are my house to dwell in. In a million eons you will still be new.
At the end of all trouble,	Anoint us, you red wounds.

In the meantime, I believe the death-streaked eyes, the spit-dripped mouth, the fire-baptized corpse, the thorn-scratched head, the furrows on the back: Until I, at the proper hour, can see in my flesh the body wounds for me, on which we build so firmly, and greet close by, the works in his hands and feet.

Hail!	Lamb of God.
Christ,	Have mercy!
Glory	To the side-wound![29]

In the face of this gory onslaught, all traces of the Enlightenment were banished from congregational discourse. Emotion and faith brought life, the intellect only betrayal. "May your astonishing simplicity make reason hateful to us!" implored the Litany. In that spirit, a group of aristocratic Brethren formed a Society of Little Fools in 1743 dedicated to spirituality of the heart and senses; as a playground for bored gentlemen, the society more than lived up to its name. Brothers and sisters strove for childlikeness, sprinkling their daily speech with diminutives like "little lamb" or "little side-hole" so frequently that, Zinzendorf eventually complained, they called everything by that term, trivializing its redeeming power. The Count himself, known to congregants as "Papa," now became "Papagen," or Little Papa. Enthusiasts coined fanciful new words like *Kreuzluftvögelein* (cross-air-bird), conveying an ethereal sense of the spirit floating to Jesus.[30]

This brand of piety would wield obvious influence on the German Romantics later in the eighteenth century. But in the 1740s, church leaders, aware that their doctrines could be perceived as controversial, tried to conceal the most graphic imagery from outside view. "Such books, letters, and hymns should be handled carefully and not communicated so freely because it is unbearable for the wounds of Jesus and similar things to be prostituted to the ridicule of the world," they warned. Word leaked out, however, helping to fuel the break with other churchmen like George Whitefield and John Wesley, with whom Zinzendorf had once had cordial relations, but who were now repelled by reports—partly exaggerated—of bloody revelry among the Brethren.[31]

At the same time, repellent as the blood and wounds theology was to many, it provided a raw, visceral appeal to thousands of people on the continent, in the Americas, and in the British Isles who sought an intensely personal relationship with Christ. Exaltation of the wounds was the devotional engine that drove the overseas missions. And in Herrnhaag, Rebecca and other brown and black worshippers became insiders when they lifted their voices to the wounds. The side-hole was the great spiritual and social equalizer, the blood of Jesus the universal cleanser. In emotional as well as practical terms, to swear fealty to the side-hole was to secure a place in this spiritual universe.[32]

Rebecca stayed on in Herrnhaag as one year turned into two. She became a regular at many of the councils where church matters were discussed—the *Pilger* or missionaries' conference, the Helpers' and "servants'" meetings, and the annual synods. Then, in February 1744, her daughter Anna Maria, now four, died suddenly, or "went to the Lamb," in the orphanage. The cause of death was not listed, but almost none of the children who came to Europe from St. Thomas or other tropical climates survived in the new environment more than a few years. The children's sections of the *Gottesacker*, or

God's Acre, in Marienborn and Herrnhaag already contained the graves of other black children such as Anna Gratias, Johannes, and David "the Moor," and now Anna Maria joined them as well.[33]

Rebecca's temporary status in Herrnhaag became ever more elastic as the plan to find her another husband went nowhere. Congregants were not allowed to court, and all marriages had to be arranged by the elders, who considered variables such as a prospective couple's age, social class, and spiritual progress in making matches. There were plenty of eligible men in town, but a mate for Rebecca had to be the right kind of man—a preacher, cut out, like her, for the missions. And what about his origins, his appearance? Ordinarily, pairing marriage partners in the church was a straightforward business, but her case was different. Although no discussion by the elders of potential candidates has been preserved, it is possible they were wary, in light of her history, of marrying her to another white man for further work in the West Indies. They might also have believed a match with a non-white man to be more appropriate, given their readiness to classify all non-Europeans as "Moors" with apparent spiritual and cultural affinities. True, she had married a white Brother once before, but that match had been a product of contingency on St. Thomas, and the elders seemed uneager to repeat it.

Christian Protten's arrival in Marienborn in the spring of 1745 must have seemed the perfect solution. Rebecca's counterpart in every way, he evidently represented the ideal partner in a union of God's servants, a groom for the symbolic wedding of the American and African wings of a germinating international Afro-Protestant movement. The records do not show exactly how and when a match was arranged, but it evidently took place late in 1745. Ordinarily single people, who were strictly segregated by sex and prohibited from any contact, did not even know each other before a betrothal, but that seems unlikely in Rebecca and Christian's case. As missionaries, who were considered something of an exalted separate class, they would have taken part in some of the same conferences and worship

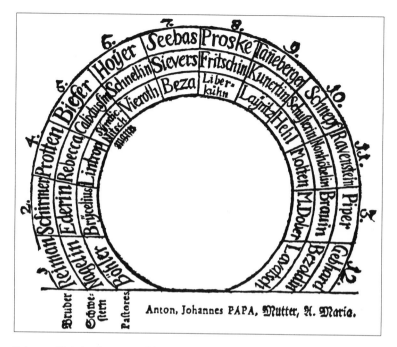

Rebecca–Christian Protten wedding circle, from *Büdingische Sammlung*, 1746.

services. Protten, who had never been married, might even have proposed a match himself, but he was not allowed to ask Rebecca directly, and the elders would have negotiated it with her after seeking the Lord's approval through the lot. As with Matthäus, she had the right to refuse, but she accepted, and on December 27, 1745, Rebecca and Christian became engaged during a lovefeast along with eleven other couples. An official diarist described them as a "mulatto couple," leaving little doubt of the importance of their shared mixed-race heritage in the minds of church leaders, and, perhaps, in their own self-perception as well.[34]

On January 6, 1746, Rebecca and Christian gathered with the eleven other engaged couples for a mass wedding in the chapel at

Marienborn. Each pair was assigned a pastor to consecrate the union; Rebecca and Christian drew Brother Lintrop. As a diagram of the occasion shows, the couples, with their pastors, stood before the altar arrayed in three concentric three-quarter circles: ministers up front, sisters in the second circle, and brothers in the third, ensuring that the betrothed would stand next to each other but not next to other single people of the opposite sex. In a long sermon interspersed with song and prayer, Zinzendorf addressed the group on the meaning of marriage, in which both spouses were "brides" of Jesus, who was the third partner in every union. "Our marriages are nothing but blessed societies, little churches, illustrations of the holy trinity. There are two people, and within them lies the third, who, through their union, is revealed by the holy guardian as a mystery, a profound and prophetic mystery." God would "send the spirit of the church, the spirit of the bride of the Lamb, of the wife who prepares her husband; and when that spirit is parceled out between husband and wife, you have all you need." Then, an account of the ceremony reports, "these 12 new couples had their hands joined by 12 ordained Brethren" and Zinzendorf blessed the group, admonishing them to "remember your bond to the congregation, to be true Vice-Christs and true daughters of the Saviour." With that, the Afro-Dane and the West Indian ex-slave became Brother and Sister Protten.[35]

After the ceremony, perhaps directly afterward, Brother and Sister Protten engaged in marital relations. But having sex in this community was no simple act of consensual privacy. It was a holy ritual, a radical celebration of the divine gift of sexuality. According to Moravian belief, because Jesus and Mary had genitalia, the sex organs were sacred and meant to be used by ordinary humans in wedlock, for procreation, certainly, but for spiritual fulfillment as well, even after a woman's childbearing years. The Brethren talked openly about sex, sang hymns about it, and issued detailed instructions about how, when, and how often to have it. While they embraced sexuality, however, they also sought to control it. Since married couples lived in separate quarters, they came together for regular conjugal visits called *Eheviertelstunden* ("marriage quarterly hourlies") scheduled by male and female "bed masters" and "curators." Couples waited their turn in line for these encounters, which generally took place once a week, or after special religious ceremonies. In some communities a bedroom in a choir house was set aside for sex, while in others, such as Herrnhaag, a "blue cabinet" or enclosed chamber served the purpose. Rebecca and Christian probably repaired to such a place after the wedding to queue up with the other eleven couples for a turn in the cabinet—their initiation to a lifetime together.[36]

As with the most graphic of their blood and wounds imagery, the Brethren tried to keep these practices secret, but word leaked out. A former church member named Jean Francois Reynier, who lived in Herrnhaag during the early 1740s before defecting in 1743 to write a salacious exposé, reported that officials such as Bishop August Spangenberg, who had befriended Rebecca on St. Thomas in 1736, watched the action through a peep hole in the cabinet, and that before weddings Count Zinzendorf fondled the brides' breasts. Whether such accounts were exaggerated is not clear; it is difficult to reconcile the image of Zinzendorf and Spangenberg, in some ways brave advocates for the slaves on St. Thomas, now reduced to gropers and peeping toms leering at their former disciple through a spy hole (and Spangenberg was in Pennsylvania at the time of Rebecca's wedding). In any case, the lurid stories contributed to a growing perception outside the church that the Moravians were a twisted cult, crazed by perverted orgies and blood lust.[37]

Inside the Herrnhaag community, however, marriage now completed Rebecca's climb up the ladder of authority and status. Just four days after the wedding, she and her fellow West Indian, Maria, were formally ordained as deaconesses along with six other women. Important positions in the church hierarchy, deacons and deaconesses "helped the preacher in *all* matters, including the administra-

Foot-washing ceremony, 1757. Courtesy of Unity Archives, Herrnhut, Germany.

tion of communion, and could, in fact, administer Communion on [their] own." Emulating Jesus' washing of the apostles' feet, they dunked their sisters' feet in water-filled wooden tubs during the foot-washing ceremony. They administered other rituals, such as the kiss of peace and the laying on of hands for new inductees. They could even preach—or at least, in the case of deaconesses, they were allowed to preach to other women.[38]

The ordination of Rebecca and Maria was thus a watershed event in three ways. They were among the earliest group of women to be ordained in the Moravian church, a highly unusual event in Christian practice at the time. What is more important, they may well have been the first black women to be ordained in western Christianity, signaling the power of this form of evangelical religion to take any and all into its bosom. Finally, it is significant that in a remote town in central Germany, a slave and a former slave now administered Communion and practiced other claims to spiritual authority over white women, including European aristocrats. Inverting the idea of mission, it was they, the women of African origin, who now schooled European women in the principles of Christianity. In these ways they took part in an emerging spiritual revolution that was quietly beginning to undermine centuries of Christian doctrine propping up the subordination of women and people of color. The irony, of course, is that the church itself supported slavery at the same time.[39]

Capturing the *Zeitgeist* on canvas was the Moravian artist Johann Valentin Haidt, who in 1747 celebrated the multi-hued character of the Unity fellowship with a large painting, nearly nine by thirteen feet, called *Erstlingsbild* or "First Fruits," a group portrait of many of the early converts. Haidt, a former goldsmith from Berlin, joined the Moravian church in London in 1739; he became a lay preacher and moved to Herrnhaag in the early 1740s, where he turned to painting. As something of an official church artist, he painted hundreds of religious scenes and portraits of important church figures before his death in the Moravian town of Bethlehem, Pennsvylania, in 1770. In Herrnhaag, the international cast from the church's mission fields provided him with the metaphorical and human inspiration to produce his most enduring and best-known work.[40]

The painting testifies to the universal saving power of Jesus, who, in an elevated throne, displays his wounds to twenty-one figures arrayed around him in various poses of blissful adoration. Two angels hover on either side of Christ, one of them reading a scroll with the key passage from Revelation 14:4: "These have been redeemed from men as first fruits for God and the Lamb." Many of the figures were among the very first converts in their own country or mission field, and were regarded as among the most sincere and discerning of the faithful. All have died and gone to meet Christ in glory, each clutching a palm branch as a symbol of triumph. Haidt imagined the features and fanciful garb of most of the figures, but he knew or had

"First Fruits" by Johann Valentin Haidt, 1747. Courtesy of Unity Archives, Zeist, Netherlands.

seen a few of them in Germany and probably portrayed their likenesses with some accuracy. Much of the visual and psychological impact of the "First Fruits" is allegorical. But also important to the work is a sense that the redeemed, far from being an abstract collection of exotic species, are individuals from particular places with specific conversion narratives, each its own record of victory now recorded in church mission lore. The legend at the bottom of the canvas identifies them carefully: "The Mingrel, Thomas Mammucha," "Guly from Persia," "David the Armenian," "Sam, the Savage from Boston," "Thomas of the Hurons," "The Carolina Negro Johannes," "Francesco from Florida," "The Hottentot Kibbodo," and others, all gathered in eternity.[41]

With four adults and four children, the Danish West Indies contingent is the largest of any group in the painting and includes several prominent participants in the St. Thomas mission. Haidt calls attention to the eight by placing them in the foreground and arranging them beneath Christ's outstretched arms at the base of the painting's central pyramid. They also appear to be the most assimilated into the church culture of any, since they are the only ones wearing European Moravian clothing. Andreas (who died in Herrnhaag in 1743), one of Friedrich Martin's first converts, gazes down on the helper Anna Maria, who holds his son, Michael, as Hanna looks on from the right. Beside them are Oly Carmel, a boy brought back to Europe by the missionary Leonhard Dober in 1734, Gratia, a young girl, and Catherina from St. John, who cradles an infant. Because she was still alive at the time, Rebecca is not shown, but she has a place in the painting anyway, for as the caption reveals, the child held by Catherine is "Rebecca's little girl," Anna Maria. Identifying her by first name only, Haidt evidently assumed that any Moravian viewing the painting would know her. While enshrining the new generation of children among the fruits of Christ's grace, the painting solidifies Rebecca's own renown in the mission pantheon.

Church records provide only scattered glimpses of the Prottens' lives between 1746 and 1749. As missionaries, their upkeep would have been supported by the church, but it is not clear whether they lived in sex-segregated housing in Herrnhaag or in some other quarters. Their days were likely filled with the elaborately plotted cycle of choir meetings, assistants' conferences, prayers, and services that crowded the congregational schedule. These devotions often reflected the international nature of the community and the Prottens' immersion in it. On one occasion, the eve of Brother Beck's departure to the mission field, a diary reported that "Brother Lintrop preached to the Danish brothers and sisters in their language, and after the usual Communion Brother Beck gave a powerful farewell speech in the Greenlander language [Inuit], whereupon Brother Protten answered him in the Accra language, and Brother Garrison gave a prayer for his journey in Spanish."[42]

In 1746 the Prottens fell out of favor with Zinzendorf, or so Christian claimed in a letter he wrote to the Count, though he didn't explain the circumstances. He struck a playfully ingratiating tone in the sentimental language of the period:

> So have Rebecca and I for more than a half year now had all assurances of Little Papa's contentment with us. [But now] Papa is not satisfied with us. Who can know and feel, that such a Little Papa as you are to us, should be displeased, and how one can give satisfaction? But what does Little Papa wish of such poor children as we are, full of bad habits and incivilities, stupid and foolish on all sides as well? . . . Now, dear Papa, show us love and what you desire for your poor mulatto couple. Open up to us, that we may have just a glimpse and become aware [of your intentions].

As far as is known, nothing came of the affair; Zinzendorf either forgave the Prottens or was never very annoyed with them to begin with. But Protten, sensitive to the Count's criticism of "Moorish" faults, sought to turn the stereotype to advantage by admitting it and asking, what else can you expect of us? The tactic might have been merely a rhetorical flourish, or it could have expressed his own internalized belief. Either way, the standard self-abasement of Pietist expression became, for Protten, a comment on his own African "nature." Another reminder of the divided selves of this Afro-European, Christian's letter begged toleration for his unworthiness by trotting out the racial clichés he sought to transcend, thereby confirming them.[43]

Rebecca was reunited unexpectedly in 1747 with her old teacher and prison mate from St. Thomas, Friedrich Martin, who returned to Germany for several months to recuperate from the pressures of his missionary work. The mission had fallen on hard times after Rebecca's departure in 1741. Her organizing skills had been missed; the islands remained a graveyard for European missionaries, and Martin, lacking enough workers to recruit and teach, gave over more authority to the helpers. Black workers, in fact, had largely kept the mission afloat by continuing to mobilize the faithful. At one point the few remaining white missionaries ran completely out of money and were kept alive only by a loan from the enslaved helper Mingo. And, ironically, the "first fruits" concept celebrated by Haidt turned out to be an obstacle for the overseas missions during the 1740s. Count Zinzendorf, increasingly dubious that most of the heathen really grasped Christianity, had told mission workers in 1742 not to strive for mass conversions but to concentrate on a handful of the most promising "first fruits." In the West Indies, many enslaved catechumens, unable to meet the rigorous standards for conversion, dropped out of the mission. The congregations retained a steady core of followers, but their numbers stagnated; whereas ninety slaves had been baptized in 1741, only ten converted during the next four years. In 1742, Martin had traveled to Bethlehem, Pennsylvania, where he stayed for a year and got married. Returning with his wife to the Caribbean, he resumed his frenzied shuttling among St. Thomas, St. Croix, and St. John, where the work remained exhausting and dangerous. Distrustful planters still occasionally roughed up preachers and worshippers until the Danish king, Frederick V, finally sent another directive in 1744 ordering the persecution to stop.[44]

Seeking rejuvenation after these trials, Martin traveled to Germany with his wife and young child in 1747. He and the Prottens attended the synod in Herrnhaag that summer, where Martin spoke out effectively against the "first fruits" ideal. After the conference the Martins and Prottens traveled together to Herrnhut, the church's original town in Saxony, for a two-month stay, and the Martins returned to the West Indies the next year. When, in 1749, Bishop Johannes von Watteville visited St. Thomas, he found a reservoir of abiding interest in Christianity among the enslaved population despite years of slack effort by the missionaries. The first fruits doctrine, he declared, "had no basis in the holy scriptures and was,

therefore, false and harmful." Thereafter, intensive efforts would resume "to preach the gospel to all people and to baptize all those who
embraced it." In effect, black evangelicals had saved the mission
when white Christians were nearly ready to abandon them. When
Martin died of a fever on St. Croix in January 1750, a throng of
mourners buried him beside their prayer house, honoring him in
apparent traditional African fashion by piling several layers of building stones "in the form of a low-lying, foreshortened pyramid" on
his grave.[45]

In Herrnhaag, meanwhile, Christian Protten was asked whether
he, along with Rebecca, intended to "throw out the net" again in Africa. There seemed to be a presumption among church leaders that
he would, or should, do so, although a panel agreed that the couple
would have to decide whether to embark on such an undertaking by
themselves or with a larger group. No decision was reached, and the
Prottens stayed on in Germany. Rebecca's circle of friends from St.
Thomas diminished as the years passed. In May 1747, "the body
of our blessed Sister, the Mooress Hanna from Guinea, was laid to
rest in God's Acre before the entire congregation." In June 1749,
Rebecca's fellow deaconess Maria "went home" in the widows' house
in Herrnhaag: "At seven in the evening our dear Mooress Maria flew
happily into the side hole after having celebrated holy communion
with several from her choir on the thirteenth. She fell asleep in the
arms of Rebecca." The death of her Dutch-speaking sister and long-
time ally left Rebecca as the last West Indian survivor in the German
congregations.[46]

These passages were overshadowed by larger changes to this
world of insular security. First, in February 1749, Count Zinzendorf
sent a reprimand to all the congregations ordering them to curtail
many of the exuberant devotional practices which he himself had
promoted but which he now believed had gotten out of hand during
the 1740s, a period generally called the Sifting Time. Concerned

that the overt physicality of many rituals evoked excessive sensual-
ism that might be condemned by outsiders, the Count ordered the
temporary suspension of foot-washings, even though they were sex-
segregated—a hint of concern about homosexuality. In addition,
he said, worshippers should not perform the Kiss of Peace—which
was also a single-sex ritual—so enthusiastically "that their lips
smack." He condemned factionalism and what he saw as a worldly
fascination with religious clothing. And, convinced that the use of
diminutives in speech had become an artificial ornamentation that
trivialized true piety, he decreed that "no one shall any longer say or
write little sweetheart, little side-hole, little foolish one, little bride."
He even discouraged the faithful from calling him "Papa." He did
not, however, renounce the emphasis on blood and wounds or
on the side-wound, which remained standard features of Moravian
doctrine through the eighteenth century. But the Count's directive
brought to a close a decade of rococo spiritualism and its creative—
if unorthodox—outburst of poetry, music, and artwork.[47]

An even greater jolt came in October 1749 when secular authorities ordered the Brethren to leave the principality of Wetterau altogether. The abrupt eviction notice came about when the Brethren's
landlord, Count Ernst Casimir of Büdingen, died and was suc-
ceeded by his son, Gustav Friedrich, who did not like Zinzendorf.
Trying to compel the Brethren to merge with the state Lutheran
church, the new Count ordered them to swear allegiance to him, as
required by law, or face expulsion. They refused and were given
three years to abandon Herrnhaag and Marienborn.[48]

Some three thousand people now had to emigrate to new homes.
Beginning in March 1750 and continuing through the next two
years, staggered waves of refugees packed their belongings and dispersed to other Moravian towns on the continent or in America.
Many ended up in Bethlehem, Pennsylvania; others were absorbed
by a new settlement called Wachovia, founded in 1753 in North

Carolina's western Piedmont. Herrnhaag's gleaming Baroque buildings were left empty, while a handful of brothers and sisters stayed
on in Marienborn until 1773.

Like everyone else, Rebecca and Christian Protten were caught
up in this exodus, though at first they did not move far. Rebecca
gave birth to a daughter in April 1750, just as the mass emigration
was beginning. Christened the day she was born, the child, like her
dead half-sister, was named Anna Maria. Church documents described her as sickly, and perhaps wishing to avoid a strenuous journey so soon, her parents moved in August to Marienborn, where
they stayed until May 1751. Then they climbed into a carriage for
the two-week trip eastward across Germany to their new home,
Herrnhut.[49]

The hill country of Upper Lusatia, fifty miles east of Dresden, was
Zinzendorf country. In this corner of Saxony, tucked between Bohemia and Silesia, the Count's tenants—serfs, really, who had no connection with the Moravian Church—worked his several-thousand-
acre estate and paid the rent that helped support his many en-
deavors. These ancestral lands remained the spiritual home of the
Brethren. It was here, in 1722, that refugees from Moravia and Bohemia, remnants of the fifteenth-century Unity of Brethren, had
found a haven with the blessing of the 22-year-old Count. They
built a town, Herrnhut, where, in 1727, they reorganized formally as
the Renewed Unity of Brethren, covenanting to live by the model of
the early Christians. Despite Zinzendorf's long years of exile and
wandering in America, England, and western Germany, the congregational ideal had never wavered in Herrnhut. The *Gemeinhaus,* or
meeting house, occupied the middle of the town square, around
which were arrayed the choir houses where most of the six hundred
congregants lived. The most important choirs were the single sisters'
and single brothers' house and garden complexes, which expanded

rapidly when the town doubled in size during the 1750s, partly to absorb refugees from Herrnhaag.[50]

The "mulatto couple," Rebecca and Christian, and their daughter Anna Maria now found refuge in this place, moving into the Pilgrims' House for missionaries, just across the street from the meeting house. They were assigned to the married people's choir, sixth class (classes were choir subgroups divided by age). There is no record of either receiving special service assignments as assistants, possibly because those positions were well filled.[51]

When Anna Maria was still an infant, most likely soon after their arrival in Herrnhut, the Prottens sat for a portrait by Johann Valentin Haidt. As the Unity's most famous family of color—and the last surviving such family in Europe—they retained high symbolic value for the fellowship. As with all his paintings of non-European brothers and sisters, Haidt's study of the Prottens sought to convey a sense of the Gospel's universal embrace and to capture in warm, glowing tones the humanity of black Christians—notable in an age when slave traders justified their ever-expanding business on the ground of African barbarity. Along with other artists of his generation, Haidt was a significant contributor to emerging European discourses about African spiritual and physical beauty that would soon aid in threatening the slave trade.[52]

Although Haidt might have wished his painting to suggest that Christianity denied the importance of ancestry or physical appearance, in fact the Prottens' "blackness" was a central motif of the work. Haidt wrote that a painter should choose the subject's clothes "according to the complexion of the person," and he composed the portrait so that the Protten family's own complexions stand out clearly against their black and white clothing and the dark background. In this, the only known representation of her, Rebecca wears a Moravian gown, *Haube,* and blue ribbon (for married women); the image of solid Europeanized piety is far different from

The Protten family by Johann Valentin Haidt, c. 1751. Courtesy of Unity Archives, Herrnhut, Germany.

the kerchief and light cotton she wore in the West Indies. All three figures were of mixed African and European descent, but Haidt carefully portrayed marked gradations in their skin tone: Rebecca was the darkest and brownest, while Christian was lighter, with a more yellow tint to his face (which may reflect a light source to his right).

Red-headed Anna Maria, sitting in the middle flanked by her parents, has the lightest skin of all. Indeed, an entry in a church register described her as "quite white." It is easily conceivable that, as the grandchild of at least one white grandparent, and probably two, her skin could have been so light, and there is no indication that Haidt shaded the truth, so to speak, of what he observed. Indeed, the artist's intent to show African physical characteristics in Anna

Maria's face is plain. The child is noticeably naked. In no other portrait or church scene is Haidt known to have portrayed any "white" child unclothed. He did depict one other naked child of African descent, the very dark-skinned Michael in "First Fruits," and the infant Jesus is naked in several of Haidt's religious scenes. The latter comparison is clearly what Haidt had in mind in this group portrait. The striking resemblance of Anna Maria to Jesus, her light color, and her prominence in the foreground convey a symbolic whitening of the family, a metaphor for the convert's journey from darkness to light—an implication that Christianity purifies the heathen in both spirit and body.[53]

Rebecca's gaze is calm, purposeful, secure in God's plan, yet tempered by a slight smile—all possibly idealized characteristics that the painter might have wished viewers to read into the portrait. Haidt's technical weaknesses as an artist are obvious—Rebecca's arm reaches around Anna Maria like a claw—but he had strong ideas about what he sought to accomplish in his work. In an undated manuscript entitled "Treatise on Art," Haidt described his philosophy of portraiture as an exercise in revealing the subject's essential personality traits. "One applies all energy to the face, so that it predominates above all. . . . Each figure must immediately show why it has been drawn. . . . A portrait is beautiful when it is a correct likeness and when one can see the essence of the person in face and action. Therefore, painters who want to paint all faces as amiable and force the mouth to smile make a mistake. The painter must look correctly at the person he wants to paint. If he has an opportunity to know the person well, it is a great help to him." At the same time, Haidt used portraits to stylize characteristics he believed were inherent in certain people or occupations: "It is very good to make observations . . . and to note well those people in whom a particular passion predominates. For example, if I wanted to portray a soldier, I would have to seek out faces which appear completely without fear and which show something resolute, as well as swiftness and stability."

The military analogy is appropriate, since missionaries were considered soldiers of the cross. Indeed, in the Prottens' resolute gaze, the portrait radiates confidence that Christianity will reach the world's untutored millions.[54]

The painting also basks in the ideal of the nuclear family, a notion which had suffered in Herrnhaag but which was perhaps finding its way back to favor after the Sifting period. Alas for Rebecca and Christian, that ideal ended again when Anna Maria died on January 22, 1754. She was, wrote a diarist, "very sickly and weak in her limbs, but had begun in the last year to walk around. Fourteen days ago she suddenly lost her strength and lay in bed with a violent cough, which finally caused convulsions, raising the chance that her captive spirit would be released, which happened this morning when death brought about a life without end. She was three years, nine months old." Two days later the congregation gathered to bury her. Starting at the *Gemeinhaus,* mourners carried her coffin around the side of the building, followed by women's, men's, and children's choirs, while a trombone band played solemn hymns. Following the road east a short way, the procession turned left up a long alley leading to God's Acre, embedded on the side of the Hutberg, a hill outside town. There, above an expanse of farming villages and fields rolling eastward toward the mountains of Silesia, Anna Maria was buried in the young girls' section of the graveyard.[55]

As her second child was lowered into German soil, did Rebecca reflect on the strange circumstances of her journey from Caribbean slavery to the pastoral remoteness of Saxony? In her era, it was almost impossible for any woman of color to find herself in Europe other than as a slave or a servant. Yet Rebecca had uncovered and exploited virtually the only way out of the traps of race and gender that snared so many women. Evangelical religion was the vehicle that carried her across geographic and cultural borders, and her skills as a leader and teacher provided an entrée to another life. In Germany she found acceptance, even authority, in the bosom of the church. Whether she sought those things, or perceived herself as savvy in exploiting opportunity, is a different matter. It seems likely that Rebecca saw any fortunes she enjoyed or suffered—from personal status to the deaths of her children—as the will of God. While Christian Protten struggled constantly to reconcile his African and European identities, Rebecca showed no such doubts. Any of life's possibilities or obstacles simply represented new chances to unite with Jesus.

CHAPTER EIGHT

Christiansborg

*M*embership in the sacred world of the Brethren meant life itself. To celebrate the radical mysteries of Christ's blood was to share the world's most fabulous secret with the closest of spiritual kin. The Atlantic wayfarers Christian and Rebecca Protten, who might otherwise be servants or oddities in Europe, were privy to the secret, gaining refuge and privilege in the inner circle of acolytes. But sweet as it was to belong, there was always the possibility of being cut off from the family—a form of social death. In 1756, the Prottens suffered that fate. By order of Count Zinzendorf, they were abruptly banned from fellowship and exiled in disgrace from Herrnhut.

The reason is not entirely clear, but Christian had angered the Count in some way. Perhaps it was the old issue of pride. In 1745 the Brethren had published a *Dank-Opfer*, or thank-offering, serving up a prayer for each congregation or mission where they had borne witness. Protten was offended that Guinea—whether inadvertently or by design—was left off the list, and he let the elders know about it. When Zinzendorf, who lived in London between 1749 and 1755, returned to Herrnhut after his nearly twenty-year banishment, Christian might have complained again, too loudly. It is also possible he committed some other offense that revealed an ungodly heart; the records do not explain what happened, but one document says he was unable to "resist the Devil." As a result, in March 1756, the Prottens were evicted from the Pilgrims' House on the square and sent to Grosshennersdorf, a village three miles to the southeast.[1]

Grosshennersdorf actually had a sacred association for the Brethren: it was where Zinzendorf had spent a crucial part of his childhood on the estate of his grandmother, Countess Henriette Katharina von Gersdorf. His father, Georg Ludwig, died just six weeks after the Count's birth in Dresden in 1700, and after his mother remarried in 1704, Zinzendorf was raised by his grandmother. A woman of learning, she befriended leaders of the Pietist movement such as August Hermann Francke and Jakob Spener and introduced her grandson to their teachings. Zinzendorf left her estate at the age of ten to attend the Pietist academy in Halle, returning to the region in 1722, where he bought his own estate at Berthelsdorf, a few miles from Grosshennersdorf, and began his life as a patron of Pietist causes. Countess von Gersdorf died in 1726, but her land stayed in the family and in the orbit of the Brethren.[2]

When Rebecca and Christian were sent there, Grosshennersdorf was far removed from the high church culture of Herrnhut. Sprawled across the bottom of a bowl of hills, it was a working Saxon estate that smelled of animals and manure. There was a palace surrounded by formal gardens and ponds, with a suite of stables and barns nearby that enclosed a huge cobbled courtyard. Angling off haphazardly from this complex were the streets of a medieval village and lanes to the fields beyond. The Brethren had a small congregation and ran a boys' school in town, but the Prottens were not connected with either organization and found themselves utterly isolated. Though the church still supported their livelihood, with no friends, nothing to do, and barred from their daily routine of services and meetings, they felt their humiliation acutely.

Rebeccca's reaction was not recorded, but the demotion was intolerable for Christian. He wrote to Zinzendorf admitting his error and pleading for forgiveness. "I have noticed that your lukewarmness has been transformed into ice coldness . . . I only ask humbly that my body no longer be left to hang as a spectacle on this scaffold, but that my *Cadaver* be restored by burial in Africa." Christian signed the letter "Your unworthy servant, Christian Protten," and added a wistful postscript: "Oh, that I could only find my *Papagen* in eternity again." Protten's reference to Africa was no mere melodramatic figure of speech. Rather than bear his shame publicly, he really did prefer to return to his homeland and seek spiritual rejuvenation by resuming the mission he had abandoned in 1741. Accordingly, in June 1756 he wrote to church elders that "as I have lost all hope, I humbly beg you to have mercy on your poor Protten and provide me with a pass (and if possible, with a few pennies) to Copenhagen." They agreed.[3]

As Protten prepared to leave, there must have been discussion of whether Rebecca should accompany him, but no record of it has survived. At some point, someone—the Count, the elders, Christian, or Rebecca herself—decided she should stay in Germany. It was an unusual decision with no ready explanation, since mission couples almost always ventured out together. One historian speculates that Protten was reluctant to bring her, having heard from his friend, Frederic Pedersen Svane, who had taken his Danish wife with him to the Gold Coast, that the lewdness of soldiers at the fort could make life rough for mission wives. Or perhaps Zinzendorf believed that since Christian's desire to go stemmed from shame, pique, and a need for personal redemption, Rebecca was not properly called to the mission as he was. In any case, Christian left Grosshennersdorf alone on August 18, 1756, bound for his homeland.[4]

Finding passage out of Copenhagen to the Gold Coast, he arrived at Fort Christiansborg in June 1757, after a long and unpleasant voyage during which the captain, Ole Eriksen, berated him daily as a scoundrelly member of a lying sect. But he found the governor of Christiansborg, Christian Jessen, to be a "very honest and civilized man" who invited Protten to his table and offered him a job as head-master of the mulatto school at the salary of ten *rixthaler* per month, which he accepted. "I am living in the castle, and quite peacefully," he wrote back to a Moravian brother in Herrnhut in August 1757, but added that he was surrounded by "great ignorance" in this "large field for the Savior." Asking for news of the congregation and of "my poor Rebecca," he implored the Brethren not to cut him off.[5]

Fort Christiansborg, in the Accra region of the Gold Coast, had been the center of Danish trade in West Africa for nearly a hundred years. The Portuguese had first built a fort in Accra in the sixteenth century, and as the Atlantic slave trade expanded the Swedes, Dutch, French, and English all contested the area before the king of Accra sold the Danes a piece of land at the coastal village of Osu in 1661. There, not far from the English outpost, James Fort, and the Dutch Fort Crevecoeur, the Danes built a small castle as a base for the West India and Guinea Company's trade to St. Thomas. Fragile relations with African rulers made for uncertain business, however. In 1680 an inland kingdom, Akwamu, launched a military offensive to the coast, defeating Accra and driving the Ga people in Osu away to re-settle at Little Popo, a hundred miles to the east on the Slave Coast. Akwamu captured Fort Christiansborg in 1693 by disguising soldiers as merchants, then executing some of the undermanned garrison. The Danes bought Christiansborg back in 1694, but, along with many coastal African states, they remained intimidated by Akwamu and dependent on its control of trading access to the interior. At the same time, the Danes profited by selling guns and powder to Akwamu, which supplied them with slaves for the West Indies.[6]

Continuing African wars kept the Danish in a series of shifting alliances. A coalition of states defeated Akwamu in 1731, flooding the market with enslaved Akwamu captives. Transported to the Caribbean, these slaves, perhaps remembering the subterfuge that was used to capture Christiansborg, would use similar trickery to take the Danish fort on St. John in 1733, igniting rebellion there. With

Christiansborg, Gold Coast, c. 1750, from Ludewig Romer, *Tilforladelig Efterretning om Kysten Guinea* [A Reliable Account of the Coast of Guinea] (Copenhagen, 1760).

the defeat of Akwamu, others vied for control of the Gold Coast—first Akim, then Ashanti, which besieged Christiansborg in 1742 and forced the Danish to pay tribute. These conflicts ensured a steady stream of slaves through the walls of Christiansborg and onto European ships to America. Yet the slave trade remained unstable and largely unprofitable for the Danish West India and Guinea Company. The Danes had relatively few ships working the triangular circuit between Copenhagen, the Gold Coast, and the Caribbean, and when they did show up they seldom found a full cargo waiting at the fort. Ships either had to wait in port to fill their capacity, which they were reluctant to do because the unhealthy conditions along the coast were often fatal to crews, or continue sailing and hope to find more slaves at other ports. Like many European traders eager to profit when they could, the Danish also sold slaves to ships from other nations. But because the trade survived only by subsidies from the crown, the king dissolved the company in 1754—along with its plantations in the West Indies—parceling out the trade to private companies.[7]

It was into this volatile society that Christian Protten was born in 1715. The arrangement by which his father, a Danish soldier, would have married, or had as a mistress, Christian's Ga mother, was standard in Christiansborg, as in other European slaving ports. Ludewig Ferdinand Romer, a Danish trader who spent years on the coast, explained the situation like this:

> Bishop Worm has granted a dispensation allowing all the Danes at Christiansborg to take to themselves a black woman, yet not more than one, and on the following conditions: (1) the husband must promise to see his heathen wife converted to Christianity; (2) when the husband returns to Europe, he will take her with him, if she wishes to go. On these conditions each man of our nation has his mistress. . . . The Negroes firmly believe that it is a great blessing to have a white child in their families, and a family, no matter how poor it is, will contribute to support the little Mulatto, supplying shirts, etc.

Danish men, Romer also contended, cared as much for their mistresses and children "as a man does who has his true wife and children in Europe. Some among the Europeans do not wish to leave their family on the Coast even if they know they could live better in Europe." Fathers paid four percent of their salary into a "mulatto fund" for the maintenance and education of their children. Under these conditions, the mulatto community in and around Christiansborg became fairly large. Children could become soldiers of the Danish crown at the age of ten, earning a salary of eight *thaler* a month; at times mulattoes were the majority of soldiers serving in the fort. As multilingual intermediaries between Europeans and black Africans, they also helped to provision the fort, smooth trade relations, and even procure slaves. These people of mixed ancestry were both a product of the slave trade and part of the system that perpetuated it.[8]

Raised in this community and educated at the Christiansborg school, Protten felt drawn to serve his fellow Afro-Europeans as a schoolmaster as his own mentor, Elias Svane, had done. So he took up his post in the castle and began to teach. Yet within a year he began to complain that he felt himself listing off course. Despite the uncomfortable terms on which he had left Germany, he remained in contact with Rebecca and church leaders (except Zinzendorf, apparently) through the slow and irregular mail service via Copenhagen, and his letters to Herrnhut reveal his spiritual malaise. "The Savior has given me an open door here. I know that I am not the man through whom the Savior can do things," he wrote in 1757. "I know that I have made a mess of everything, but I could not act differently. I still cling to our Magnet and cannot live without Him. His death and sufferings, His martyrdom and His bloody wounds are the only things left to me, since I am a poor heart, as God knows."[9]

Similarly, in May 1759, Protten confessed to a fragile emotional state brought on largely by solitude and frustration: "As for my inner condition, it is forever changing. Sometimes I hold the Savior as close as one can hold anything, sometimes there are tears, and not without cause. On those days I sing: Take me anew by the hand that lets nothing fall, and Let my soul never out of your trusting arms. So I cry, I laugh, I am quiet, and am still here in this country quite alone, alone." He complained that Danish Brethren in Copenhagen had received him with a "cold attitude" and that Eriksen, the ship captain, had denounced him "long before my arrival as a Herrnhuter *Apostell*." As a result, "in body I am still fairly healthy, yet dejected and melancholy, because among so many people I must continually live like a hermit . . . the enemy has accomplished nothing, but I have been placed between two seats." In using the German phrase "between two seats" *(zwischen zwei Stühle)* to describe his sensation of being trapped between two positions, Christian invoked an apt metaphor for his entire life experience.[10]

Perhaps the analogy resonated with him because of its African connotation of royal power symbolized by the king's throne, or stool. Protten was surrounded by reminders that he himself was of royal blood and might, under different circumstances, have been heir to the line of succession. His grandfather was apparently the Ga king Ofori, who, in 1680, after years of fighting between the Ga and Akwamu in the Accra region, retreated with his people before the Akwamu advance. They settled in Little Popo, a hundred miles east, and founded the kingdom of Glidji. Ofori's daughter was Christian's mother; his son (Christian's uncle) was Ofori Bembeneer, who ruled from 1694 to 1733. Ofori Bembeneer's son (Christian's cousin), Assiambo, also known as Ashangmo or Assiongbon Dandjin, took the throne in 1733 and ruled for many years, becoming an exceptionally powerful figure in the military and political affairs of the Slave Coast. Assiambo had served in the army of Dahomey, a large inland kingdom that exerted hegemony over a number of smaller states on the coast, but fearing execution by a jealous king, he fled in 1737, and a Ga force annihilated a Dahomian army that was pursuing him. This victory marked Assiambo's ascendancy as the dominant power on the western Slave Coast, capable even of destroying Dahomey, in the opinion of the Danish trader Romer: "The reason Assiamboe did not completely destroy the Dahomeys is that his free Negroes, or subjects, refused to follow up their victory in the land of the Dahomeys, fearing that if Assiamboe became more powerful he, like other great African kings, would become a tyrant—and they were certainly right." Assiambo aided other kingdoms that resisted Dahomey, waged war against several smaller states, and challenged his rival's commercial supremacy by becoming an important player in the slave trade.[11]

Assiambo was still on the throne when Christian Protten, his cousin, arrived in Christiansborg in 1757. Though the king's seat of power was still at Little Popo, he maintained good relations with the Danes a hundred miles away. Protten wrote that Assiambo wanted him to visit Popo, but he decided to wait. Romer, who dealt with Assiambo and considered him a friend, gave this eyewitness testimony of his authority, although it was not without European condescension:

> [Africans] have another custom that is rarely seen. It is celebrated when they are building a house, and the clay for the walls must be moistened with brandy, or, which is less desirable, with palm wine. The king at Little Popo, Assiamboe, has not only had his entire residence, which is of great size, built with brandy, but at every half-span of the walls he has stuck on all manner of European goods, such as cotton [cloth], Silesian linen, etc. This widely renowned residence, in which I lodged for six weeks, looks dreadful. Rain has washed some of the clay walls away from the exterior, exposing the [textile] fibers. It much resembles a great heap of sweepings. The patches hanging exposed there are so bleached that one cannot see what color they originally were. The Negroes at Popo called this residence a fortress, and I believe it has cost easily as much as a fort. Assiambo has four cannons without their gun carriages. Shortly before I arrived there, he had caught four of his enemies (Dahomey Negroes), whose heads he had cut into small pieces, placed them in the cannons, and shot them away. He told me his enemies would have to hunt for a long time before they could recover their heads.[12]

It was Romer who also suggested that Protten might once have claimed some form of inheritance in the royal line. "We have seen instances of black royal women destined to bring into the world only heirs to the throne, who have married a soldier," he wrote. "Although Mulattos cannot inherit the throne, they can inherit their mother's brother's wealth," which, in Christian's case, meant the estate of his uncle, Ofori Bembeneer. Christian was "actually heir to the wealth of Assiamboe at Little Popo, and had he been black, would have been heir to his throne as well. Indeed, according to the law of the Blacks, Christian Prott[en] ought to have the kingdom of Afolli [Ofori Bembeneer], who was Assiamboe's predecessor and Prott's mother's brother, but Prott[en] was not present in the country when Afolli died, and Assiamboe took everything." If Christian ever regretted his lost opportunities for riches or power, he left no indication, writing only of his desire for spiritual peace. Nonetheless, despite its contradictory claims about how much Protten, as a mulatto, might have inherited, Romer's description is an important reminder of his bicultural, and royal, heritage.[13]

In Christiansborg, the Protestant evangelist connected again with his African lineage. He began serious study of African spirituality, comparatively observing and describing the hierarchy of African divinities in different cultures, from supreme god to several strata of lesser "national or family gods" such as snakes, tigers, rivers, and plants. He witnessed sacred ceremonies, such as the sacrifice of a goat, whose "blood was mixed with palm oil and salt, which was then applied to the foreheads of the entire company." He took field trips to visit—or intrude on—secret holy spaces. On one occasion, he "saw some words at the edge of a village. In front of the entrance to it, there hung a mat curtain. He was tempted to go in, despite the pleadings of the Negroes who tried to discourage him from doing so by warning him that it was the dwelling place of a powerful spirit who could kill anyone who earned his displeasure. Upon entering, he found it to be a very lovely secluded spot, which he continued visiting many times after that." There is no indication that Protten ever felt tempted to engage in African worship practices, but he seemed fascinated by them. Was there an element of wistfulness in his fixation? Did he consider himself an ethnographer of this culture—his culture—from the outside or from within? He didn't say.[14]

Protten found members of his family, many of whom still lived in nearby villages, particularly in Osu, near the Danish castle, and around the Dutch fort of Crevecoeur, and even as far away as Capo Corso, the English fort fifty miles west along the Gold Coast. Tette, the chief, or cabuceer, of the Tessing region, was "a blood relative of mine, and fairly close by, very pious, and as a genuine person, better than I," Christian wrote. It is not certain how warmly his relatives welcomed him, but they might have seen him as a valuable multilingual go-between, and he was eager to claim his connections with them.[15] He found his mother, though where she lived is unclear; she was evidently shocked to the point of disbelief at seeing her son again. Christian must have written to Rebecca describing the reunion, for she mentioned it in a response to him on September 2, 1760. She had read his melancholy reports from the field, and now, writing in a phonetic, half-German, half-Dutch scrawl, she tried to buck up her husband's wavering spirits four thousand miles away:

> This letter has been a long time in the writing, I hardly know what to say, that I should have made you wait so long before writing. You know well that I love you and that I will never forget it. That I promise, but, poor me, what will your poor heart do in these times. Turn to Him, who has everything. The Lord blesses and protects you and meets you and clothes you with mercy. I received your last letter, from 12 May 1759, with joy and with sorrow. Dear heart, what should I say? My heart, the Lord shows us mercy, that we may turn ourselves over to Him. We know his great heart well, and He has also taught us that a great heart is patient. I want to say something to you, and I put before you this example, that if your mother had known that she would see you again, that when it happened, I think you believed it, but your poor mother could not believe it and didn't know where to find the faith [to believe it]. I believe you feel that too.

Rebecca also referred to a secret of Christian's, which, in the sharing, might have drawn the cords of empathy even tighter between them—the revelation that, all his life, he carried around thoughts of his father. Almost nothing is known of that Danish soldier who, like all the others, married into an African family and produced a mixed-race son. After Christian left the Gold Coast for Copenhagen at age twelve in 1727, it is not known whether his father died at Christiansborg, returned to Denmark, or ever saw his son again. Yet, as Rebecca's letter reveals, Christian never forgot him:

> O, that He would lead us so far for us to comprehend the basis of our faith. The dear Savior suffers with you at your beside and strengthens the faith by which you have worked in this world. Namely, one day your father will let go of you and not help any more. Then it may come about that we will have to cling to each other now, as you once did to your father.

Christian, it seems, was suspended between the memory, or the image, of an admired but long-lost Danish father, and an African mother who could not quite accept that her son had returned. As an "Atlantic Creole," the product of the complex interchange between Africa and Europe, his multilingualism and ability to cross cultures served him well. But as he showed, it was also possible to be a casualty of that system: in all his passages between Denmark, Germany, and the Gold Coast, he never felt fully accepted in any place or among any group of people.[16]

Perhaps Christianity was the only thing left to this uprooted child of the slave trade. But faith, for him, was not always the panacea it was for his wife. Rebecca not only found fortitude in the Gospel; it was the vehicle by which she expressed a tenaciously strong will. Of course she must have had insecurities and fears, but she betrayed none in any of her few writings or in the record of her public actions. The conviction that she had a divine destiny, steeled by her imprisonment and trial years earlier, stayed with her for life. Christian, more restless, did not necessarily question his faith, but neither did it often allay his self-doubt. He, too, believed he had an appointment from God to preach, but his spirit fluttered in the winds of uncertainty. Still, the intimacy of their surviving fragmentary correspondence shows that Rebecca and Christian loved each other despite the odds against an arranged marriage succeeding on that level. Their obvious similarities evidently created real empathy, while her strength was a counterpoint to his fragile, though probably charismatic, temperament.

Rebecca had fared well enough in Christian's absence. Because she had been banished only because of her connection with him, she was recalled from exile in 1757 and was again living in Herrnhut, worshipping with the congregation. She wrote at least twice to Christian with chatty details about friends and choir activities, mentioning also that armies marched through the town during the Seven Years' War, often demanding food and shelter. The Prussians even quartered in town for two months. The big news, however, was the death of Count Zinzendorf in May 1760. The Count's wife had died in 1756, and he married the Single Sisters' leader, Anna Nitschmann, the next year. But he became reclusive and his health began to fail, and the death of the magnetic figure who had dominated the church for more than thirty years marked a sharp break for the Brethren.[17]

Christian had never reconciled with the Count, and the news of Zinzendorf's death might not even have reached him when his own depressed state of mind was jolted by disaster in February 1761. He was cleaning a gun when he accidentally shot and killed a young student in the mulatto school, Friedrich Magnus. At least, that was his explanation to the Danish authorities who arrested and imprisoned him. He sat in jail for six weeks while the case was investigated, receiving daily visits from Anna, the governor's mulatto mistress, "who often cried over my misfortune, because she believed it was an accident and not intentional." To emphasize his lack of intent in shooting the child, Christian wrote in his diary that the student's father had "died in my arms" in 1758. In a letter written to

King Frederik V of Denmark, long afterwards, Christian described what happened after the shooting: "The Governor and council looked into the whole matter themselves, recognized my innocence, and released me from imprisonment; but at the same time, after I paid the child's relatives 32 Reichsthaler, they ordered me to remove myself from there and to have nothing to do with the child's friends in the future." Exonerated but again disgraced, Christian left the place that was to have been his salvation and returned to Europe. He arrived in Copenhagen in the spring of 1762 and, broke, walked back to Herrnhut, a journey of 300 miles.[18]

Apart from Rebecca's presumable joy, the sight of the prodigal son returning after yet another botched mission inspired mixed reactions among the Brethren. Protten had left on bad terms five years earlier, and his latest misfortune, though ruled accidental, furnished more evidence of an unsteady character. It is not clear whether he was accepted back into the fold, because documents from 1762 again place him in Grosshennersdorf rather than Herrnhut. Still, church leaders recognized that he still had a role to play in Africa and that he wanted to embrace it. They questioned him closely about the Gold Coast, sizing up the prospects of expanding the mission there. He drew up several reports describing the flora and geography of the country as well as the economic and political apportionment of power among the Danish, Dutch, and English traders. In his opinion, indigo could be grown quite well along the coast, should the Brethren wish to start a settlement, although he seems not to have discussed the question of labor. No doubt flattered by the attention, Christian emphasized his family connections, especially with the cabuceer Tette, and said they might prove hospitable for establishing an outpost. The elders were impressed.[19]

In October 1762, Christian wrote to Frederik V asking to be reinstated in Christiansborg. "I am resolved to visit my fatherland Guinea again to serve God and my fellow men by bringing *Information* and instruction to the poor, largely forsaken mulatto children," he insisted. Christian's effort to rehabilitate—or reinvent—himself again worked. The king granted the request, announcing late in the year that because "Christian Protten is a very useful person, in that he understands the language of the country and has already been active in instructing the mulatto children," he would be pardoned in order to resume his post. If Christian felt himself divided between his African and European selves, it was this binary quality that still made him "useful" to the crown despite all his problems. No European was master of African languages like Protten; none could straddle cultural divides so easily, as the king recognized. And this time, by agreement of the church elders, Rebecca would accompany him to help in the mulatto school. After years away from the missions, she was going back, into the heart of the slave trade itself, back to the land of her own origins, to do what she had done thirty years earlier—teach.[20]

The king's ruling completed Christian's reconciliation with church leaders. Though he was to be officially employed by the crown, the Brethren considered his work part of their cause, and as he and Rebecca prepared to leave in March 1763, several elders wrote to wish him well and outline their expectations. "You and your dear Rebecca are going back to Guinea with the blessing and peace of our Savior and his congregation," they assured him. The Prottens should build a house outside the Christiansborg walls that could be the hub of a "Negro village for the Lord," just close enough to the fort to gain refuge in times of war, but far enough away from the Europeans' unholy ways. This little settlement, the elders wrote, would be a beachhead for a larger mission to inland peoples, with additional teams of evangelists to come later. They gently tried to dissuade Christian from surging off on his own to preach among the Ga on the Slave Coast. "We know that Popo, where your cousin is king, is near to your heart. We don't say you should disregard it altogether, but that you should prepare the way with the mulatto children for the Brethren who will come later." Wishing the Prottens to go "with the escort of a thousand angels," they sent along a letter in Dutch to the cabuceer Tette, offering salutations, the Brethren's friendship, and promising a gift from "our friend" Protten and his wife—"zyne Vrouwe Rebecka." On March 28, the couple set out for the Gold Coast.[21]

Rising from a rock cliff along the shore of Africa, Christiansborg castle was built to intimidate. The original 1661 fort had been enlarged several times, so that voyagers approaching by ship saw several rings of high, whitewashed walls four feet thick, a thicket of bastions and towers, and guns bristling at them from the ramparts. Waving in the wind high above the walls, a huge Danish flag—white cross on a red background—was visible from miles out at sea. The fort, defended by "30 Europeans and 300 Africans," was described as "invincible and impregnable against all the forces of the Africans so far known on Gold Coast—even if the Africans were united." All this Christian and Rebecca would have seen when their ship, *Christiansborg*, a slaver that sailed the triangular route between Denmark, the Gold Coast, and the Caribbean, pulled up offshore on May 10, 1765.

The fortifications, however, were not the most dangerous threat that travelers faced. The rugged coastline offered no good place for ships to anchor; shallow jagged rocks lurked just below the water, and breakers pounded the shore. "There is at that place a most vile harbor for landing, so that thereby many Christians have suffered injuries both of their persons and their goods when trying to land," one visitor wrote. African boatmen were expert at maneuvering canoes through the waves, shuttling goods, slaves, and passengers between anchored ships and the castle. A captain would say a few words to the sea, sprinkling several drops of brandy as an offering, and paddlers would slice through the waves at the right moment. But when the Prottens disembarked and tried to land, they fell victim to the violent surf. Perhaps European boatmen rather than Africans were steering; in any event, their canoe lost control and capsized. Although they were rescued and taken to the fort, they lost all their belongings in the ocean, including Christian's papers.[22]

Sadly, it was a fitting end to their journey after an extraordinarily frustrating two years since their departure from Germany. They had traveled first by mail coach to Zeist, the Brethren's congregation in Holland near the coast south of Amsterdam. There they tried to book passage on a Dutch ship to Africa, but they had virtually no money. Officials in Herrnhut had given them little, and the administrators in Zeist refused to pay their fare, arguing that it was the responsibility of the Danish crown. Thus began an excruciating period of wandering, as the Prottens borrowed small sums of money to travel back and forth between churches in Zeist, Amsterdam, and Heerendijk, pleading their cause to unsympathetic ears. They even journeyed to London but met the same reception. Why the Brethren should have treated them so coldly is not altogether certain. Church leaders complained that Christian was drinking heavily, and they might have concluded again that he could not be trusted. Perhaps he drank in response to their intransigence. But perhaps here, as well, was the key to Christian's troubled relationship to the church all along, the reason for his censure and banishment. Was it his drinking that Papa Zinzendorf and the others had equated with "Moorish" pride and lack of self-control? Now, in Holland, Christian put his anger into his diary, at one point writing that someone's words of rejection "were like a knife in my heart." Finally, in desperation, after more than a year of inaction, the Prottens traveled to Copenhagen in the summer of 1764 to seek help from the crown.[23]

Back in the familiar town of his adolescence, Protten was able to salvage something from the fiasco. As if to confirm his own value, and to thank the king, he wrote and submitted a manuscript that was published in Copenhagen in 1764 with the Danish title *En nyttig Grammaticalsk Indledelse til Tvende hinindtil gandske ubekiendte Sprog, Fanteisk og Acraisk,* or *A Useful Grammatical Intro-duction to Two Completely Unknown Languages, Fante and Ga.* A ma-jor work of scholarship that Protten must have partly drafted, or made notes for, in Christiansborg, the book is considered the earliest written example of the Ga language, and it also supplements a cate-chism written in Fante by Johannes Capitein in 1744. The 64-page text, in Danish, provides a basic vocabulary, an overview of Ga and Fante grammatical structures, and translations of key biblical texts such as the Lord's Prayer, the Ten Commandments, Luther's Cate-chism, and the sacrament of baptism. Though his orthography is now obsolete, Protten established himself in his time as a pioneer in the exceptionally difficult task of translating European and African languages into each other.[24]

The book's introduction was also instructive of the author's in-tent and his view of his own role in the work. "It would be very use-ful for Mulatto children around Fort Christiansborg, on the Accra coast in Guinea," he told readers, "to grasp and understand the Danish language, preferably written, or as it is contained in books, if it could be expanded and elucidated through the country's language and their own mother tongue." Europeans might also find the book useful in "gaining some insight into these two so singularly different languages." The Accra, or Ga, language, he explained, was difficult to learn, because "one must have got the correct pronunciation with one's mother's milk, or from one's child-legs and youth on up." As a result, Ga was spoken only within a range of about ten miles of Christiansborg. The easier Fante, on the other hand, was the lingua franca along the entire sixty-mile length of the Gold Coast and for many miles inland. Although foreigners could understand and even speak both languages well, Protten wrote, previous attempts to tran-scribe them had failed because the writers were not native speakers.[25]

The proclamation of his African identity thus shadowed the en-tire project, but in ways that again showed his divided heritage. Mu-latto children were to be the main beneficiaries of the work, the better to help them learn Danish and Christianity. On the other hand, in claiming the expertise of a native whose knowledge derived from his "mother's milk," Protten undercut the authority of European interpreters of Africa. By suggesting that only Africans could truly understand their own cultures, he prepared the way for Afro-European writers such as Olaudah Equiano who, a few years later, would lay similar claim to native authority as a basis for attacking the slave trade. Though Protten had no such overt intent in his own work, he was making a new, embryonic argument that African-centered knowledge had to lie at the heart of any discussion about Africa. His book was printed and distributed in Copenhagen, and he took copies with him when he and Rebecca finally left Copenhagen on the king's account in late 1764 or early 1765. Alas, those copies were lost in the breakers at Christiansborg.[26]

"Arriving in this land is like arriving in a different world," wrote the Danish merchant Ludewig Romer, "where one sees different objects, different people and a different way of life." So it must have seemed to Rebecca when she climbed a set of stairs and passed through the gates of Christiansborg's whitewashed walls. But she would also have recognized immediately many of the images that assaulted her senses: the tropical climate and landscape, the heavily protected fortress, the handful of armed Europeans engulfed in an African world, the slave mart, the busy streets and colorful markets outside the fort, the bright clothing of the people—she knew them all too well from the West Indies. She would have heard Danish, Dutch, and several familiar Akan languages, remembered the filed teeth and the ethnic patterns of lines and circles etched onto African faces, nodded in recognition at the gait and demeanor of her new neighbors.[27]

The fort's impressive exterior, wrote one visitor, belied its cramped, uncomfortable interior. The walls enclosed an inner courtyard, paved with light-brown local sandstone, around which the life of the fort revolved. A stone cistern in the courtyard with an octagonal Baroque design stored up to four hundred barrels of rain water. Around the interior walls were a series of small cubicles for the soldiers, so low they could not even stand up, and with windows so small they did not permit a cooling cross-draft. "It is easy to understand that this place alone is enough to breed contagious illness," the visitor concluded. Disease and heat could drive Europeans insane. In 1755, a Danish pastor began to sing and dance and picked a fight with a sentry. When African medicines failed to cure him, he was confined to a room, where "sometimes he climbs up to the window, puts his legs out between the wooden bars, and bleats like a goat or crows like a cock." European soldiers and administrators excelled in three diversions, "Bacchus, gaming, and Venus," knowing their life span on the coast was bound to be short.[28]

The focal points of the courtyard—indeed, the very reason for Christiansborg's existence—were the two slave dungeons enclosed behind heavy iron grille doors. Slaves who had marched from inland to the coast, often hundreds of miles from their capture or sale, ended the first part of their journey in these cramped and poorly ventilated chambers, where they might stay for months until a ship came to pick them up. The stench that poured out into the courtyard was said to be overpowering. It was here, in the dungeons of Christiansborg, that many of the people Rebecca worshipped with on St. Thomas had huddled before crowding onto slave ships bound for the Caribbean. And the dungeons were continually replenished. By the time Rebecca arrived in Christiansborg, St. Thomas had been surpassed by the much larger island of St. Croix as the Danish West Indies' major plantation society and sugar producer; the demand for slaves had intensified, and the Danish slave trade accelerated accordingly. Whereas in the 1730s about 270 people were exported annually from Christiansborg and Fredensborg, the other major Danish Gold Coast fort built in 1737, that number had grown to 350 annually in the 1750s and to 600 per year in the 1770s, nearly eleven percent of the total exports from the Gold Coast. From behind their bars in the Christiansborg jail the slaves could look out onto a solitary tree in the courtyard, which, during the rainy season, held hundreds of migratory birds who "twitter and sing from morning to evening, so you can scarcely hear yourself speak." Virtually the last sound many captives heard in Africa, before marching to canoes that would take them to the slave ships, was the raucous clamor of the birds.[29]

Here, in the fort, is where the Prottens were to live and hold school as the slave trade swirled around them. But nothing, it seems, was ever simple with Christian. If he thought his return would be a triumphant redemption after a disastrous exile four years earlier, he was wrong. Once again his legitimacy came under attack, this time when a Danish Lutheran minister, Hagerup, challenged his appointment by the king. Christian probably lost his letter of authorization during the landing and had no other proof, so on March 26, two weeks after his arrival, he answered by letter a series of questions from the minister. The trade board in Copenhagen, he explained, had appointed him and Rebecca to come to Christiansborg to instruct the mulatto children. He would teach the boys reading and writing, while Rebecca would teach the girls household skills such as sewing and washing laundry. His annual salary had been set at 250 gold *Rixthaler*, plus an additional 150 *thaler* to provide for the poorest children, all to be paid on the king's account at the fort. He was to provide a reckoning of his expenses for the poor. Protten evidently made a convincing case to the governor, for he and Rebecca were allowed to proceed.[30]

They began asking pesky questions of their own, however. First, Rebecca protested that the kitchen in the fort, provided to her by the Christiansborg administrator, was inadequate to meet her task of cooking for the schoolchildren, especially the indigent. The kitchen had been fine for previous ministers and even a governor, replied the administrator. Showing again her famous stubbornness, Rebecca still refused to use it. The complaint was apparently unresolved when the Prottens asked permission sometime later in 1765 to build a house in the *Negeriet,* or Negro village, of Osu outside the fort walls, where they would live with children from the school. That was exactly the plan that Christian had discussed with the Moravian elders two years earlier. Despite his subsequent struggles with the church, he still apparently wanted to build a mission base, and he believed the children could be schooled better away from the fort. But the commandant, Carl Gottleb Resch, rebuffed the proposal, saying the Prottens should be content with their two rooms and kitchen in the fort, and that the school children "should not live among the heathen." School had always been held in the fort, he said, and there it would stay.[31]

In making his case for his appointment, Protten revealed some of the underlying assumptions governing his and Rebecca's task in the school, which had about forty pupils. These children of mixed unions were to be educated to serve the interests of the Danish government and the fort. Boys would enter the militia at age ten, while girls were to become the wives of European and, presumably, mulatto men. Rebecca's job, therefore, was to instruct girls in the skills they would need in European-style patriarchal households. Since the children were all baptized Christians, instruction in the faith was a crucial part of their education, which involved a steady diet of biblical passages, prayers, and a catechism. It was a challenging assignment because many mulattoes, with a foot in both cultures, continued to worship African deities as well. In the 1740s Anna Sophia Peterson, the wife of a Danish soldier, offered a bottle of brandy as a sacrifice to a Ga oracle, who refused it, and instead, according to the merchant Romer, "he farted, and damned her with these words, 'Your memory shall be obliterated.'" Mulattoes passed up burial in the Christian cemetery in favor of the African custom of burial in the household compound, often deceiving the preacher by "bringing an empty coffin or exhuming the body at night after the burial." It seemed to one Danish pastor that, by partaking in the customs of both Africans and Europeans, mulattoes were "equally despised by both; by the first because they proudly lifted themselves above them, by the latter, because they wanted to lift themselves up to their level."[32]

Educating girls had proven particularly frustrating for Danish ministers, who complained that they ignored teachings about pre-marital chastity and adultery. Most African societies placed little stigma on premarital sex, and the culture of Christiansborg encour-aged a freewheeling sexuality that shoved aside traditional Christian morality. "As soon as a young man arrives from Europe, fornicating women offer their body to him for a mere bottle of brandy, and co-habit with him as long as he is in the land, and then look out for an-other one," wrote Romer. European men often had several wives, and premarital pregnancies were not uncommon among mulatto girls and women.[33]

The perceived advantage of liaisons with European men made very difficult any attempt to teach against such practices, and it is not clear whether Rebecca sought to do so. There is little informa-tion about the regimen she conducted in class, or whether read-ing and writing were part of her religious instruction. What can be said is that both she and Christian had a strong spiritual and emo-tional investment in the school. They saw themselves as driving an opening wedge for the planting of Protestant Christianity in Africa. The school was an extension of the work in female education that Rebecca had begun in the western hemisphere thirty years ear-lier, and of what Christian had been trying to achieve, on and off, since then himself. In working with mixed-race children, more-over, they operated in the seam where Europe and Africa met and merged. Though Christian knew the Gold Coast more intimately than Rebecca did, she understood that intersection well, having lived her life within it.

Rebecca would have readily grasped the need to make adapta-tions, such as in language. She could have spoken to the girls in

Danish, but they understood little. How, then, was she to communicate with them? In 1769, a Lutheran minister at Christiansborg named Feldtmann complained that Christian spoke only Ga with the students, and he added that, because the girls spoke Danish so poorly, he had to address them through an interpreter. The remark raises the intriguing prospect that Rebecca learned Ga, Fante, or both, to reach the students. She had an adept verbal facility with languages, and Christian might have reconstructed some of his lost translations to help her. Perhaps she knew something of a few Gold Coast languages from the West Indies. By teaching them in their own tongue, Christian preferred to interact with students on African terms, and Rebecca, skilled in gliding between cultures, may well have accepted the idea as simply part of adjusting to another new place in the way she had learned Dutch, Creole, and German in previous life stages.[34]

Christian could not escape his personal demons, however, which, according to Danish officials, began to undermine his effectiveness as a teacher. It appears that he sought to withdraw from European Christiansborg and melt back into Africa. For obscure reasons, he was drawn to the Afro-Dutch sector around Fort Crevecoeur, the Dutch fort a few miles away. In October 1766 the Prottens, with permission from the governor, left the fort to stay at the home of Oto Brafo, chief of Accra, who was an important broker for the Dutch, though whether he was a relative of Christian is unknown. Then Protten asked to be allowed to move into the *Neegerie,* the African village beside Crevecoeur. The governor of Christiansborg objected, accusing Christian of missing school and church the day before, and threatening consequences if he didn't return. The controversy passed for a time, but on December 15, 1766, Christian went visiting in the *Neegerie,* and when he returned late at night he was arrested for shooting his gun in Osu outside Christiansborg. With the consent of the governor, the Africans in Osu fined Protten 16 *thaler,* and he responded by shouting and cursing at the governor, according to a complaint. His rifle and powder were confiscated and he was locked up in the fort, though apparently not for long.[35]

What were the administrators to do about their vexing employee? Few were happy with him, but it would take trouble to revoke his royal appointment. Christian virtually stopped writing back to the Brethren during these years—or at least any letters he wrote have not survived—so the reports of Danish officials, all negative, are the principal source of information about him. Jacob Meder, a Moravian missionary based in Copenhagen who was in correspondence with the Danes, wrote back to the Brethren in Herrnhut that the director of the Danish slave trading company was disgusted with Protten. He was Henning Bargum, a merchant who had gained a royal charter in 1765 to operate the trade out of Christiansborg with his company, the "Slave Trade Society," or Bargum's Trading Society. As a businessman, Bargum had little patience with the school's mission, or the antics of its headmaster. "Mr. Bargum says no good things about him, and he tells me he [Protten] is much given to drink, so that he cannot fulfill his duty as Mulatto schoolmaster," Meder reported in September 1767, adding that Bargum "would like to be rid of him."[36]

A dissenting opinion came from Ludewig Romer, the Danish merchant and Christiansborg veteran who was living in Copenhagen and working for the Moravians as an agent for African affairs. "Do not give up on Protten," he advised later that year. "He can still be of great service to you. His kinship with noble Accras, especially Asiambo, can still be very useful for your good purpose." Still, Romer admitted, Protten made life difficult for himself and those around him.[37]

As Romer suggested, the Brethren were still determined to press on with an African mission. The slave trade was their golden chance, in Jacob Meder's opinion. "It is well known that Negro slaves are brought from more than two or three hundred miles inland to the coast," he wrote in January 1768. "We should take the opportunity, when we preach the gospel to them, to say that many of their nation, and possibly their cousins, in the West Indies have come to know the grace of Him who died for all mankind." The idea that exhausted and battered survivors would find solace, after a 300-mile trek, in knowing that their kinfolk had converted to Christianity an ocean away, was a measure of the Brethren's vigorous optimism as well as their naiveté. It also stamped them as still resolutely unable or unwilling to criticize the business of slavery. At a time when Protestant activists on both sides of the Atlantic, both white and black, were beginning to use Christianity to attack human bondage, the Brethren wanted only the chance to proselytize those about to begin an ocean voyage to an infinity of servitude.[38]

Protten would probably be useless in this project, contended Meder, who, writing from four thousand miles away in Denmark, even painted Rebecca with the same critical brush. "We believe Protten, like his wife, would be a hindrance and a detriment to us. One must consider that they have already lived long outside our fellowship, that he is a peculiar man, that he is surrounded by bad examples, and that he has been very poorly treated." Though not entirely unsympathetic, Meder could find little of redeemable value in the couple.[39]

As the criticism intensified, Christian and Rebecca felt abandoned by friends in Europe, cut off from their support in Christiansborg, and impoverished. Christian revealed their distress in a "pretty confused letter" to a Moravian brother in Copenhagen in April 1768, "filled with loud complaints about the government there, that he is being impeded and persecuted in his task of instructing the mulatto children, and that he and his wife are about to perish from hunger and worry. He wishes to be relieved of his duty and writes, 'I wish I could end my life in Popo, where my cousin is king, if I had permission from the congregation to move there.'" His sense of persecution was no doubt real, but Christian refused to admit responsibility for any of his troubles, including the difficult position he had put Rebecca in. Typically, he straddled the problem that had bedeviled him his entire life: he again proclaimed, almost defiantly, his blood ties to African royalty, but he sought permission to embrace that kinship from the Europeans who had forsaken him. As for Rebecca, there is no glimpse of how she dealt with the double burden of pressure from the government and her husband's personal problems. She had always responded to tribulation by trusting Jesus, and probably she did so again, but that resolve was not reflected in Christian's desperate outburst.[40]

Though Christian complained of poverty, his salary of 250 *thaler* compared favorably with that of many others at the fort. In 1753, the commandant earned 800 *thaler,* the bookkeeper and the chaplain 240 each, a head clerk 168, a surgeon 192, a sergeant 192, and a private 84. Those figures could be deceptive, however, since the economy of Christiansborg was almost always in shambles. The West India and Guinea Company had lost money on the slave trade, as did private companies that took over the trade after 1754. When a new governor, Christian Tychsen, arrived in 1766, he found the accounts in a mess, the fort in terrible repair, and a garrison complaining of starvation and close to mutiny. Because money was scarce, employees received some of their pay in the form of goods, which they were expected to sell back to Africans. Protten was among a group of employees who wrote to the governing council protesting that, of the goods they received as salary, only the Danish brandy sold well, and a tax increase drained their profits further. Life was already hard on the Coast, the petitioners argued, and the chance of returning home alive slim.[41]

The high mortality rate kept coffin makers in steady business, and Christian did have enough money to buy belongings of the dead regularly at auction. Perhaps it was a survival strategy with the intention of reselling the items, but many of the things he bought had little value, and perhaps he wanted them for his own or Rebecca's use. At one auction he bought some old stockings, a silk scarf, two pewter plates and a pewter pot, a bottle of ink, and several quills; at another he bought twenty quarts of Danish brandy; at a third he bought a pair of old English shoes, bottles, glasses, buttons, and conch shells. And when Governor Tychsen died in early 1768, Christian bought from his estate thirty-four feet of embroidered taffeta, six Dutch books, ten Latin books, and twenty-five French books. Whatever the whimsical or practical reasons may have been for buying many items, Christian seems to have wanted books to keep alive his, and perhaps his wife's, humanistic interests in a place where learning was difficult.[42]

In the spring of 1768 four Moravian evangelists set out from Copenhagen for the Gold Coast. Arriving at Christiansborg in July, the group—leader Jacob Meder accompanied by Gottfried Schulze, Johann Kleffel, and Johann Lembke—was filled with idealism at the prospect of launching the long-promised mission to new heathen frontiers. Christian and Rebecca, despite their strained relationship with the church, must have been glad to see some familiar faces enter the fort, a kind of affirmation that they still mattered. Inspecting the situation on the coast, Meder moderated the critical views he had held in Copenhagen, writing to Romer of his favorable impression of Rebecca and of his optimism that Christian would right himself and support the mission. It hardly mattered. Within two months Meder and two of the others came down with fever and died. Of Meder, the Danes wrote that his death caused "no inconsiderable loss to us in respect to many things, not only of company, science, and moral matters, but even in being of assistance to us in the prescription of medicines, tending the sick, nay he was agreeable and serviceable to all men." Five more missionaries sent in 1769 did succeed in establishing a mission at Ningo, a village near the Danish fort of Fredensborg, further east along the coast. But two years later all five, as well as the lone survivor from 1768, were dead. The church sent no more martyrs to the Gold Coast.[43]

They were joined by one more, however. In the middle of the string of deaths, Christian Protten himself died in 1769 at the age of fifty-four. The news came in a letter to the Brethren from Rebecca. "Dear congregation," she wrote, "I cannot neglect to inform you that on August 22 my husband became sick with a sore throat, which developed into a high fever, and on the 25th he passed out of time. I send greetings to the entire congregation. I am your poor widow, Rebecca Protten." The letter was printed in the *Gemein Nachrichten,* a sort of Unity newsletter sent out to Moravian congregations around the world, but there was no other attempt to remember the troubled life of this "first fruit." For a church keenly aware of its own history, in which almost everyone left a memoir and official writings eulogized the mission soldiers, the omission was telling. No matter what gloss might have been put on it, Protten's narrative followed no triumphalist script, fulfilled no expectation for a joyful meeting with Jesus. He remained an unreconciled alloy of two worlds, dying, after a lifetime of seeking, in the place of his birth that never fully received him back. In Christiansborg, the Danish logbooks mentioned the schoolmaster's passage, but if anyone felt relief, it was kept quiet.[44]

Having buried her second husband, Rebecca was alone again. Fifty-one years old in 1769, she had long since lost the vigorous step that had once spirited her along the roads of St. Thomas. The Christiansborg governing council described her as "old and weak," and "no longer capable of working." The council voted, in accordance with the law, to give her a pension of 10 *Rixthaler* a month for one year. In July 1770, when the year was about to expire, the council recommended to the directors of Bargum's Company that the pension be extended "since she has, especially in her age and weakness, nothing at all to live from." Whether the proposal was approved is uncertain; Rebecca's name appears alongside her 10-*thaler* monthly payment in the company's account ledger between August 1769 and July 1770, but no payments are recorded thereafter. What, then, became of the twice-widowed evangelist? Did Bargum, or the crown itself, approve a pension that never made it into the books? Did the Moravian Church send her money from afar? Or did she seek help from Protten's African family—her own relatives-in-law— or other African officials nearby? Any of these is possible; whatever the resolution, she disappeared from view in the records for several years.[45]

Then, in 1773, the Brethren wrote to Rebecca offering a chance to return to the West Indies. The company endorsed the plan. "The directors have promised, as in our letter to Rebecca, the widowed Protten, to send her on the next ship free of charge to St. Thomas," wrote church leader Abraham von Gersdorf in Germany on October 13, 1773. "If she is still alive, she will accept the offer with joy." Here was a solution agreeable to everyone: the church would fulfill its responsibility, the company would be rid of the old woman and could concentrate on trading slaves, and she would return home after a thirty-year absence, completing the Atlantic triangle circuit back to the Caribbean and the whitewashed church on St. Thomas.[46]

Either because of delays in transmitting messages, or because she couldn't decide at once, two years passed before Rebecca gave her answer. In 1776 the company ship, *Ada,* was to leave Christiansborg for the West Indies, and the directors pressed to know whether she would be a passenger. Their report told the story:

Rebecca, the widow of the departed teacher Protten, is still alive and has been given the letter sent her by the honorable board of directors. She answered orally: Since she is now old and frail and could not endure the travel to St. Croix in the West Indies, she has decided to stay in this country for the rest of her life. She is very thankful to the honorable board for the kindness that she could go on the ship *Ada* and enjoy free passage. It was her wish that, according to an application to the said high offices, she could receive a small pension annually for her support, since she is poor, has nothing to live from and can no longer earn a living by working.

There the matter stayed. The *Ada* departed with a load of slaves, and Rebecca was not on board. The company directors must have been disappointed, and no record indicates whether her pension request was granted. But someone, somehow, supported her, and she lived on, perhaps tucked into a corner of the fort or shuffling through the streets of the *Negeriet,* stopping for a word with the Dutch-speaking villagers. Or perhaps not: war broke out between the Dutch, Danish, and their African allies in the mid-1770s, and fighting raged around Christiansborg and Crevecoeur for several years. Wherever she stayed, Rebecca's scope of movement was probably quite limited.[47]

And so, one day in 1780, a bit of non-military news made its way to a Christiansborg official, who wrote a letter that a ship carried to Copenhagen, where a Moravian brother opened it and forwarded the news overland by coach to Herrnhut. There, in July 1781, the tidings were broadcast in the *Nachrichten:* "From Guinea by way of Copenhagen we have received the report that the well-known Christian Protten's widow Rebecca has herself gone to the Savior a year ago." She was sixty-two. As with her husband, there was nothing else to say, it seemed, about the well-traveled sister who went to meet Jesus in obscurity a world away.[48]

Rebecca died far from the place of her greatest triumphs. Her achievements in Africa, like Christian's, are difficult to assess. Teaching and nurturing pupils as she had done for a lifetime, she probably left an imprint on some, or many, of the girls who passed through the Christiansborg school, though how deeply that influence was felt is impossible to say. A priestly woman to the end, she continued her cause of female education as she had done in America and Europe. In a region consumed by the traffic in slaves, however, the Prottens ignited no widespread interest in Christianity on the Gold Coast. Absorbed into the very machinery of the trade itself, they were not in a position to oppose it, nor, perhaps, did they seek to do so. That was a struggle that others were preparing to wage.

The important thing is that Rebecca made it to Africa at all. That she carried out a ministry in three distinct parts of the world was, for a free woman of color in the eighteenth century, virtually unique. She lived as a kind of reverse cultural bridge across the Atlantic during the period of the overwhelming one-way flow of Africans to America. Alert to the options open to her while aware of the limitations within which she worked, she forged a distinctively international persona—obedient to a calling, yet adept at negotiating life's possibilities, resourceful in any setting or language. Stamping her personality on whatever situation she encountered, she crossed, and sometimes threatened, boundaries between slavery and freedom, whiteness and blackness, male and female activity.

In the end, the image that remains—the one that matters—is that of the preacher, the solitary figure walking the roads, taking the word to workers in the sugar cane fields of America.

Epilogue: Rebecca's Shadow

*J*ust outside the walls of Christiansborg castle stretches a green field rimmed with palm trees—the site of the Danish graveyard where Rebecca Protten was probably buried. Though the pastoral landscape has survived since the eighteenth century, Christiansborg and its environs have changed. The fort's interior courtyard with its cistern and slave dungeons still exists, but the former center of the Danish slave trade is the remodeled, gleaming white government headquarters of the modern nation of Ghana. Where once the village of Osu nestled in the stronghold's shadow, the bastions now look out over the capital city of Accra and its one million people. The great African-American scholar and activist W. E. B. Du Bois, who made his home in Ghana when he died in 1963, was once buried on the grounds of Christiansborg, though his grave was later moved; but no graves remain of the eighteenth-century soldiers, governors, and missionaries who lived and died there. Any traces of Rebecca's memory have vanished from the land.[1]

The erasure is symbolic, for her story of shifting fortunes and adroit maneuvering through the Atlantic littoral has likewise faded from view. That obscurity is scarcely surprising. Historians have only recently begun to examine seriously women's roles as cultural innovators and transmitters, particularly in the diaspora of African peoples during the era of the slave trade. And because she spent nearly all her life among Germans, Danish, Dutch, and Africans, Rebecca has remained largely unknown to the English-speaking world. Once in a while someone will mention the mixed-race woman who married a white man, defying the mores of a colonial slave society. "Her importance lay in her marriages," particularly the interracial union to Matthäus Freundlich, concludes one historian, describing Rebecca also as a "dutiful wife to the easily excitable Protten."[2] Apart from the archaic idea that a woman's significance is defined through her relationships with men, the sum of Rebecca's life well exceeded that modest appraisal. In fact, she stood where the three main currents of the eighteenth-century black Atlantic world flowed together: the dramatic expansion of the slave trade, the Afro-Atlantic freedom struggle, and the rise of black Christianity. Her life illustrates the interconnectedness of Africa, Europe, the Caribbean, and North America, and of one person's ability to navigate those connections. Rebecca was at the eye of a social storm that swirled back and forth across the ocean during the eighteenth century, gathering the momentum to touch, and change, virtually every society on either side.

Though she died seemingly alone and forgotten, Rebecca was in fact celebrated in print during her lifetime. In trying to remake their image in the outside world, her fellow worshippers in the Moravian Church began writing their own history, and as they did, the story of the evangelist's early years and the movement she helped to spearhead unfolded.

Although the Brethren's mission efforts had long been recognized, many churchmen on the continent and in Britain scorned the group as bizarre cultists or dangerously disturbed peddlers in free will. As a result, after Count Zinzendorf's death in 1760, church elders began a concerted effort to rehabilitate their reputation and project themselves into the Protestant mainstream. They destroyed or suppressed embarrassing evidence from the "Sifting" years. They scaled back controversial practices such as the prominent leadership role of women. They befriended important religious leaders, especially in Britain. And they launched a campaign to publicize their evangelism more broadly as the signature of their identity, commissioning Moravian authors to write the histories of key missions. To investigate the history of the Danish West Indian project, church leaders chose Christian Georg Andreas Oldendorp.[3]

Born in 1721, Oldendorp joined the Brethren in the early 1740s, living in Marienborn and Herrnhaag at the same time as Rebecca and Christian. He knocked around in service to various congregations on the continent before receiving, in 1767, the writing assignment that would dominate his life for a decade. Wanting to see firsthand the scene of his study, he sailed to the West Indies, landing on St. Croix on March 22, 1767; for the next eighteen months, as both missionary and scholar, he shuttled among St. Croix, St. Thomas, and St. John gathering materials for his history. With a comprehensiveness and curiosity rare for students of slavery in his, or any, generation, he interviewed dozens of African and Creole workers, many of whom were original converts from the 1730s. He asked about their experiences as Christians, to be sure, but he wanted to embed his story in a larger context of slavery and Afro-Caribbean culture, so he probed them about their lives in Africa, their pre-Christian religious beliefs, their experiences in the slave trade, their work and living conditions on the plantation. Refusing to categorize all Africans as alike, Oldendorp developed a sophisticated understanding of distinctions among the peoples who were siphoned into the Danish slave trade, primarily from the Gold Coast and Kongo. He made a close study of the Dutch Creole language, providing corresponding translations and rudimentary phonetic transcriptions of key words in more than twenty African languages. He witnessed and wrote a harrowing description of a slave auction on St. Croix. A respectable artist, he drew pictures of Caribbean flora and congregational scenes from the Brethren's own plantations.

Then he took his notes and headed back to Germany where, surrounded in the church archives by thousands of pages of mission diaries, letters, and reports, he wrote.[4]

And wrote. Oldendorp worked for five years, submitting in stages, during the early to mid-1770s, a manuscript of several thousand pages. The first volume alone, focusing on African cultures and the plantation system in the Danish West Indies, was huge; the even more unwieldy next volume, divided into three parts, covered the mission from the early 1730s to the late 1760s. Oldendorp turned out to be a gifted and passionate writer, though he made it clear that his historical and ethnographic methods served a larger purpose. Patiently amassing his data, he depicted the mission as a momentous struggle between light and darkness, pitting white preachers and their Afro-Caribbean allies against idolatry and planter brutality. A thread of divine destiny coils through the narrative: here, another African begs the Brethren for baptism; there, another bullying planter relents. Friedrich Martin and other missionaries receive plenty of attention, but the heroes of the book manifestly are the black converts who risked, and endured, awful punishment for the Gospel. Oldendorp lovingly sketched these men and women in fine, humanistic detail, showing eighteenth-century readers a group of enslaved people who were not barbarians or nameless drudges but mighty strivers fortified by God's word against terrible odds. Peter, Mingo, Andreas, Anna Maria, Magdalena, and many others—these were the stars in a black book of Acts.[5]

Of course, much about Oldendorp's book raises red flags for the modern scholar. His use of oral testimony is often suspect, as when he quotes Africans praising their enslavement because it brought them to Jesus. Because his book was intended partly as a promotional tract to entice planters to engage the Brethren's services, he put his own proslavery opinions in full view. He repeatedly emphasized the power of the Gospel to overcome what he called the inherently sinful, thieving, and lying nature of unconverted Africans and render them better slaves. And his tone of Christian triumphalism can obscure the slaves' motives for embracing the mission as enthusiastically as Oldendorp contended.[6]

Nonetheless, his achievement was to emphasize the ability of unknown people to claim spiritual authority for themselves, and a central player in the drama was Rebecca. The two knew each other from their years in Herrnhaag, though how well is uncertain (in his writing Oldendorp referred to Christian Protten as a friend). It is quite possible that Rebecca told him something of her life on St. Thomas that helped frame the description he wrote of her twenty-five years later. Echoing Friedrich Martin's diaries, Oldendorp portrayed her as a searching young evangelist who found her way among the Brethren and went on to become a dynamic and indispensable leader. In his narrative, her imprisonment and trial—along with that of Martin and Freundlich—was a defining moment in the history of the church, if not of western Christianity, and Oldendorp depicted Rebecca, like the Apostles, as willing to follow the providential script to martyrdom if necessary. Oldendorp saw all his characters as actors on a divine stage and wrote their parts accordingly. But it is not likely that, in doing so, he distorted Rebecca's motivation, since Danish trial records and her own words confirm that she saw herself in exactly that light. In any case, he cast her as essential to the unfolding momentum of God's plan.

When Oldendorp turned in the last of his manuscript in 1775, church elders thanked him and handed it over to an editor, Johann Jakob Bossart, who spent two more years pruning it to publishable size. When it was finally published in 1777 as *Geschichte der Mission der evangelischen Brüder auf den caraibischen Inseln S. Thomas, S. Croix, und S. Jan (History of the Mission of the Evangelical Brethren on the Caribbean Islands of St. Thomas, St. Croix, and St. John)*, Oldendorp's opus was only about one-third of its original length. Appalled at the butchery, the author protested, but it did no good. Bossart had stripped down the relentless mass of detail that

Oldendorp had worked so hard to compile. Still, the essentials of the story remained, and even in abridged form, Oldendorp's book became a standard part of church lore. Whether anyone ever sent Rebecca a copy in Christiansborg is unknown, and her story probably never became widely known outside Germany. Parts of Oldendorp's book were translated into English for a limited abolitionist audience but were not widely published, although the book did inform mission histories in English by other authors. As a result, the roots of one of the eighteenth century's major intellectual and social transformations, as explored by Oldendorp, remained mostly obscure to English readers.[7]

That transformation was the embrace of Christianity by people of African descent. Perhaps "the single most significant event in African American history," contend the historians Sylvia Frey and Betty Wood, it "created a community of faith and . . . provided Afro-Atlantic peoples with an ideology of resistance and the means to absorb the cultural norms that turned Africans into African Americans." The process had begun long before Rebecca's time, but she occupied a pivotal place in the continuum, for she and her cohort of preachers helped usher in a radical new stage.[8]

Before the 1730s, to be black and Christian almost certainly meant being Catholic. Apart from scattered black Protestants in North America, the British and Dutch Caribbean, and Europe itself, the great preponderance of African converts were found in Kongo, Brazil, and Spanish and French America. When Rebecca and other brown and black preachers took to the Path, St. Thomas suddenly became the Americas' new axis for Afro-Protestant conversion. In their zeal to extend what they regarded as Christ's liberating grace to people of African descent, these women and men put themselves at the forefront of an indigenous black movement that was birthed in the slave quarters. From dozens of converts, to hundreds, then thousands, within just a few years, the movement became a mass popular upsurge in the face of violent opposition. Had black exhorters not carried the word onto plantations and into homes, taught literacy—secretly, if necessary—and even written bold petitions to the king and queen of Denmark, the efforts of white missionaries would have shriveled on the vine. The genesis of the movement was keyed to the moment Rebecca threw herself into it, even before the missionaries' arrival, by recruiting, teaching, and leading enslaved women.

St. Thomas proved to be the model for the spread of evangelical religion through New World slave communities. From there, black Pietism radiated outward across the Caribbean. Black preachers accompanied white missionaries to St. John and St. Croix, where new congregations flourished. In the Danish West Indies, the Moravian Church registered 4,560 converts by 1768, 7,000 by 1790. Emboldened by these successes, the church set up missions in Surinam and the British West Indies. By the 1780s, Antigua alone claimed another 6,000 enslaved converts, making the island one of the single largest concentrations of Afro-Protestants in the world. While those figures represented just a small fraction of the black population in the Protestant Americas, they reveal the burgeoning of a hemispheric movement for black self-organization.[9]

Keenly watching the experiment, other evangelicals emulated what they saw in the Danish and British islands. White Methodist and Baptist itinerant preachers ventured into the plantation country of Virginia and South Carolina in the 1740s and 1750s, urging slaves toward an emotional conversion of the heart in the language of religious egalitarianism. Responding eagerly like their counterparts in St. Thomas, black men and women formed prayer groups, worshipped side-by-side with white brothers and sisters, and broadcast the word themselves. African-American interest in Christianity had been steadily building from within slave quarters on the mainland by the middle of the eighteenth century, and so all this might have happened without the impetus of the black Caribbean evangelists. Still, the influential example of their teaching and organizing is hard to overlook. By the time of the American Revolution, black Chris-

Afro-Caribbean worshippers at the Moravian plantation of Friedensthal, St. Croix, by C.G.A. Oldendorp, c. 1767. Courtesy of Unity Archives, Herrnhut, Germany.

tians were among the vocal advocates for African-American spiritual and social equality. In places like Williamsburg, Savannah, Pine Bluff, South Carolina, and Philadelphia, they created North America's first black churches.[10]

At the same time, Rebecca, Christian Protten, and other carriers of the Gospel were the earliest harbingers of what would become an international evangelicalism spanning the Atlantic in multiple directions. From St. Thomas, a handful of black brothers and sisters shipped out to Pennsylvania and Germany in the 1740s to live in interracial Moravian communities. Though most died within a few years, the prominence of Rebecca and Maria demonstrated a visible and vocal presence for black Christian women in some wings of European evangelical leadership. Similarly, from Africa itself came Christians like Protten, the Afro-Dutch Jacobus J. C. Capitein, and the Anglican Philip Quaque, all highly educated and well-placed advocates for African missions. Their own years back on the Gold Coast were filled with frustration and scant results. Still, joined by Rebecca herself, in the era of the slave trade they pioneered the idea that people of African origin could return there as part of a larger intellectual agenda. In tentative and decentralized ways, they envisioned an Afro-Christian community of faith encompassing America, Europe, and Africa—a sort of spiritual triangle trade.

As Rebecca continued her own witness in Germany and Africa, the movement she had helped kindle spread with increasing fervor into many corners of the Americas. By the time of her death, British evangelical societies influenced by the Moravian example launched a new flurry of missions in the Caribbean. Here again, Rebecca's example presaged the centrality of women to this diffusion. On Antigua, for example, enslaved women reached out to the Methodists with particular vigor. By the early nineteenth century almost all of the colony's 3,516 Methodists were black women, some of whom were said to "have good gifts in Prayer and hold prayer meetings." The free black sisters Anne and Elizabeth Hart instructed and shepherded hundreds of Afro-Methodist women on Antigua, the "favorite of heaven," as one evangelical termed it, and from there the faith vaulted to other islands in the British West Indies.[11]

Of course, enslaved converts continually negotiated the tensions between Christianity and traditional African beliefs, and between the doctrines of freedom and subordination in the Gospel. The role of the planters too had changed: many no longer opposed or feared the spread of Christianity among bondpeople. Unequivocally proslavery, Moravian missionaries advertised that their teachings would make slaves more docile, a claim echoed in the 1780s by the Methodists and Baptists in the West Indies and, slightly later, in North America. Planters now welcomed the missionaries eagerly, implicating them deeply as ideological buttresses for the plantation system. Whether Christianity did indeed make enslaved workers more pliant is harder to ascertain. Certainly they were instructed that to be a good Christian was to obey one's master, and mission disciplinary codes reinforced that message. It is quite possible that some black Christians believed it. On the other hand, the Gospel would never have spread among the slaves if it taught them only to bow. Its increasing popularity suggests that they took something greater from the Bible, some affirmation, perhaps, that Jesus died for them, a fundamental sense that their affliction made them God's chosen people. Many slave uprisings in the Caribbean and North America in the late eighteenth and early nineteenth centuries were fueled in part by a messianic belief that Christian freedom and equality should extend to the body as well as the spirit. At the very least, religion was a flash point for the slaves' continuing debates about submission and resistance.[12]

Religion also became a fulcrum for the germinating antislavery movement. Although this connection went far beyond anything Rebecca is known to have articulated or even intended, it was part of her legacy as well. In the 1780s, a new generation of Christian Afro-Atlantic writers such as Ignatius Sancho, Ottobah Cugoano, and Olaudah Equiano gave powerful impetus to the antislavery movement in Britain and the United States by bearing witness to the evils of an unchristian slave trade. Their testimony undergirded the arguments of prominent white British opponents of slavery such as Granville Sharp, James Ramsay, and William Wilberforce, evangelicals for whom the notions of religion and freedom for black folk were entwined.[13]

The example of Afro-Christianity that most inspired these activists was that of the Moravians, despite the white Brethren's own slaveholding. Parts of Oldendorp's *History* were translated and circulated among British activists, who seized on its moral of black improvement to make a broader point. James Ramsay's influential and controversial *An Essay on the Treatment and Conversion of African Slaves in the British Sugar Colonies,* published in 1784, praised the missions on the Danish islands and Antigua. The benefits to the slaves were "a considerable degree of religious knowledge, an orderly behavior, a neatness in their persons and clothing, a sobriety in their carriage, a sensibility in their manner, a diligence and faithfulness in their stations, industry and method in their own little matters, an humility and piety in their conversation." Ramsay's argument was couched in the patronizing language of paternalism toward Africans. But he also contended that for blacks to enjoy the full benefits of Christian religion and civilization, the slave trade, and slavery itself, must end.[14]

Similarly, when the ceramic artist Josiah Wedgwood produced in 1788 a relief of a chained black man, kneeling in supplication, beneath the motto "Am I Not a Man and a Brother?" he drew inspiration in part from the Brethren's vision of spiritual equality. The image became an instantly recognizable and often-reproduced emblem of the antislavery movement, and its theme was a centerpiece of the parliamentary debates of the 1790s that ended in Britain's outlawing of the slave trade in 1808. Thus, black Christianity—the spiritual freedom that the enslaved claimed for themselves—was fundamental to the antislavery politics of the late eighteenth century.[15]

Denmark actually became the first nation to ban the slave trade to its West Indian colonies in 1792. The impetus came from Count Ernst Schimmelmann, the Danish minister of finance, owner of several plantations and many slaves on St. Croix, who was part humanitarian and part imperialist. As chair of a commission investigating the trade, Schimmelmann was moved by the piety of his enslaved workers, many of whom were Moravian converts. He believed the high death rate among slaves would end if the trade were abolished, forcing masters to treat workers better; new plantations could then be created on the Gold Coast, cultivated by African slaves who would be spared the transatlantic voyage. Nothing came of the idea, although Schimmelmann won the trade ban. During the ten years between its enactment and the time it took effect in 1802, slave imports climbed sharply as planters stockpiled African workers. Still,

Denmark inaugurated the policy that Britain would impose on a much larger scale a few years later.[16]

Religion and antislavery merged with the nascent African colonization movement when Sierra Leone was founded in 1787 by British and American abolitionists. Free black American evangelicals and antislavery activists like John Marrant, Paul Cuffee, Lemuel Haynes, and African-born Thomas Peters joined forces with Cugoano and Equiano to advocate the emigration to Sierra Leone of black refugees of the American Revolution living in Nova Scotia, as well as impoverished blacks in Britain. The project had its share of the Christian condescension toward Africa that would undergird the European colonization of the continent in the nineteenth century. In its time, however, the return-to-Africa movement represented a spiritual linking of America, Europe, and Africa, an attempt to reverse the slave trade even as it still drained Africa of its people. From seeds the Prottens and others had planted years earlier, the black evangelical outreach branched in ways they had not imagined, forging a new kind of reciprocal cultural exchange across the Atlantic. For better or worse, that, too, was a fruit of Rebecca's revival. And in the nineteenth-century United States, a new generation of female African-American preachers such as Rebecca Cox Jackson, Jarena Lee, and Sojourner Truth emerged from the shadows to testify and to help provide a guiding moral light in the struggle against slavery.[17]

In Charlotte Amalie, the port town of St. Thomas where thousands of Africans ended their voyage to the New World, vestiges of slavery are not widely advertised these days, but they are easily visible. The vegetable and fruit market downtown is the place where slaves were once sold, including, perhaps, the young child who one day became Rebecca. At the old Danish Fort Christian, a colorful tourist destination by the bay, rebellious slaves were flogged or executed, and it was there that Rebecca spent four months in prison. Close by, a tree-ringed public green, Emancipation Park, commemorates the freeing of slaves in the Danish West Indies on July 3, 1848. The dramatic decree by Governor Peter von Scholten followed one of the hemisphere's truly successful—and bloodless—slave uprisings. When eight thousand enslaved men and women on St. Croix marched on the local fort demanding freedom, the government, remarkably, capitulated instead of shooting them.[18]

A road leaves Charlotte Amalie to the east, winding about six miles through gaps in the hills toward the coast. Formerly the Path, the road passes through the heart of the colonial plantation country, much of it now built over with homes and shopping malls. Just off to one side, straddling a ridge above a stand of trees, is the whitewashed meeting hall, now called New Herrnhut Moravian Church, built by black congregants in the 1740s on the old Posaunenberg estate. The site was once crowded with buildings of a working sugar plantation—stables, barn, forge, kitchen, boiler house, slave quarters. Of these, only a few foundations remain, the archaeological stubble of three hundred years; the rest is overgrown, and the meeting house is the last building left. The church has remained constant—through the end of slavery and into freedom, through the purchase of the Danish colonies by the United States in 1917, and through the advent of the Virgin Islands' tourism economy, people have come here to worship. Parishioner James Francis, born in 1916 when St. Thomas was still a Danish colony, recalled that well into the twentieth century people still walked to church from miles around, following the same network of roads their ancestors did: "They walked barefoot to save their shoes, then washed their feet and put shoes on for service." Nowadays parked cars line the dirt lane up the hill that once led past fields of cane.[19]

Churchgoers walk past a cemetery as the lane hairpins to the church. Old stone slabs mark the graves of the many missionaries who died here, but the plots of black brothers and sisters are largely overgrown, and few are marked. In front of the meeting house hangs an old plantation bell that, in slavery times, summoned work-ers to the fields; after emancipation it tolled only for prayer. Two hundred or more people fill the benches inside the spare white room. Many years ago, the hall echoed with songs and sermons in Dutch Creole. James Francis's mother and grandparents spoke Creole at home "when they didn't want the children to understand," but the language fell into disuse on the island years ago. Now, in English, a succession of speakers bear witness to the faith. "There's trouble all around," one woman testifies. "How do you function in a society like that? God is our refuge. Whatever crisis, whatever trou-bles you, Jesus wants to bring comfort to our hearts." Between les-sons, a swaying gospel choir and band lead the assembly in hymns.

The service ends, and the congregants exchange hugs and hand-shakes. Lingering in the cross-breeze that flutters through open doors, they visit for another moment on the threshold; then, step-ping out into the sun, they slowly file downhill and flow back out onto the old Path.

MA-NP	Moravian Archives, Northern Province, Bethlehem, Pennsylvania
Oldendorp, *CM*	*A Caribbean Mission.* Christian Georg Andreas Oldendorp, *History of the Mission of the Evangelical Brethren on the Caribbean Islands of St. Thomas, St. Croix, and St. John,* ed. Johann Jakob Bossart, English trans. and ed. Arnold R. Highfield and Vladimir Barac (Barby, 1777; republished, Ann Arbor, 1987)
Oldendorp, *Historie*	Christian Georg Andreas Oldendorp, *Historie der caribischen Inseln Sanct Thomas, Sanct Crux und Sanct Jan. Kommentiere Edition Des Originalmanuskriptes,* vol. 1, ed. Gudrun Meier, Stephan Palmié, Peter Stein, and Horst Ulbricht (Berlin, 2000); vol. 2, parts 1–3, ed. Hartmut Beck, Gudrun Meier, Stephan Palmié, Aart H. van Soest, Peter Stein, and Horst Ulbricht (Berlin, 2002)
RA	Rigsarkivet, Copenhagen
UA	Unitätsarchiv, Herrnhut, Germany
VGK-KKA	Vestindisk Guineisk Kompagni, Kompagniets Kobenhavnske Arkivalier, Rigsarkivet, Copenhagen
WMQ	*William and Mary Quarterly*

NOTES

PROLOGUE

1. The United States bought St. Thomas, along with its companion colonies of St. John and St. Croix, from Denmark in 1917, and the three now constitute the U.S. Virgin Islands. Fort Christiansborg is in Accra, the modern capital of Ghana.

2. The only previous writings about Rebecca are Arnold R. Highfield, "Rebekka Freundlich: A Moravian Life," *Conference Proceedings of the Society of Virgin Islands Historians,* ed. Robert V. Vaughn (St. Croix, 1992), 51–61, and Hans Werner Debrunner, *Presence and Prestige: Africans in Europe, a History of Africans in Europe Before 1918* (Basel, 1979), 108–109.

3. For overviews of the origins of black Protestantism in the Americas, see Sylvia R. Frey and Betty Wood, *Come Shouting to Zion: African American Protestantism in the American South and British Caribbean to 1830* (Chapel Hill, N.C., 1998); and Albert Raboteau, *Slave Religion: The "Invisible Institution" in the Antebellum South* (New York, 1978).

4. Recent scholarship on women in the African Atlantic diaspora includes such works as Jennifer Morgan, *Laboring Women: Reproduction and Gender in New World Slavery* (Philadelphia, 2004); David Barry Gaspar and Darlene Clark Hine, eds., *More Than Chattel: Black Women and Slavery in the Americas* (Bloomington, Ind., 1996); Hilary McD. Beckles, *Centering Woman: Gender Discourses in Caribbean Slave Society* (Kingston, Jamaica, and Princeton, N.J., 1999); and Patricia Morton, ed., *Discovering the Women in Slavery: Emancipating Perspectives on the American Past* (Athens, Ga., 1996).

5. As an amalgamation of cultures, and in her ability to cross bound-

aries of race, nationality, and language, Rebecca was an example of what Ira Berlin has termed "Atlantic creoles" of the early modern period. See Berlin, "From Creoles to African: Atlantic Creoles and the Origins of African-American Society in Mainland North America," *WMQ,* 3rd ser., 53 (1996), 251–288.

6. See Henry Louis Gates, Jr., and William L. Andrews, eds., *Pioneers of the Black Atlantic: Five Slave Narratives from the Enlightenment, 1772–1815* (Washington, D.C., 1998). For examples of nineteenth-century African-American women's narratives, see Andrews, *Sisters of the Spirit: Three Black Women's Autobiographies of the Nineteenth Century* (Bloomington, Ind., 1986); Mary Prince, *History of Mary Prince, a West Indian Slave,* and Harriet A. Jacobs, *Incidents in the Life of a Slave Girl,* reprinted in Henry Louis Gates, Jr., *The Classic Slave Narratives* (New York, 1987); and Margaret Washington, ed., *Narrative of Sojourner Truth* (New York, 1993).

7. This study is based primarily on original manuscripts housed in the archives of the Renewed Unity of Brethren, or Moravian Church, in Herrnhut, Germany. Translations of these documents from German are by the author in collaboration with Werner Sensbach. An indispensable eighteenth-century work based on those same documents is Christian Georg Andreas Oldendorp, *Geschichte der Mission der evangelischen Brüder auf den Caribischen Inseln S. Thomas, S. Croix und S. Jan* (Barby, 1777). A modern English translation and edition of that volume is cited here as Oldendorp, *CM.* Oldendorp's vast original manuscript was severely pared down by editor Johann Jakob Bossard for publication in 1777, but an annotated edition of Oldendorp's text has since restored the deleted material, including a wealth of information about Africans in the Americas. See Oldendorp, *Historie.* For a description of that editing project, see Gudrun Meier, "Preliminary Remarks on the Oldendorp Manuscripts and Their History," in Stephan Palmié, ed., *Slave Cultures and the Cultures of Slavery* (Knoxville, 1995), 67–77. For the convenience of readers, I have generally cited the English edition, supplementing it when necessary from the restored German text.

I   A BAPTISM OF BLOOD

1. Pierre J. Pannet, *Report on the Execrable Conspiracy Carried Out by the Amina Negroes on the Danish Island of St. Jan in America 1733,* trans. and

ed. Aimery P. Caron and Arnold R. Highfield (Christiansted, St. Croix, 1984).

2. J. L. Carstens, *St. Thomas in Early Danish Times: A General Description of all the Danish, American or West Indian Islands,* trans. and ed. Arnold R. Highfield, originally published in the 1740s as *En almindelig Beskrivelse om alle de Danske, Americanske eller West-Indiske Eylande* (St. Croix, 1997), 38, 81–82. While authorship of the anonymous book has been attributed to the Danish Creole planter Johan Lorentz Carstens, inconsistencies in the text make it almost certain that he did not write it.

3. Pannet, *Report on the Execrable Conspiracy,* 17–18.

4. Waldemar Westergaard, *The Danish West Indies Under Company Rule (1671–1754)* (New York, 1917), 318–319; Carstens, *St. Thomas in Early Danish Times,* 81–82; Oldendorp, *CM,* 230–232.

5. Carstens, *St. Thomas in Early Danish Times,* 39. Condemning a man to die alongside a hapless dog seems to have implied a peculiar degradation. Two slaves, Gomas and George, were executed in this fashion after a rebellion on St. Croix in 1759; one survived half an hour, the other three hours. Waldemar Westergaard, "Account of the Negro Rebellion on St. Croix, Danish West Indies, 1759," *Journal of Negro History,* 11 (1926), 51–61.

6. Pannet, *Report on the Execrable Conspiracy,* 13. The basic secondary account of the uprising is found in Westergaard, *Danish West Indies,* 168–178, which draws on Pannet and other sources.

7. Pannet, *Report on the Execrable Conspiracy,* 14–16.

8. Ibid., 15–16.

9. The standard work on the early colonization of St. Thomas remains Westergaard, *Danish West Indies,* 1–44 ("John Indian" on pp. 33–34). Also important is Georg Norregard, *Danish Settlements in West Africa, 1658–1850* (Boston, 1966).

10. Westergaard, *Danish West Indies,* 37–39.

11. Ibid., 41.

12. Neville T. Hall, *Slave Society in the Danish West Indies: St. Thomas, St. John, and St. Croix,* ed. B. W. Higman (Mona, Jamaica, 1992), 6–7.

13. During its 131 years in the transatlantic slave trade, Denmark ferried approximately 126,000 Africans to the New World—about two percent of the entire trade. See Arnold R. Highfield, "The Danish Atlantic and West

Indian Slave Trade," in George F. Tyson and Arnold R. Highfield, eds., *The Danish West Indian Slave Trade: Virgin Islands Perspectives* (St. Croix, 1994), 11–32; Svend Erik Green-Pedersen, "The Scope and Structure of the Danish Negro Slave Trade," *Scandinavian Economic History Review*, 19 (1971), 149–197; and Per O. Hernaes, *Slaves, Danes, and African Coast Society: The Danish Slave Trade from West Africa and Afro-Danish Relations on the Eighteenth-Century Gold Coast* (Trondheim, Norway, 1998). On the Dutch trade, see Johannes Postma, *The Dutch in the Atlantic Slave Trade, 1600–1815* (New York, 1990).

14. On the founding of St. John, see Aimery P. Caron and Arnold R. Highfield, trans. and ed., *The French Intervention in the St. John Slave Revolt of 1733–34* (Occasional Paper No. 8, Bureau of Libraries, Museums, and Archaeological Services, St. Thomas, 1981), 1–8.

15. Ray A. Kea, "'When I die, I shall return to my own land': An 'Amina' Slave Rebellion in the Danish West Indies, 1733–34," in John Hunwick and Nancy Lawler, eds., *The Cloth of Many Colored Silks: Papers on History and Society, Ghanaian and Islamic in Honor of Ivor Wilks* (Evanston, Ill., 1996), 159–167; Ivor Wilks, "The Rise of the Akwamu Empire, 1650–1710," *Transactions of the Historical Society of Ghana*, 3, pt. 2 (1957); John K. Thornton, *Warfare in Atlantic Africa, 1500–1800* (New York, 1999); Caron and Highfield, eds., *French Intervention*, 51 n. 13; Oldendorp, *CM*, 163.

16. Kea, "'When I die,'" 168; Sandra E. Greene, "From Whence They Came: A Note on the Influence of West African Ethnic and Gender Relations on the Organizational Character of the 1733 St. John Slave Rebellion," in Tyson and Highfield, eds., *Danish West Indian Slave Trade*, 51–56; Caron and Highfield, eds., *French Intervention*, 51 n. 13; Oldendorp, *CM*, 235.

17. Carstens, *St. Thomas in Early Danish Times*, 68–69.

18. Ibid.; Oldendorp, *CM*, 188; "Character einiger Nationen der Schwarzen," undated manuscript, R15.Ba.27, p. 1, UA.

19. Pannet, *Report on the Execrable Conspiracy*, 12, 17; Kea, "'When I die,'" 174–180; Greene, "From Whence They Came," 47–67.

20. Pannet, *Report on the Execrable Conspiracy*, 17.

21. Oldendorp, *CM*, 219–220.

22. Ibid., 220, 246.

23. Oldendorp, *CM,* 225–226; Carstens, *St. Thomas in Early Danish Times,* 61–75, quote on p. 74; Kea, "'When I die,'" 159–160.

24. This account follows the similar narrative format of Westergaard, *Danish West Indies,* 165–168; Kea, "'When I die,'" 172–173; Caron and Highfield, eds., *French Intervention,* 14–15.

25. Westergaard, *Danish West Indies,* 171–172.

26. *South Carolina Gazette,* Feb. 23–March 2 and March 2–9, 1734. The example of the St. John revolt was one of several factors that influenced the Trustees of Georgia to ban slavery in the fledgling colony in 1735. See Peter H. Wood, *Black Majority: Negroes in Colonial South Carolina from 1670 through the Stono Rebellion* (New York, 1974), 220–221, 222; Betty Wood, *Slavery in Colonial Georgia, 1730–1775* (Athens, Ga., 1984), 3–10.

27. Gardelin to Champigny, March 21, 1734, and d'Orgueville to the Minister, April 16, 1734, in Caron and Highfield, eds., *French Intervention,* 26, 35.

28. Champigny to the Minister, April 16, 1734, and Longueville to the Minister, June 21, 1734, in Caron and Highfield, eds., *French Intervention,* 37, 41–42.

29. Longueville to the Minister, June 21, 1734, and Orgueville to the Minister, July 1, 1734, in Caron and Highfield, eds., *French Intervention,* 42–43, 46–47.

30. Westergaard, *Danish West Indies,* 176; Kea, "'When I die,'" 187.

31. Thomas J. Davis, *A Rumor of Revolt: The "Great Negro Plot" in Colonial New York* (New York, 1985), 148–149, 158–160; this draws on Daniel Horsmanden, *A Journal of the Proceedings in the Detection of the Conspiracy formed by Some White People, in Conjunction with Negro and other Slaves, for Burning the City of New-York in America, and Murdering the Inhabitants* (New York, 1744), republished as Thomas J. Davis, ed., *The New York Slave Conspiracy* (Boston, 1971), 206, 212, 265. On the cycle of slave revolts in the 1730s, see Peter Linebaugh and Marcus Rediker, *The Many-Headed Hydra: Sailors, Slaves, Commoners, and the Hidden History of the Revolutionary Atlantic* (Boston, 2000), 193–198; Wood, *Black Majority,* 221–224; and David Barry Gaspar, "A Dangerous Spirit of Liberty: Slave Rebellion in the West Indies during the 1730s," *Cimarrons,* I (1981), 79–91.

2 REBIRTH AND REMEMBRANCE

1. J. L. Carstens, *St. Thomas in Early Danish Times: A General Description of all the Danish, American, or West Indian Islands,* ed. and trans. Arnold R. Highfield, originally published in the 1740s as *En Almendelig Beskrivelse om alle de Danske, Americanske eller West-Indiske Eylande* (St. Croix, 1997), 21. The girl's name is identified as "Schelli" in the Herrnhut congregation's Married Choir Catalog for 1752–53, R27.124.39-86, UA, and in the *Diener-Blätter* (Missionaries' Pages) of Christian and Rebecca Protten, UA.

2. Oldendorp, *CM,* 219 (quotes). For guides to the literature on the Atlantic slave trade, see David Eltis, *The Rise of African Slavery in the Americas* (New York, 2000); David Eltis and David Richardson, eds., *Routes to Slavery: Direction, Ethnicity, and Mortality in the Transatlantic Slave Trade* (London, 1997). On the workings of the slave market, in another time and place, see Walter Johnson, *Soul by Soul: Inside the Antebellum Slave Market* (Cambridge, Mass., 2000).

3. David Barry Gaspar, *Bondmen and Rebels: A Study of Master-Slave Relations in Antigua* (Durham, N.C., 1986), 83. Shelly's birthplace is identified as Antigua in the Herrnhaag congregation register, Jan. 6, 1746, R8.35.a, UA; and Oldendorp, *CM,* 314.

4. Oldendorp, *CM,* 314. On West Indians of mixed European and African ancestry, see Gaspar, *Bondmen and Rebels,* 105; Barbara Bush, *Slave Women in Caribbean Society, 1650–1838* (Bloomington, Ind., 1990); and Hilary Beckles, "Sex and Gender in the Historiography of Caribbean Slavery," in Verene Shepherd, Bridget Brereton, and Barbara Bailey, eds., *Engendering History: Caribbean Women in Historical Perspective* (New York, 1995), 133.

5. Oldendorp, *CM,* 314. On smuggling out of Antigua, see Gaspar, *Bondmen and Rebels,* 86.

6. Oldendorp, *CM,* 314; Waldemar Westergaard, *The Danish West Indies Under Company Rule (1671–1754)* (New York, 1917), 38; Hugo Ryberg, "A List of the Names of Inhabitants, Danish West Indian Islands, from 1650–1825," pp. 22–25 of typescript in Von Scholten Collection, Enid M. Baa Library, St. Thomas; Landslister for St. Thomas, 1727, Nos. 90 and

127, VGK, RA. Lucas van Beverhout appears to be different from someone by the same name on the Dutch colony of Curacao in the early eighteenth century; see Cornelis Ch. Goslinga, *The Dutch in the Caribbean and in the Guianas, 1680–1791* (Assen/Maastricht, The Netherlands, and Dover, N.H., 1985), 129. My thanks to Betty King, historian of the Reformed Church on St. Thomas, for supplying me with additional information on the van Beverhout family.

7. Carstens, *St. Thomas in Early Danish Times,* 45–46, 55.

8. Oldendorp, *CM,* 157.

9. Carstens, *St. Thomas in Early Danish Times,* 54–55. Many of these observations were echoed by visitors to Dutch colonies such as Surinam. See, for example, Goslinga, *The Dutch in the Caribbean and in the Guianas,* 312–374, esp. 342–344. On the evolution of Dutch slaveholding, see Goslinga, *The Dutch in the Caribbean and on the Wild Coast* (Gainesville, Fla., 1971), 339–370.

10. Oldendorp, *CM,* 157; Carstens, *St. Thomas in Early Danish Times,* 10–11.

11. Oldendorp, *CM,* 225.

12. Carstens, *St. Thomas in Early Danish Times,* 64–65; Hans West, *Description of St. Croix with a Brief Overview of St. Thomas, St. John, Tortola, Spanishtown and Crab Island* (Copenhagen, 1793), excerpted in George F. Tyson and Arnold R. Highfield, eds., *The Kamina Folk: Slavery and Slave Life in the Danish West Indies* (St. Croix, 1997), 128. See also Hilary McD. Beckles, *Centering Woman: Gender Discourses in Caribbean Slave Society* (Kingston, 1999), 125–139; Marietta Morrissey, *Slave Women in the New World: Gender Stratification in the Caribbean* (Lawrence, Kans., 1989), 64–67; and Barbara Bush, *Slave Women in Caribbean Society, 1650–1838* (Bloomington, Ind., 1990).

13. Oldendorp, *CM,* 314. Dutch, of course, was the first language of Sojourner Truth, who grew up among Dutch-American settlers in rural New York. See Nell Irvin Painter, *Sojourner Truth: A Life, A Symbol* (New York, 1995), 7.

14. Dokumenter vedk. de maeriske brodre pa St. Thomas, 1737–49, Document 5, No. 4, "Extract from the Town Court of St. Thomas," Dec. 15, 1738, VGK-KKA, No. 185, RA (trans. Louise Sebro). On Dutch atti-

tudes toward the conversion of slaves, see Goslinga, *The Dutch in the Caribbean and on the Wild Coast,* 368–369 (quote); Allison Blakely, *Blacks in the Dutch World: The Evolution of Racial Imagery in a Modern Society* (Bloomington, Ind., 1993), 202–224.

15. Two somewhat different versions of the same source discuss this subject: Oldendorp, *CM,* 314; and Oldendorp, *Historie,* part II, vol. 1, 177–178.

16. Oldendorp, *CM,* 314.

17. Ibid., 314, 264.

18. Landlister for St. Thomas, 1730, No. 90, VGK; Document 5, No. 5, "Extract from the Town Court of St. Thomas," Dec. 22, 1738, VGK, KKA, No. 185, RA (trans. Louise Sebro); Oldendorp, *CM,* 322; Carstens, *St. Thomas in Early Danish Times,* 61.

19. Governor Gardelin to Marquis de Champigny, March 21, 173, and Monsieur d'Orgueville to the Minister, July 1, 1734, in Aimery P. Caron and Arnold R. Highfield, trans. and ed., *The French Intervention in the St. John Slave Revolt of 1733–34* (Occasional Paper No. 8, Bureau of Libraries, Museums, and Archaeological Services, St. Thomas, 1981), 26, 46, 48.

20. Neville A. T. Hall, "'An Intermediate Sort of Class': The Emergence and Growth of the Freedman Population," in Hall, *Slave Society in the Danish West Indies: St. Thomas, St. John, St. Croix,* ed. B. W. Higman (Mona, Jamaica, 1992), 138–156; Carstens, *St. Thomas in Early Danish Times,* 61–63; David W. Cohen and Jack P. Greene, eds., *Neither Slave Nor Free: The Freedmen of African Descent in the Slave Societies of the New World* (Baltimore, 1972); Arnold A. Sio, "Marginality and Free Coloured Identity in Caribbean Slave Society," *Slavery and Abolition,* 8 (1987), 166–182.

21. Oldendorp, *CM,* 314; St. Thomas Diary, May 7, 1738, R15 Ba.2b, UA. On manumission of enslaved domestic workers, see Morrissey, *Slave Women in the New World,* 66–67, 70–73. Clothing of free blacks is discussed in Carstens, *St. Thomas in Early Danish Times,* 61–63.

3   A PRIESTLY WOMAN

1. Friedrich Martin diary, Sept. 26, 1736, R15.Ba.10, UA.

2. Two nearly identical accounts by Martin, written two years later, describe the first meeting with Rebecca: his diary, May 4, 1738, R15.Ba.10, UA; and "Ein Zeugniss von 2 Gliedern Jesu, ihrer Verehelichung: M. T. F en Rebecca" ["Bericht von der Trauung des Br. Matth. Freundlich mit der

Mulattin Rebecca"], July 3, 1739, R15.Ba.31, UA. Similarly, Dutch missionaries in the Cape Colony of South Africa had relied on a converted Khoikhoi woman named Eva to evangelize among other Khoikhoi in the early 1670s, although she later abandoned the mission and died tragically. See Jonathan N. Gerstner, "A Christian Monopoly: The Reformed Church and Colonial Society under Dutch Rule," in Richard Elphick and Rodney Davenport, eds., *Christianity in South Africa: A Political, Social, and Cultural History* (Berkeley, 1997), 28.

3. A standard account is Kenneth G. Hamilton and J. Taylor Hamilton, *History of the Moravian Church: The Renewed Unitas Fratrum, 1722–1957* (Bethlehem, Pa., 1967).

4. On the origins of early Moravian congregation towns, see Elisabeth Sommer, *Serving Two Masters: Moravian Brethren in Germany and North Carolina* (Lexington, Ky., 2000), 1–32.

5. Peter Vogt, "A Voice for Themselves: Women as Participants in Congregational Discourse in the Eighteenth-Century Moravian Movement," in Beverly Mayne Kienzle and Pamela Walker, eds., *Women Preachers and Prophets Through Two Millennia of Christianity* (Berkeley, 1998), 229–231.

6. Ibid., 229–241, quotes on pp. 229, 238; Sommer, *Serving Two Masters,* 27.

7. For expanded versions of this oft-repeated story, see Oldendorp, *CM,* 270–278; Hamilton and Hamilton, *History of the Moravian Church,* 19.

8. Ernst Benz, "Pietist and Puritan Sources of Early Protestant World Missions (Cotton Mather and A. H. Francke)," *Church History,* 20 (1951), 28–55; Daniel Jeyaraj, *Inkulturation in Tranquebar: der Beitrag der frühen dänisch-halleschen Mission zum Werden einer indisch-einheimischen Kirches (1706–1730)* (Neuendettelsau, Germany, 1996). Thanks to Mark Peterson for sharing his ideas on this subject as well.

9. John Thornton, *Africa and Africans in the Making of the Atlantic World, 1400–1680* (New York, 1998), chap. 9; Thornton, "On the Trail of Voodoo: African Christianity in Africa and the Americas," *The Americas,* 44 (1988), 261–278; James H. Sweet, *Recreating Africa: Culture, Kinship, and Religion in the African-Portuguese World, 1441–1770* (Chapel Hill, N.C., 2003).

10. Sylvia R. Frey and Betty Wood, *Come Shouting to Zion: African*

American Protestantism in the American South and British Caribbean to 1830 (Chapel Hill, N.C., 1998), chaps. 1–3; Albert Raboteau, *Slave Religion: The "Invisible Institution" in the Antebellum South* (New York, 1978); Annette Laing, "'Heathens and Infidels'? African Christianization and the Anglican Mission in the South Carolina Low Country, 1700–1750," *Religion and American Culture,* 12 (2002), 197–228; Harry J. Bennett, *Bondsmen and Bishops: Slavery and Apprenticeship on the Codrington Plantations of Barbados, 1710–1838* (Berkeley, 1958).

11. Oldendorp, *CM,* 279–281.

12. August Spangenberg, "Kurze Nachricht von einigen in St. Thomas erweckten Negern und von dem Segen des Herrn unter ihnen," unpublished diary from August through October, 1736; quote from Oct. 11, R15.Ba.17, UA. Diaries and correspondence by Dober and Nitschmann between 1732 and 1735 (R15.Ba.1 and 2b, UA) would furnish material for an extended study of the earliest years of the mission, which is beyond my scope here. The critical support of Johann Lorentz Carstens for the mission is discussed in Arnold R. Highfield's introduction to J. L. Carstens, *St. Thomas in Early Danish Times: A General Description of all the Danish, American, or West Indian Islands,* ed. Highfield (St. Croix, 1997), xix–xxi.

13. *Dienerblätter* (Missionaries' Pages) of Martin and his sister, Susanna Nitschmann, UA; Oldendorp, *CM,* 308.

14. Martin's St. Thomas diary, 1736, esp. Oct. 8, 30, and 31, R15.Ba.2b, UA; Spangenberg, "Kurze Nachricht," Sept. 30 and Oct. 18, 1736; Oldendorp, *CM,* 307, 317–319.

15. Spangenberg, "Kurze Nachricht," Sept. 30 and Oct. 10, 1736; Oldendorp, *CM,* 281, 318. On the appeal of literacy for Africans enslaved in the Americas, see the introduction to Henry Louis Gates, Jr., and William L. Andrews, eds., *Pioneers of the Black Atlantic: Five Slave Narratives from the Enlightenment, 1772–1815* (Washington, D.C., 1998), 1–29.

16. Spangenberg, "Kurze Nachricht," Sept. 10, 17, and 29, 1736.

17. Ibid., Sept. 14, 1736; Martin's St. Thomas diary, Oct. 8, 1736, R15.Ba.2b; Oldendorp, *CM,* 328.

18. Oldendorp, *CM,* 322; Spangenberg, "Kurze Nachricht," Sept. 16, 1736.

19. John P. Meier, *The Vision of Matthew: Christ, Church and Morality in*

the First Gospel (New York, 1979), quote on p. 223; Hans Dieter Betz, *The Sermon on the Mount: A Commentary on the Sermon on the Mount, Including the Sermon on the Plain (Matthew 3:3–7 and Luke 6:20–49)* (Minneapolis, 1995); Theophus H. Smith, *Conjuring Culture: Biblical Formations of Black America* (New York, 1994), 3.

20. Spangenberg, "Kurze Nachricht," Sept. 19, 1736; Martin's St. Thomas diary, Sept. 12 and 30, 1736; Oldendorp, *CM,* 317.

21. Spangenberg, "Kurze Nachricht," Sept. 16 and 19, 1736; Martin's St. Thomas diary, Sept. 17, 1736. Excerpts of conversations with Marotta are found in Oldendorp, *CM,* 312–313.

22. Spangenberg, "Kurze Nachricht," Sept. 27, 1736.

23. Ibid., Sept. 30, 1736.

24. Peter Stein, "When Creole Speakers Write the Standard Language: An Analysis of Some of the Earliest Slave Letters from St. Thomas," in Martin Puetz and Rene Dirven, eds., *Wheels Within Wheels: Papers of the Duisburg Symposium on Pidgin and Creole Languages* (Frankfurt, 1989); and "Bemerkungen zur Edition der 'Sklavenbriefe' aus St. Thomas, 1737–1768," in N. Boretzki, W. Enninger, and T. Stolz, eds., *Akten des 1. Essener Kolloquiums über "Kreolsprachen und Sprachkontakte" vom 26.1.1985 an der Universität Essen* (Bochum, 1985), 135–142; Oldendorp, *CM,* 330.

25. Letter from Rebecca in "Briefe von Neger-Geschwistern, 1737–1765," R15.Ba.15, UA, trans. Sanneryn Jansen. Part of this letter is translated, along with those of several other converts, in Oldendorp, *CM,* 330, 411–413.

26. Comparisons with contemporary female New Light spiritual narratives from New England are drawn from Catherine A. Brekus, *Strangers and Pilgrims: Female Preaching in America, 1740–1845* (Chapel Hill, N.C., 1998), 39–40.

27. None of these letters is a full-fledged memoir, a standard genre in the Moravian Church. Congregants were expected to compose a *Lebenslauf,* or life story, describing their worldly lives, spiritual resurrection, and refuge in the church. See Katherine Faull Eze, "Self-Encounters: Two Eighteenth-Century African Memoirs from Moravian Bethlehem," in David McBride, Leroy Hopkins, and C. Aisha Blackshire-Belay, eds., *Crosscurrents: African Americans, Africa, and Germany in the Modern World* (Co-

lumbia, S.C., 1998), 29–52; idem, *Moravian Women's Memoirs: Their Related Lives, 1750–1820* (Syracuse, 1997); and Daniel B. Thorp, "Chattel with a Soul: The Autobiography of a Moravian Slave," *Pennsylvania Magazine of History and Biography*, 112 (1988), 433–451.

28. Vogt, "A Voice for Themselves," 238–239. On the best-known example of Quaker women prophesying in the early modern period, see Phyllis Mack, *Visionary Women: Ecstatic Prophecy in Seventeenth-Century England* (Berkeley, 1992); and Rebecca Larson, *Daughters of Light: Quaker Women Preaching and Prophesying in the Colonies and Abroad, 1700–1775* (Chapel Hill, N.C., 1999).

29. Astrid Billes Beck, "Rebekah," in *The Anchor Bible Dictionary*, 6 vols. (New York, 1992), vol. 5, 629–630.

30. Jacquelyn Grant, "Womanist Theology, Black Women's Experience as a Source for Doing Theology, with Special Reference to Christology," in Gayraud S. Wilmore, ed., *African American Religious Studies: An Interdisciplinary Anthology* (Durham, N.C., 1989), 209–227; Jean M. Humez, "'My Spirit Eye': Some Functions of Spiritual and Visionary Experience in the Lives of Five Black Women Preachers, 1810–1880," in Barbara J. Harris and JoAnn K. McNamara, eds., *Women and the Structure of Society* (Durham, N.C., 1984), 129–143, 275–281; Nell Irvin Painter, *Sojourner Truth: A Life, A Symbol* (New York, 1996); Bettye Collier-Thomas, *Daughters of Thunder: Black Women Preachers and Their Sermons* (San Francisco, 1998).

31. Spangenberg to Zinzendorf, Oct. 25, 1736, R15.Ba.10, UA.

32. Oldendorp, *CM*, 322; Spangenberg, "Kurze Nachricht," Oct. 13, 1736.

33. Martin letter to Zinzendorf, Sept. 19, 1737, R15.Ba.10, UA; Oldendorp, *CM*, 318.

4   THE PATH

1. Oldendorp, *CM*, 319.

2. J. L. Carstens, *St. Thomas in Early Danish Times: A General Description of all the Danish, American or West Indian Islands*, ed. and trans. Arnold R. Highfield, originally published in the 1740s as *En Almendelig Bekrivelse om alle de Danske, Americanske eller West-Indiske Eylande* (St. Croix, 1997), 16, 20; Oldendorp, *CM*, 52.

3. Oldendorp, *CM,* 132–133, 221–222; Carstens, *St. Thomas in Early Danish Times,* 72–73. For an overview of rural slavery in the Danish islands, see Neville A. T. Hall, *Slave Society in the Danish West Indies: St. Thomas, St. John and St. Croix* (Mona, Jamaica, 1992), 70–86. On slave housing, see William Chapman, "Slave Villages in the Danish West Indies: Changes of the Late Eighteenth and Early Nineteenth Centuries," in Thomas Carter and Bernard L. Herman, eds., *Perspectives in Vernacular Architecture,* IV (Columbia, Mo., and London, 1991), 108–220. On West Indian provision grounds, see Woodville K. Marshall, "Provision Ground and Plantation Labor in Four Windward Islands: Competition for Resources during Slavery," in Ira Berlin and Philip D. Morgan, eds., *Cultivation and Culture: Labor and the Shaping of Slave Life in the Americas* (Charlottesville, Va., 1993), 203–220.

4. Oldendorp, *CM,* 31; Carstens, *St. Thomas in Early Danish Times,* 50; Neville A. T. Hall, "Slavery in Three West Indian Towns: Christansted, Fredericksted and Charlotte Amalie in the Late Eighteenth and Early Nineteenth Century," in B. W. Higman, ed., *Trade, Government and Society in Caribbean History 1700–1920* (Kingston, 1983), and "Slaves' Use of Their 'Free' Time in the Danish Virgin Islands in the Later Eighteenth and Early Nineteenth Century," *Journal of Caribbean History,* 13 (1979), 21–43; Karen Fog Olwig, *Cultural Adaptation and Resistance on St. John: Three Centuries of Afro-Caribbean Life* (Gainesville, Fla., 1985); and Sidney Mintz and Douglas Hall, "The Origins of the Jamaican Internal Marketing System," *Papers in Caribbean Anthropology,* 57 (New Haven, 1970), 3–26.

5. Carstens, *St. Thomas in Early Danish Times,* 16–17, 74. Oldendorp, *CM,* 115–134, discusses vegetation on St. Thomas. On maroons, see Neville A. T. Hall, "Maritime Maroons: *Grand Maronnage* from the Danish West Indies," *WMQ,* 3rd ser., 42 (1985), 476–498.

6. Oldendorp, *CM,* 226 *(Baas),* 313, 341, 403, 419, 422, 486; Oldendorp, *Historie,* vol. II, part 1, 105–106; Arnold R. Highfield, "Patterns of Accommodation and Resistance: The Moravian Witness to Slavery in the Danish West Indies," *Journal of Caribbean History,* 28 (1994), 151; Highfield, "Introduction," in Carstens, *St. Thomas in Early Danish Times,* xx.

7. Oldendorp, *CM,* 328; letter signed by Martin, Matthäus Freundlich, Rebecca, Peter, Andreas, and Magdalena, April 11, 1738, R15.Ba.10, UA.

8. Oldendorp, *CM*, 418–419.

9. Ibid., 376, 424–427.

10. Ibid., 328; St. Thomas diary, March 30 and May 28, 1737, R15.Ba.10, UA.

11. Martin to Johann Decknatel, Feb. 13, 1737, R15.Ba.10, UA. On black female catechists, see Sylvia R. Frey and Betty Wood, *Come Shouting to Zion: African American Protestantism in the American South and British Caribbean to 1830* (Chapel Hill, N.C., 1998), 104–105, 126–128, 169–172, and 187–189; and Emily Clark and Virginia Meacham Gould, "The Feminine Face of Afro-Catholicism in New Orleans, 1727–1852," *WMQ*, 3rd ser., 59 (2002), 409–448.

12. St. Thomas diary, April 14, 1737, R.15.Ba.10, UA; Rebecca's confirmation in Oldendorp, *Historie*, vol. II, part 1, 224.

13. St. Thomas diary, March 3, 1737, and April 29, 1738, R.15.Ba.10 and R.15.Ba.2b, UA.

14. St. Thomas diary, May 1 and 27, 1738, R.15.Ba.2b, UA; Nell Irvin Painter, *Sojourner Truth: A Life, a Symbol* (New York, 1995).

15. St. Thomas diary, July 1, 1737, R.15.Ba.2b, UA.

16. Ibid., June 28, 1737, R.15.Ba.2b, UA.

17. Ibid., April 27, July 15, 1738, R.15.Ba.2b, UA.

18. The term "geography of faith" was kindly suggested to me by Sylvia Frey.

19. Oldendorp, *CM*, 329–330, 389, and *Historie*, vol. II, part 1, 233–235. On shipmates, see Sidney Mintz and Richard Price, *The Birth of African American Culture: An Anthropological Approach* (1976; reprint, Boston, 1992), 22–23.

20. Oldendorp, *CM*, 328; "Kirchen-Buch der Evangelischen Brüder-Gemeine in St. Thomas, St. Crux und St. Jan, 1736–1759," baptismal data for years 1738–1741, R15.Ba.16b, UA.

21. Oldendorp, *CM*, 327, 354, 420.

22. Ibid., 163, 321, 327.

23. Virgin Islands Mission, Church Register 1737–1750 ("Ein Apendix zum Kirchen-Buch der Evangelischen Brüder-Gemeine in St. Thomas, Crux u. Jan"), West Indies Catalogues Box, MA-NP. See also Karen Fog Olwig, "African Cultural Principles in Caribbean Slave Societies: A View

from the Danish West Indies," in Stephan Palmié, *Slave Cultures and the Cultures of Slavery* (Knoxville, Tenn., 1995), 23–39, and "African Culture in the Danish West Indies: The Slave Trade and Its Aftermath," in George F. Tyson and Arnold R. Highfield, eds., *The Danish West Indian Slave Trade: Virgin Islands Perspectives* (St. Croix, 1994), 69–87.

24. John K. Thornton, "The Development of an African Catholic Church in the Kingdom of Kongo, 1491–1750," *Journal of African History,* 25 (1984), 147–167; Linda M. Heywood, ed., *Central Africans and Cultural Transformations in the American Diaspora* (New York, 2001), 71–90; Mary Karasch, *Slave Life in Rio de Janeiro, 1808–1850* (Princeton, N.J., 1987); James H. Sweet, *Recreating Africa: Culture, Kinship, and Religion in the African-Portuguese World, 1441–1770* (Chapel Hill, N.C., 2003).

25. Oldendorp, *CM,* 200–203, 312–313, 540; St. Thomas diary, June 6, 1737, April 8, 1738, R.15.Ba.2b, UA. A full account of the confrontation of African and Moravian beliefs in the Danish West Indies through the eighteenth century is beyond the scope of this book.

26. Oldendorp, *CM,* 390; Nikolaus Ludwig von Zinzendorf, "Heidenkatechismus zum Gebrauch für die Boten," in Zinzendorf, *Texte zur Mission* (Nürnberg, 1748; repub. Hamburg, 1979), 61–69. See also Robin Law, "Human Sacrifice in Pre-Colonial West Africa," *African Affairs,* 84 (1985), 53–87. On the comparable attractiveness of Christ's blood to Delaware and Mahican Moravian converts in eighteenth-century Pennsylvania, see Jane T. Merritt, *At the Crossroads: Indians and Empires on a Mid-Atlantic Frontier, 1700–1763* (Chapel Hill, N.C., 2003), 112–116.

27. Oldendorp, *CM,* 199–200, 264, 332; St. Thomas diary, May 17, 1738, R.15.Ba.2b, UA; "Kirchen-Buch der Evangelischen Brüder-Gemeine in St. Thomas, St. Crux und St. Jan, 1736–1759," 73–75, R.15.Ba.16b, UA; Michael A. Gomez, "Muslims in Early America," *Journal of Southern History,* 60 (1994), 671–710.

28. August Spangenberg, "Kurze Nachricht von einigen in St. Thomas erweckten Negern und von dem Segen unter ihnen," unpublished diary, September and October, 1736, quote from Sept. 28, R15.Ba.17, UA; Oldendorp, *CM,* 329; John Thornton, *Africa and Africans in the Making of the Atlantic World 1400–1680,* 2nd ed. (New York, 1998), chap. 9, esp. 240–242.

29. Oldendorp, *CM,* 573, 171. For European accounts of African reli-

gions on the Gold Coast, see Adam Jones, *Brandenburg Sources for West African History, 1680–1700* (Stuttgart, 1985).

30. Oldendorp, *CM*, 551; Olwig, "African Cultural Principles," 33–37; Highfield, "Patterns of Accommodation and Resistance," 153–154; Hall, *Slave Society in the Danish West Indies*, 115–121. On African elections in America, see Elizabeth W. Kiddy, "Who Is the King of Congo? A New Look at African and Afro-Brazilian Kings in Brazil," in Heywood, ed., *Central Africans and Cultural Transformations*, 153–182; Robert Dirks, *The Black Saturnalia: Conflict and Its Ritual Expression on British West Indian Slave Plantations* (Gainesville, Fla., 1987).

31. St. Thomas diary, July 19, 1738, R.15.Ba.2b, UA.

32. Spangenberg, "Kurze Nachricht," Sept. 17, 1736; Oldendorp, *CM*, 171–172, 333–334, 454. I am grateful to Daniel Thorp for calling my attention to the last citation.

33. Oldendorp, *CM*, 332–335.

34. Ibid., 334. See also Highfield, "Patterns of Accommodation and Resistance," 138–164; and Frey and Wood, *Come Shouting to Zion*, 83–87.

35. Oldendorp, *CM*, 220, 263. See also Olwig, "African Cultural Principles" (quote on p. 28). For examples of women's religious roles in West Africa, see Sandra E. Greene, *Gender, Ethnicity, and Social Change on the Upper Slave Coast: A History of the Anlo-Ewe* (Portsmouth, N.H., 1996); Edna G. Bay, *Wives of the Leopard: Gender, Politics, and Culture in the Kingdom of Dahomey* (Charlottesville, Va., 1998); and Margaret W. Creel, *"A Peculiar People": Slave Religion and Community-Culture Among the Gullahs* (New York, 1988), 288–292.

36. Oldendorp, *CM*, 584. On Afro-Catholic confraternities, see Karasch, *Slave Life in Rio de Janeiro;* Elizabeth W. Kiddy, "Ethnic and Racial Identity in the Brotherhoods of the Rosary of Minas Gerais, 1700–1830," *The Americas*, 56 (1999), 221–252.

37. Oldendorp, *CM*, 335, 376, 541, 605. On black Christian godparents and similar practices in Afro-Catholic Latin America, see Jon F. Sensbach, *A Separate Canaan: The Making of An Afro-Moravian World in North Carolina, 1763–1840* (Chapel Hill, N.C., 1998), 137–143; and Clark and Gould, "The Feminine Face of Afro-Catholicism."

38. Oldendorp, *CM*, 487, 457–458. On helpers in the early Moravian

church, see Hanns-Joachim Wollstadt, *Geordnetes Dienen in der christlichen Gemeinde* (Göttingen, 1966), 155–161, 213–215.

39. "Plicht van Een helper Broeder en Suster," undated document, R15.Ba.27 (trans. Sanneryn Jansen). A report from 1760 by the missionary Georg Weber describes all the helpers on St. Thomas, St. John, and St. Croix—fifty-four men and women, in all; R15.Ba27.11, UA. The most famous was the multilingual Cornelius van de Companie; see Christian Degn, *Die Schimmelmanns im Atlantischen Dreieckshandel: Gewinn und Gewissen* (Neumünster, 1974), 338–345.

40. Oldendorp, *CM*, 333.

41. Ibid., 353, 691 n. 3. On the origin and organization of bands, see Wollstadt, *Geordnetes Dienen in der christlichen Gemeinde,* 93–99; quote on p. 96.

42. List of bands given in "Konferenz-Protokolle von St. Thomas," Sept. 8, 1740, R15.Ba.1, UA; Oldendorp, *CM*, 388.

43. Oldendorp, *CM*, 412.

44. Ibid., 327.

45. Martin letter, April 11, 1738, R.15.Ba, UA.

46. List of bands given in "Konferenz-Protokolle von St. Thomas," Sept 8, 1740, R15.Ba.1, UA; Oldendorp, *CM*, 388. The predominance of African-American women in both biracial and all-black churches in the U.S. South during the late eighteenth and early nineteenth centuries is noted in Frey and Wood, *Come Shouting to Zion,* 163–164.

5   WITNESS

1. Description of Christiansfort in Johann Lorentz Carstens, *St. Thomas in Early Danish Times: A General Description of all the Danish, American, or West Indian Islands,* trans. and ed. Arnold R. Highfield, originally published in the 1740s as *En almendelig Beskrivelse om alle de Danske, Americanske eller West-Indiske Eylande* (St. Croix, 1997), 33–38. The fort exerted an intimidating presence well into the twentieth century. A psychologist writing about St. Thomas in 1943 noted that the last execution had occurred on the island in 1864, but that "whippings were generously administered" along with a "period of time in the cool dungeons of the Fort" to those convicted of crimes. As a result, "To many St. Thomians the fort is

an object of considerable fear, and they will not go near it unless summoned by the police." Albert A. Campbell, "St. Thomas Negroes—A Study of Personality and Culture," *Psychological Monographs,* 55:5 (1943), 1–90, quote on p. 49.

2. For summaries of the complex Moravian views on marriage and sexuality, see Peter Vogt, "'*Ehereligion*': The Moravian Theory and Practice of Marriage as Point of Contention in the Conflict between Ephrata and Bethlehem," *Communal Societies,* 21 (2001), 37–48, quotes on pp. 44–45; and Craig D. Atwood, "Sleeping in the Arms of Christ: Sanctifying Sexuality in the Eighteenth Century Moravian Church," *Journal of the History of Sexuality,* 8 (1997), 25–51. The idea of Rebecca's marriage as *Streiterehe* is also put forth in Arnold Highfield, "Rebekka Freundlich: A Moravian Life," *Conference Proceedings of the Society of Virgin Islands Historians,* ed. Robert V. Vaughn (St. Croix, 1992), 51–61.

3. Oldendorp, *CM,* 345; St. Thomas diary, Jan. 12, 1738, R15.Ba.2b.10, UA. On procedures for arranging marriage, see Elisabeth Sommer, *Serving Two Masters: Moravian Brethren in Germany and North Carolina, 1727–1801* (Lexington, Ky., 2000), 70–78 and passim; Gillian Lindt Gollin, *Moravians in Two Worlds: A Study of Changing Communities* (New York, 1967), 52–62, 110–127.

4. Oldendorp, *CM,* 338–339; Martin, "Ein Ehe-Zeugnis von 2 Gliedern von Jesus," May 4, 1738, also found in his St. Thomas diary, May 4, 1738, both in R15.Ba.10, UA.

5. Martin, "Ein Ehe-Zeugnis."

6. St. Thomas diary, April 18, May 2, May 5, 1738; Martin, "Ein Ehe-Zeugnis." Part of this description is also drawn from court testimony on St. Thomas, Nov. 24, 1738, in Dokumenter vedk.de maeriske brodre pa St. Thomas, 1737–1749, VGK, KKA, No. 185, RA. All translations from the Danish in this set of documents were done by Louise Sebro.

7. Examples of Rebecca's activities reported in Martin's St. Thomas diary, May 5, 19, 22, 24, June 1, 4, 22, 24, 29, July 6, 26, 1738, R15.Ba.2b, UA; Oldendorp, *CM,* 339.

8. A basic narrative of this transaction is provided in Oldendorp, *CM,* 339–340, but important additional details are described in St. Thomas diary, July 10, 1738, R15.Ba2.b, and Georg Weber, "Wie die Mährischen

Glieder zur Plantage mit Sclaven gekommen" ("Copie Eines Documents was ich von unders seeligen Br. Friedrich Martins eigen Hand hier aufgehoben vom Jahr dem 10ten July 1738"), July 23, 1755, R15.Ba3.31, and R15.Ba.10.85, UA.

9. St. Thomas diary, July 10, 28, Aug. 9–12, 1738, R15.Ba.2b, UA; Oldendorp, *CM,* 340–341.

10. Martin did not actually own the slaves himself, but rather acted as trustee for the Unity of Brethren, which held title to them. There is no evidence that the missionaries considered buying slaves and emancipating them to work as wage laborers, but they did not really have that option anyway. The government controlled private manumissions, wanting to limit the number of freed people on the island. Neville A. T. Hall, *Slave Society in the Danish West Indies: St. Thomas, St. John, St. Croix* (Mona, Jamaica, 1992), 140.

11. Statutes banning interracial marriage are mentioned in Hall, *Slave Society in the Danish West Indies,* 151, 252 nn. 43, 44. One black (presumably enslaved) congregant named Maria, baptized in 1750, was listed in a Moravian church register as having a white husband, although it was probably not a legally recognized marriage. Virgin Islands Mission, Church Register, 1737–1750 ("Ein Apendix zum Kirch-Buch der Evangelischen Brüder-Gemeine in St. Thomas, St. Crux, u. St. Jan"), No. 482, West Indies Catalogues Box, MA-NP.

12. Oldendorp, *CM,* 331–332, 343–344, 685 n. 2.

13. Ibid., 345; VGK, KKA-185, extract from Sept. 30, 1738, RA. VGK, KKA-185, court affidavit of Oct. 20, 1738, RA.

14. Martin's diaries and letters from Sept. 1738 to Jan. 1739, R15.Ba.10, UA; Oldendorp's account in *CM,* 345–356, and a longer version in *Historie,* vol. II, part 1, 273–322; and Danish court extracts in VGK, KKA-185. In reconstructing the series of court hearings, I have relied on the two firsthand accounts—Martin's and that of the court documents—whenever possible, falling back on Oldendorp when no primary document is available.

15. VGK, KKA-185, extract from Oct. 6, 1738, RA.

16. Martin letter to Zinzendorf, Oct. 30, 1738, R15.Ba.10, UA.

17. Ibid.

18. Ibid.

19. Ibid.

20. Ibid.

21. Matthäus's response to judge in hearing of Nov. 24, 1738, in VGK, KKA-185, RA; Oldendorp, *CM,* 354; Martin letter to Zinzendorf, Oct. 30, 1738, R15.Ba.10, UA. Martin ended his letter to Germany as follows: "We greet all of you. I will write again as soon as possible. Rebecca kisses all the brothers and sisters with a holy kiss. Under arrest in St. Thomas, Oct. 30, 1738."

22. Oldendorp, *Historie,* vol. II, part 1, 291.

23. Oldendorp, *CM,* 348–349.

24. St. Thomas diary, Nov. 21, 1738, R.15.Ba.10, UA.

25. Ibid., Dec. 5, 1738. The medicinal uses of onions are described in Laurel Thatcher Ulrich, *A Midwife's Tale: The Life of Martha Ballard, Based on Her Diary, 1785–1812* (New York, 1990), 50, 51, 357. Herbs and other plants used for folk treatments on St. Thomas are described in Oldendorp, *CM,* 115–118. See also Richard Sheridan, *Doctors and Slaves: A Medical and Demographic History of Slavery in the British West Indies, 1680–1834* (London, 1985).

26. St. Thomas diary, Nov. 21, 1738., R.15.Ba.10, UA.

27. Hearing of Nov. 24, 1738, VGK, KKA-185, RA; Oldendorp, *CM,* 348–349.

28. Hearing of Nov. 24, 1738, VGK, KKA-185, RA. For dramatic effect I have rephrased this exchange, which is recorded in the document in the third person ("They were asked whether they . . ." "They answered that they . . ."). Remarkably, the testimony matches, nearly point by point with minor variations, the exchange between prosecutor and defendants that Martin reported in his own diary. Martin was not at the hearing and must have gotten his information from Matthäus and Rebecca, whose own version followed closely that of the court scribe. St. Thomas diary, Nov. 24, 1738; and Oldendorp, *Historie,* vol. II, part 1, 298–301.

29. Hearing of Dec. 15, 1738, VGK, KKA-185, RA. Aquilin referred to a Danish statute that stipulated: "Anyone suspected of living a loose or scandalous life together should be ordered to stay away from each other, and if they have no [professional] bonds they should be sent out of the town and parish away from each other or else submit to the discipline of the church

and be punished by their master." *Christian den Femtes Lov* [Danish Law by Christian VI] (Copenhagen, 1683), 936.

30. Hearing of Dec. 22, 1738, VGK, KKA-185, RA.

31. St. Thomas diary, Dec. 11, 1738, R.15.Ba.10, UA; Oldendorp, *CM*, 344, 353.

32. Carstens' account reported in Oldendorp, *CM*, 355.

33. Oldendorp, *CM*, 354–356.

34. Synod at Zeist, May–June, 1746, R.2.A.12, UA.; Oldendorp, *CM*, 357–358.

35. Oldendorp, *Historie*, vol. II, part 1, 326.

36. Synod of 1739, R.2.A.2, UA.

37. Letter from Rebecca to Anna Nitschmann, Feb. 16, 1739, R15.Ba.11, UA; translated by Marjoleine Kars.

38. Second letter from Rebecca to Anna Nitschmann, Feb. 16, 1739, R15.Ba.11, UA; translated by Marjoleine Kars.

6 THE DEVIL'S BARGAIN

1. Moth to Danish West India and Guinea Company, March 24, 1739, in Dokumenter vedk. de maehriske brodre pa St. Thomas, 1737–1749, VGK, KKA-185, RA. All translations from the Danish in these documents were done by Louise Sebro. An example of a vigorous polemic against Zinzendorf in his own time is Henry Rimius, *A Candid Narrative of the Rise and Progress of the Herrnhuters, Commonly Called Moravians or Unitas Fratrum* (London, 1753).

2. August Gottlieb Spangenberg, *Leben des Herrn Nikolaus Ludwig Grafen von Zinzendorf und Pottendorf* (Barby, 1773–1775); Erich Beyreuther, *Nikolaus Ludwig von Zinzendorf* (Hamburg, 1965); Otto Uttendörfer, *Zinzendorfs Weltbetrachtung: eine systematische Darstellung der Gedankenwelt des Begrunders der Brüdergemeine* (Berlin, 1929); John Weinlick, *Count Zinzendorf* (New York, 1956).

3. J. Taylor Hamilton and Kenneth G. Hamilton, *History of the Moravian Church: The Renewed Unitas Fratrum, 1722–1957* (Winston-Salem, N.C., and Bethlehem, Pa., 1967), 60–70.

4. Oldendorp, *CM*, 358–359; letter from Zinzendorf, Feb. 11, 1739, R15.Ba.1, UA.

5. Extract of conversation between Schonneman and Zinzendorf, Feb. 11, 1739, in VGK, KKA-185, document 11, RA.

6. Letter from A. Willemsen to Governor Moth, Feb. 20, 1739, in VGK, KKA-185, document 5:1, RA.

7. Albin Theodor Feder to Leonhard Dober, Aug. 4, 1739, R15.Ba.11, UA. On the cycle of slave rebellions in the 1730s, see Peter Linebaugh and Marcus Rediker, *The Many-Headed Hydra: Sailors, Slaves, Commoners, and the Hidden History of the Revolutionary Atlantic* (Boston, 2000), 193–198; David Barry Gaspar, "A Dangerous Spirit of Liberty: Slave Rebellion in the West Indies During the 1730s," *Cimarrons,* 1 (1981), 79–91; and Peter H. Wood, *Black Majority: Negroes in Colonial South Carolina from 1670 Through the Stono Rebellion* (New York, 1974).

8. On the relationship between Methodists and Moravians, which oscillated between hostility and reconciliation for much of the eighteenth century, see Clifford W. Towlson, *Moravian and Methodist: Relationships and Influences in the Eighteenth Century* (London, 1957); and Colin Podmore, *The Moravian Church in England, 1728–1760* (Oxford and New York, 1998), 80–88.

9. Sylvia R. Frey and Betty Wood, *Come Shouting to Zion: African American Protestantism in the American South and British Caribbean to 1830* (Chapel Hill, N.C., 1998), 91–95. On the Bryan affair, see also Harvey H. Jackson, "Hugh Bryan and the Evangelical Movement in Colonial South Carolina," *WMQ,* 3rd ser., 43 (1986), 594–614; and Alan Gallay, *The Formation of a Planter Elite: Jonathan Bryan and the Southern Colonial Frontier* (Athens, Ga., 1989), 38–47.

10. Oldendorp, *CM,* 359–360.

11. Spangenberg, *Leben des Zinzendorf,* 1166–1167.

12. Zinzendorf's conference minutes, St. Thomas, Feb. 11, 1739, R15.Ba.1, UA. A synopsis of these minutes appears in Oldendorp, *CM,* 360–361.

13. *Stundenbeter* (hourly watchers') list in Zinzendorf's conference minutes, St. Thomas, Feb. 11, 1739, R15.Ba.1, UA; Oldendorp, *CM,* 364, 377.

14. Oldendorp, *CM,* 360.

15. Zinzendorf's address to slaves, Feb. 15, 1739, Dutch manuscript copy, R15.Ba.1, UA; English translation in Oldendorp, *CM,* 361–363.

16. The interplay of these ideas in medieval and early modern Christianity is explored in David Brion Davis, *The Problem of Slavery in Western Culture* (Ithaca, 1966); Winthrop D. Jordan, *White Over Black: American Attitudes Toward the Negro, 1550–1812* (Chapel Hill, N.C., 1968); Forrest G. Wood, *The Arrogance of Faith: Christianity and Race in America from the Colonial Era to the Twentieth Century* (New York, 1990); and Benjamin Braude, "The Sons of Noah and the Construction of Ethnic and Geographical Identities in the Medieval and Early Modern Periods," *WMQ,* 3rd ser., 54 (1997), 103–142.

17. Oldendorp, *CM,* 363.

18. Ibid., 363–364.

19. Letter to King of Denmark, Feb. 15, 1739, R15.Ba.1, UA.

20. Manuscript letters in the name of Damma and Marotta (Magdalena), in an African language, Dutch Creole, and German, are found in R15.Ba.1, UA. On this episode, see also Angelita Reyes, *Mothering Across Cultures: Postcolonial Representations* (Minneapolis, 2002), 113–123. Though the phonetic spelling of the eighteenth-century orthography differs from modern techniques, the language appears to be Fon, a colloquial branch of Ewe still spoken in parts of modern Benin. Bernard Gadagbui to the author, Oct. 27, 2002.

21. "Der erweckten *Negros* in St. Thomas Schreiben an Ihro Majest. den König in Dännemarck, An. 1739," and "Der Aeltestin der Gemeine der *Negros* in St. Thomas Schreiben an die Königen von Dännemarck, An. 1739," *Büdingische Sammlung,* vol. 4 (Büdingen, 1741), in Nikolaus Ludwig von Zinzendorf, *Ergänzungsband,* VII (Hildesheim, 1965), 483–487.

22. "A Translation of two Letters from some *Negroes* in the American Island of St. Thomas, belonging to the King of Denmark, which are brought to the Communion of the Gospel of our Blessed Lord and Saviour, and baptised by the Ministry of some Meravian Bretheren," *The Christian Monthly History,* IV (1744), 58–60. I am grateful to Doug Winiarski for calling this citation to my attention.

23. St. Thomas diary, Feb. 16 and 22, 1739, R15.Ba.2b, UA; Oldendorp, *CM,* 367.

24. Martin's St. Thomas diary, Feb. 23, 1739, R15.Ba.2b, UA; some details also derive from the description of another eyewitness, missionary

from Georg Weber, in a letter to Leonard Dober, May 5, 1739, R15.Ba.11, UA. Oldendorp used these accounts for his description in *CM*, 367–368.

25. Weber letter to Dober, May 5, 1739, R15.Ba.11, UA; Martin's St. Thomas diary, Feb. 23, 1739, R15.Ba.2b ("... door in our face?" translates from the German "Macht ihr die Tür vor unserer Nase zu?"), UA.

26. Martin's St. Thomas diary, Feb. 23, March 11 and 18, 1739, R15.Ba.2b; Weber letter to Dober, May 5, 1739, R15.Ba.11, UA. Meanwhile, at the governor's request, Martin was called to testify in court against the attackers of February 23. They denied his charges and filed a slander suit against him. At the urging of the planter Johann Carstens, all charges were eventually dropped. Martin's diary, Feb. 25–March 25, 1739; Oldendorp, *CM*, 369, 377.

27. Veronica Löhans to Anna Nitschmann, April 26, 1739, R.15.Ba.11, UA.

28. Löhans to Nitschmann, July 20, 1739, R15.Ba.11, UA. After Valentin died in 1742, Veronica married the missionary Johann Böhner and served the West Indian mission until her death in 1765. Oldendorp, *CM*, 387, 611–613. See also Horst Ulbricht, "Zum Beispiel Elisabeth Weber: Die Frauen in den ersten Jahren der Karibik-Mission," *Unitas Fratrum*, 45/46 (1999), 103–112.

29. Zinzendorf to St. Thomas, Sept. 1741, R15.Ba.1, UA.

30. St. Thomas diary, Oct. 1, 1740, R15.Bb.2, UA.

31. A letter of support for the Brethren by Governor Moth dated March 24, 1739, and the decree of King Christian IV of Denmark permitting the missionaries to preach, dated March 13, 1739, are located in KKG, VGK-185, items 1 and 24.

32. "Register derer von unsern Brüdern in Diesen Eilanden getauften weissen," in Kirchen-Buch der Evangelischen Brüder Gemeine in St. Thomas, St. Crux und St. Jan, 1736–1759, p. 55, R15.Ba.16b, UA.

33. Minutes of Helpers' Conference [Helfer-Conferenz], Aug. 30, 1740, R15.Bb.2; Christian Gottlieb Israel to Jacob Till, April 17, 1740, R15.Ba.11; St. Thomas diary, Feb. 20 and April 19, 1740, R15.Bb.2; Martin to Isaac LeLong, May 18, 1740, R15.Ba.11, UA.

34. Oldendorp, *Historie*, vol. II, part 1, 434, 444.

35. St. Thomas diary, April 25 and 26, 1741, in *Büdingische Sammlung,*

vol. 5, 561–563, 597–598; Oldendorp, *CM*, 404–405. The diaries of the missionary Christian Gottlieb Israel between Sept. 23 and Dec. 16, 1740, and those of Friedrich Martin between Feb. 11 and May 8, 1741, published in the *Sammlung*, 561–628, are an excellent sample of daily activities in the mission. Other examples of masters punishing slaves for worship are found on pp. 561, 565, and 588.

36. These activities are sketched out in minutes of Helpers' Conferences from Aug. 24, Aug. 30, and Sept. 8, 1740, R15.Bb.2 and R15.Ba.1, UA. A summary is provided in Oldendorp, *CM*, 385–390.

37. Oldendorp, *CM*, 385–386. Oldendorp's description is drawn from the Helpers' Conference minutes, Aug. 24, 1740, items 7–9, R15.Bb.2, UA.

38. Oldendorp, *CM*, 390.

39. St. Thomas diary, Nov. 10–15, 1739; extract of letter to the governor, St. Thomas, Nov. 13, 1741, VGK, KKA-185, item 24; Oldendorp, *CM*, 398.

40. Johann Christian Erhardt, "Freundlichs Reise von St. Thomas nach Marienborn," June 5, 1742, R15.Ba17.15, UA; Oldendorp, *CM*, 398–399.

41. Erhardt, "Freundlichs Reise."

42. Ibid.; Wetterau diary, June 3, 1742, R8.33.b; Herrnhaag diary, June 3, 1742, R8.33.b, UA.

7   A PILGRIM IN EUROPE

1. On Protten, see Hans Werner Debrunner, *Presence and Prestige, Africans in Europe: A History of Africans in Europe before 1918* (Basel, 1979), 82–83; Ludewig Ferdinand Romer, *A Reliable Account of the Coast of Guinea (1760),* trans. and ed. Selena Axelrod Winsnes (Oxford and New York, 2000), 186; Hans Werner Debrunner, *A History of Christianity in Ghana* (Accra, 1967), 62–63, 74–75, 92; Peter Sebald, "Christian Jacob Protten Africanus (1715–1769)—Erster Missionar Einer Deutschen Missionsgesellschaft in Schwarzafrika," in Wilfried Wagner, ed, *Kolonien und Missionen: Referate des 3. Internationalen Kolonialgeschichtlichen Symposiums 1993 in Bremen* (Hamburg, 1994), 109–121; and Jacob Elisa Johannes Capitein, *The Agony of Asar: A Thesis on Slavery by the Former Slave,* trans. and ed. Grant Parker (Kingston and Princeton, 2001), 148–150.

2. Debrunner, *Presence and Prestige*, 82–83. A church register identifies Protten's birthplace, probably incorrectly, as Capo Corso, a British slaving

fort further west on the Gold Coast. Herrnhaag Kirchenbuch, Jan. 6, 1746, R8.35.a, UA.

Although a full account of Protten's life story is beyond the scope of this book, his written legacy is far larger than Rebecca's, since he wrote hundreds of pages of diaries and letters between the 1730s and 1760s which are preserved in the Unitätsarchiv in Herrnhut (UA). On Afro-European communities in West African port towns, see Ira Berlin, "From Creoles to African: Atlantic Creoles and the Origins of African-American Society in Mainland North America," *WMQ,* 3rd ser., 53 (1996), 251–288.

3. Protten, "Des Malatten C. J. Prottens Schreiben um die Aufnahme in die Evange. Mährische Brüder-Gemeine" ["The Mulatto C. J. Protten's Description of his Admission to the Evangelical Moravian Brethren's Congregation"], in *Büdingische Sammlung* (Büdingen, 1741), reprinted in Nikolaus Ludwig von Zinzendorf, *Ergänzungsband VII* (Hildesheim, 1965), vol. 4, 418–419. On Frederik Svane, see Debrunner, *Presence and Prestige,* 84–85.

4. Protten, "Des Malatten C. J. Prottens Schreiben," 419.

5. Peter Martin, *Schwarze Teufel, edle Mohren: Afrikaner in Geschichte und Bewusstsein der Deutschen* (Hamburg, 1993); Sue Peabody, *"There Are No Slaves in France": The Political Culture of Race and Slavery in the Ancien Régime* (New York, 1996); Alison Blakely, "Problems in Studying the Role of Blacks in Europe," *Perspectives,* 35 (May/June 1997), 1, 11–13; David Northrup, *Africa's Discovery of Europe, 1450–1850* (New York, 2002), 141–165; Vera Lind, "Africans in Early Modern German Society: Identity—Difference—Aesthetics—Anthropology," *Bulletin of the German Historical Institute,* 28 (Spring 2001), 74–82.

6. W. E. Abraham, "The Life and Times of Anton Wilhelm Amo," Historical Society of Ghana, *Transactions,* VII (1964), 60–81; and F. L. Bartels, "Jacobus Eliza Johannes Capitein, 1717–47," Historical Society of Ghana, *Transactions,* IV (1959), 3–13. For the best evaluation of Capitein's life and work, see Grant Parker's introduction to Capitein, *The Agony of Asar,* 3–78, quote on p. 49.

7. Protten, "Des Mallatten C. J. Prottens Schreiben," 419–420.

8. Ibid., 420–421. For a different version of Svane's departure for Africa, see Debrunner, *Presence and Prestige,* 84–85. At Christiansborg Svane

served as a catechist for mulatto children between 1735 and 1746, when, frustrated by his lack of support and success, he returned to Denmark. Debrunner, *History of Christianity in Ghana,* 61, 63, 68, 70, 73–74.

9. Sebald, "Christian Jacob Protten Africanus," 117–118; Debrunner, *Presence and Prestige,* 82–83. On the etymology of "Moor," see Jack D'Amico, *The Moor in English Renaissance Drama* (Tampa, Fla., 1991), esp. 224 n. 8; Winthrop D. Jordan, *White over Black: American Attitudes Toward the Negro, 1550–1812* (Chapel Hill, N.C., 1968), 5–6; Elliott H. Tokson, *The Popular Image of the Black Man in English Drama, 1550–1688* (Boston, 1982); Sander L. Gilman, *On Blackness without Blacks: Essays on the Image of the Black in Germany* (Boston, 1982), xii.

10. Minutes of Marienborn Synod, 1740, R.2.A.3.A.1, UA; Sebald, "Christian Jacob Protten Africanus," 117–118.

11. On Philip Quaque, see F. L. Bartels, "Philip Quaque," *Transactions of the Gold Coast and Togoland Historical Society,* I (1955), 153–177; and Debrunner, *Presence and Prestige,* 81–82. On the African joining of Christian mission and antislavery in the eighteenth century, see Lamin Sanneh, *Abolitionists Abroad: American Blacks and the Making of Modern West Africa* (Cambridge, Mass., 1999), chaps. 1–2.

12. Debrunner, *History of Christianity in Ghana,* 62–63; Oldendorp, *Historie,* vol. II, part 1, 539–540.

13. Herrnhaag Diary extract, April 15, 1745, R.8.33.d, UA.

14. Herrnhaag Diary, Feb. 9, 1744, R.8.33.d, UA.

15. J. Taylor Hamilton and Kenneth G. Hamilton, *History of the Moravian Church: The Renewed Unitas Fratrum, 1722–1957* (Bethlehem, Pa., 1967), 60–75; Hans-Walter Erbe, "Herrnhaag: Eine religiöse Kommunität im 18. Jahrhundert," *Unitas Fratrum,* 23/24 (1988), 4–222, and "Herrnhaag: Tiefpunkt oder Höhe punkt der Brüdergeschichte?" *Unitas Fratrum,* 26 (1989), 37–51.

16. Paul Peucker, "Aus Allen Nationen: Nicht-Europäer in den Deutschen Brüdergemeinen des 18. Jahrhunderts," unpublished manuscript, 2003. I am grateful to Dr. Peucker for sharing his work with me.

17. For a similar black Christian transatlantic migration from the Caribbean to England toward the end of the eighteenth century, see John Saillant, "Antiguan Methodism and Antislavery Activity: Anne and Eliza-

beth Hart in the Eighteenth-Century Black Atlantic," *Church History,* 69 (2000), 86–115. The role of sailors in binding together a black Atlantic consciousness is discussed in W. Jeffrey Bolster, *Black Jacks: African American Seamen in the Age of Sail* (Cambridge, Mass., 1997); and Julius Scott, "Afro-American Sailors and the International Communication Network: The Case of Newport Bowers," in Colin Howell and Richard J. Twomey, eds., *Jack Tar in History: Essays in the History of Maritime Life and Labour* (New Brunswick, 1991).

18. Protokolle der Aeltesten Conferenz in Herrnhaag, Sept. 10, 1742, R.8.36.C1, UA; Stundebeter Einrichtung zu Herrnhaag, R.8.36.C, UA.

19. Peucker, "Aus Allen Nationen." Moravian clothing is discussed in Elisabeth W. Sommer, "Fashion Passion: The Rhetoric of Dress within the Eighteenth Century Moravian Brethren," in Michele Gillespie and Robert Beachy, eds., *Pious Pursuits: German Moravians in the Atlantic World* (forthcoming).

20. On the development of the choir system in the early Moravian fellowship, see Gillian Gollin, *Moravians in Two Worlds: A Study of Changing Communities* (New York, 1967), 67–109; Elisabeth W. Sommer, *Serving Two Masters: Moravian Brethren in Germany and North Carolina, 1727–1801* (Lexington, Ky., 2000), 29–32.

21. Beverly Prior Smaby, "Female Piety Among Eighteenth Century Moravians," *Pennsylvania History,* 64 (supplement, Summer 1997), 151–167; Peter Vogt, "A Voice for Themselves: Women as Participants in Congregational Discourse in the Eighteenth-Century Moravian Movement," in Beverly Mayne Kienzle and Pamela J. Walker, eds., *Women Preachers and Prophets through Two Millennia of Christianity* (Berkeley, 1998), 227–247; and Aaron Spencer Fogleman, "Jesus Is Female: The Moravian Challenge in the German Communities of British North America," *WMQ,* 3rd ser., 60 (2003), 295–332, esp. pp. 318–319 on Anna Nitschmann.

22. Protokolle der Aeltesten-Conferenz in Herrnhaag, April 3, 1743, R.8.36.C1, UA; Herrnhagisches Kirchenbuch, Feb. 9, 1744, p. 186, R8.35.a, UA. On Zinzendorf's theory of child-rearing and the role of the children's choirs, see Gollin, *Moravians in Two Worlds,* 74–75, 80–83; Otto Uttendörfer, *Zinzendorf und die Jugend: Die Erziehungsgrundsätze Zinzendorf's und der Brüdergemeine* (Berlin, 1923).

23. Herrnhaag Diary, Dec. 9, 1742, R.8.33c, UA; Peucker, "Aus Allen Nationen."

24. Herrnhaag Diary, June 24, 1743, R.8.33.c, UA; Protokoll der Hirschberger Synode, June 30–July 7, 1743, R.2.A.8, pp. 1–3, UA.

25. Protokoll der Hirschberger Synode, July 7, 1743, R.2.A.8, p. 127–169, UA.

26. Craig D. Atwood, "Deep in the Side of Jesus: Zinzendorfian Piety in Colonial America," in Gillespie and Beachy, eds., *Pious Pursuits;* Erbe, "Herrnhaag: Eine religiöse Kommunität"; Craig D. Atwood, "Zinzendorf's 1749 reprimand to the *Brüdergemeine,*" *Transactions of the Moravian Historical Society,* 29 (1996), 59–84; Paul Peucker, "'Blut auf unsre grünen Bändchen': Die Sichtungszeit in der herrnhuter Brüdergemeine," *Unitas Fratrum,* 49/50 (2002), 41–94; Caroline Walker Bynum, "Violent Imagery in Late Medieval Piety," *Bulletin of the German Historical Institute,* 30 (Spring 2002), 3–36.

27. Erbe, "Herrnhaag: Eine religiöse Kommunität."

28. Atwood, "Deep in the Side of Jesus," 8–24; Craig D. Atwood, "Sleeping in the Arms of Jesus: Sanctifying Sexuality in the Eighteenth-Century Moravian Church," *Journal of the History of Sexuality,* 8 (1997), 25–51; Fogleman, "Jesus Is Female."

29. Craig D. Atwood, "Zinzendorf's Litany of the Wounds," *Lutheran Quarterly,* 11 (1997), 189–214.

30. Erbe, "Herrnhaag: Eine religiöse Kommunität," 82–94; Atwood, "Zinzendorf's 1749 Reprimand," 65, 70–71.

31. Atwood, "Deep in the Side of Jesus," 19. Much of Atwood's evidence comes from the Moravian settlement of Bethlehem, Pennsylvania, which was founded in 1741, but it applies equally well to the European congregations.

32. On the rising popularity of the church in England during this period, see Colin Podmore, *The Moravian Church in England, 1728–1760* (New York and Oxford, 1998); and J. C. S. Mason, *The Moravian Church and the Missionary Awakening in England, 1760–1800* (Woodbridge, Suffolk, and Rochester, N.Y., 2001).

33. Examples of Rebecca's attendance at meetings are noted in minutes of the Diener-Conferenz, Dec. 11, 1744, R.2.A.13.4; Pilger-Conferenz, Jan.

4, 1745, R.2.A.14;, and Helfer-Conferenz, Dec. 10–23, 1745, R.2.A.13.3, all UA; Anna Maria's death is noted in Herrnhaagisches Kirchenbuch, Feb. 9, 1744, p. 186, R.8.35.a, UA.

34. Marienborn Diary, Dec. 27, 1745, R.8.33.d, UA.

35. "Die Trauung von zwölf Paar Geschwister, den 6 Jan. 1746 in Marienborn" ["The Wedding of Twelve Pairs of Brothers and Sisters, Jan. 6, 1746, in Marienborn"], in Nikolaus Ludwig von Zinzendorf, *Materialen und Dokumente: Band XXIV.2. Herrnhut im 18. und 19. Jahrhundert. Teil 2.* (Hildesheim, 2000), 229–240, quotes on pp. 235–236, 239.

36. Fogleman, "Jesus Is Female," in Gillespie and Beachy, eds., *Pious Pursuits,* 24–27; Atwood, "Sleeping in the Arms of Christ," 25–51.

37. Fogleman, "Jesus Is Female," in Gillespie and Beachy, eds., *Pious Pursuits.* Two versions of Reynier's account, one censored and the other not, were published in 1746 and 1748 by enemies of the Moravians, Johann Philip Fresenius and Alexander Volck. According to Fogleman, Reynier, Fresenius, and Volck probably stretched the truth in describing some of these sexual practices, but were accurate in depicting the line of couples waiting outside the cabinet.

38. Sommer, *Serving Two Masters,* 27.

39. See Peucker, "Aus Allen Nationen."

40. See Vernon Nelson, *John Valentine Haidt,* exhibition catalogue, Abby Aldrich Rockefeller Folk Art Collection (Williamsburg, Va., 1966); Nelson, "Johann Valentin Haidt und Zinzendorf," in *Graf Ohne Grenzen: Leben und Werk von Nikolaus Ludwig Graf von Zinzendorf* (Herrnhut, 2000), 152–158; Garth Howland, "John Valentine Haidt, A Little Known Eighteenth Century Painter," *Pennsylvania History,* 8 (1941), 304–313; and John F. Morman, "The Painting Preacher: John Valentine Haidt," *Pennsylvania History,* 20 (1953), 180–186.

41. Although no extended analysis of the "First Fruits" has ever been done, see Nelson, *John Valentine Haidt,* 22, and Hugh Honour, *The Image of the Black in Western Art,* Part IV: *From the American Revolution to World War I,* vol. 1: *Slaves and Liberators* (Cambridge, Mass., and London, 1989), 58–59, 313–314. Haidt painted at least three other different versions of the "First Fruits." One was destroyed by fire in 1758; another, which hung in the Herrnhut prayer hall, was destroyed when the advancing Soviet army

torched the town in 1745; a third survives in Bethlehem, Pennsylvania. The earliest version, from Herrnhaag, is now in Zeyst, the Netherlands.

42. Conference in Marienborn, Feb. 28, 1746, R.8.36.a, UA.

43. Protten to Zinzendorf, Dec. 6, 1746, Guinea Mission Papers, R.15.N.2, UA.

44. Oldendorp, *CM,* 402–403, 433; on Zinzendorf's "first fruits" idea, see pp. 414–417; on the helpers' persistent organizing efforts, see pp. 418–420.

45. Oldendorp, *CM,* 433–434, 443–455, 466; notations of July 27 and Oct. 23, 1747, in Jüngerhaus Diarium, 1747, vol. 1, pp. 305, 407, UA; Mason, *The Moravian Church and the Missionary Awakening in England,* 96–97.

46. Zeist Synod, May-June 1746, R.2.A.12, UA; Gemein Haus Diarium, Herrnhaag, May 9, 1747, and June 17, 1749, R.8.33.f and R.8.33.c, UA.

47. Atwood, "Zinzendorf's 1749 Reprimand to the *Brüdergemeine*"; Erbe, "Herrnhaag: Eine religiöse Kommunität"; Peucker, "'Blut auf unsre grünen Bändchen.'"

48. Hamilton and Hamilton, *History of the Moravian Church,* 105–106; Erbe, "Herrnhaag: Eine religiöse Kommunität," 149–154.

49. Emigrations-Tabellen, R.8.33.g5, UA; notation of Aug. 31, 1750, in Gemein-Diarium von Herrnhaag, R.8.34.f, UA; notations of May 7, 1751, in Jüngerhaus Diarium, 1751, vol. 6, and May 19, 1751, Jüngerhaus Diarium, 1751, vol. 2, UA.

50. The narrative of the building of Herrnhut and the consecration of the Renewed Unity of Brethren has been told many times; for summaries see Hamilton and Hamilton, *History of the Moravian Church,* chaps. 1–2, and Sommer, *Serving Two Masters,* 1–32.

51. Classen des Ehe-Chors, 1754, R.27.124.63, UA.

52. Honour, *Image of the Black in Western Art.* Although the portrait is officially attributed to the Moravian painter Abraham Brandt, the foremost authority on Haidt, Vernon Nelson, credits the painting to Haidt because of its stylistic consistency with his work.

53. "John Valentin Haidt's Treatise on Art," trans. and ed. Vernon H. Nelson (typescript, MA-NP), p. 28; description of Anna Maria in notation of Jan. 22, 1754, in Herrnhuter Kirchenbuch, 1722–1758, R.6.A.b.a1, UA.

54. Nelson, ed., "Haidt's Treatise on Art," 5, 27, 28; see also Vernon H. Nelson, "John Valentin Haidt's Theory of Painting," *Transactions of the Moravian Historical Society,* 23, parts III, IV (1984), 71–77.

55. Herrnhut Congregation Diary, Jan. 22 and 24, 1754, R.6.A.b.19a, UA.

8   CHRISTIANSBORG

1. Berthelsdorf Synod, June 8–July 5, 1756, R.2.A.39.B, UA.

2. Kenneth G. Hamilton and J. Taylor Hamilton, *History of the Moravian Church: The Renewed Unitas Fratrum, 1722–1957* (Bethlehem, Pa., 1967), 16–22; F. Ernst Stoeffler, *German Pietism during the Eighteenth Century* (Leiden, 1973), 40–47.

3. Protten to Zinzendorf, March 16, 1756, R.15.N.2, UA; Protten to Unity Elders, June 25, 1756, R.15.N.2.57, UA.

4. Notation of Aug. 18, 1756, in Jüngerhaus Diarum, 1756, Band III, Beilage, p. 964; Hans W. Debrunner, *A History of Christianity in Ghana* (Accra, 1967), 68.

5. Protten to Lorenz Praetorius, Aug. 14, 1757, R.15.N.2, UA. Captain Eriksen, incidentally, had been the subject of an investigation in 1748 when 174 of 334 slaves died on board his ship, *Jaegersborg,* en route to America. A surgeon determined they had been given too much water. Georg Norregard, *Danish Settlements in West Africa, 1658–1850* (Boston, 1966), 88.

6. Norregard, *Danish Settlements,* 42–45, 58–59, 75; Albert van Dantzig, *Forts and Castles of Ghana* (Accra, 1980), 31–32. The standard overview of Gold Coast society and politics during the period is Ray A. Kea, *Settlements, Trade, and Politics in the Seventeenth-Century Gold Coast* (Baltimore and London, 1982).

7. Norregard, *Danish Settlements,* 79–80, 90–93, 113. For a superb account of European slave-trading practices in eighteenth-century West Africa, see Robert Harms, *The Diligent: A Voyage Through the Worlds of the Slave Trade* (New York, 2002). Similarly, an account of a Danish slaving vessel that regularly ferried Africans from the Gold Coast to the Caribbean is Leif Svalesen, *The Slave Ship Fredensborg* (Bloomington, Ind., 2000).

8. Ludewig Ferdinand Romer, *A Reliable Account of the Coast of Guinea (1760),* ed. and trans. Selena Axelrod Winsnes (Oxford and New York,

2000), 185–186; Selena Axelrod Winsnes, *Letters on West Africa and the Slave Trade: Paul Erdmann Isert's Journey to Guinea and the Caribbean Islands in Columbia (1788)* (Oxford and New York, 1992), 157; Ira Berlin, "From Creoles to African: Atlantic Creoles and the Origins of African-American Society in Mainland North America," *WMQ,* 3rd ser., 53 (1996), 251–288.

9. Protten to Lorenz Praetorius, Aug. 14, 1757, R.15.N.2., UA; also quoted in Debrunner, *A History of Christianity in Ghana,* 74–75.

10. Protten to P.J., May 14, 1759, R.15; UA. Part of this letter is extracted in a notation of Aug. 6, 1760, in Jüngerhaus Diarium, 1760, Band 2, Beilage, p. 600.

11. N. L. Gayibor, "Les Rois de Glidji: Une Chronologie Revisée," *History in Africa,* 22 (1995), 197–222; Romer, *Reliable Account,* 186, 202; Robin Law, *The Slave Coast of West Africa, 1550–1750* (Oxford and New York, 1991), 316–318, 322.

12. Protten to Lorenz Praetorius, Aug. 14, 1757, R.15.N.2, UA; Romer, *Reliable Account,* 180–181.

13. Romer, *Reliable Account,* 186. See editor Winsnes's important suggestion in n. 240 that Romer might have confused Akan matrilineal practices with Ga patrilineal ones.

14. Oldendorp, *CM,* 189, 191. Protten's diary from 1756 to 1761 would permit a far more extensive examination of these issues than space permits here. R.15.N.8, UA.

15. Undated document by Protten, R.15.N.8., UA.; summary of Protten's observations about the Gold Coast, Aug. 11, 1762, R.15.N.8, UA.

16. Rebecca to Protten, Sept. 2, 1760, R.15.N.8, UA. On European-African interchanges during the era of the slave trade, see Berlin, "From Creoles to African," and David Northrup, *Africa's Discovery of Europe, 1450–1850* (New York, 2002), both of which survey large literatures.

17. Rebecca's readmission into the congregation is reflected in choir lists from the late 1750s; Catalogus von Ehe-Chor, 1757–1760, R.27.125.2, 3, 11, 12, 24, UA. On the Seven Years' War in Herrnhut and the death of Zinzendorf (followed by his second wife's death just twelve days later), see Hamilton and Hamilton, *History of the Moravian Church,* 115–117.

18. Prottens Reise-Diarium (Protten's travel diary), 1756–1761, Feb. 12,

1761, R.15.N.8, p. 131, UA; Protten to Frederik V, Oct. 30, 1762, R.15.N.8.3, UA.

19. Prottens Nachricht von einigen mitgebrachten u. übergebenen africanischen Sachen, March 3, 1762, R.15.N.8, UA; summary of Protten's observations about the Gold Coast, Aug. 11, 1762, R.15.N.8., UA.

20. Protten to Frederik V, Oct. 30, 1762, R.15.N.8, UA; Frederik V to West Indies and Guinea Company, Dec. 31, 1762, R.15.N.8, UA.

21. Johannes von Watteville, Leonhard Dober, and Joseph Spangenberg to Christian Protten, March 27, 1763, R.15.N.8., UA.

22. Norregard, *Danish Settlements,* 43; Dantzig, *Forts and Castles of Ghana,* 31–32; Winsnes, ed., *Letters on West Africa: Isert's Journey,* 28; Romer, *Reliable Account,* 212; Svalesen, *Slave Ship Fredensborg,* 66–67; Debrunner, *Christianity in Ghana,* 72. Christian Protten's arrival listed in 248 G. B. Journal, Litr. A, Generaltoldkammeret, Vestindiske-Guineiske Sager, RA (translations from the Danish in this and subsequent citations from this collection were done by Louise Sebro); Jacob Meder to Brethren's Directorate, Sept. 12, 1767, in "Neue Guineische Akten, 1767–73," no. 65, R.15.N.8.1e, UA.

23. Protten's travel diary, 1763–1764, R.15.N.8, UA.

24. H. M. J. Trutenau, ed., *Christian Protten's 1764 Introduction to the Fante and Accra (Ga) Languages* (London, 1971).

25. Ibid., 4–8.

26. Paul Edwards, "Introduction," in *The Life of Olaudah Equiano, or Gustavus Vassa, the African* (London, 1969), v–lxxii; Vincent Carretta, "Olaudah Equiano or Gustavus Vassa? New Light on an Eighteenth-Century Question of Identity," *Slavery and Abolition,* 20 (1999), 96–105; Debrunner, *Christianity in Ghana,* 72.

27. Romer quoted in Svalesen, *Slave Ship Fredensborg,* 68.

28. Romer, *Reliable Account,* 212; Winsnes, ed., *Letters from West Africa: Isert's Journey,* 29–30, 156; Svalesen, *Slave Ship Fredensborg,* 213–215; Norregard, *Danish Settlements,* 169.

29. Svalesen, *Slave Ship Fredensborg,* 213–215; Norregard, *Danish Settlements,* 86; Romer, *Reliable Account,* 213. Figures on the Danish slave trade are from Per O. Hernaes, *Slaves, Danes, and African Coast Society: The Danish Slave Trade from West Africa and Afro-Danish Relations on the Eighteenth-*

Century Gold Coast, No. 6 Trondheim Studies in History (Trondheim, Norway, 1998), 335. Larger holding pens for slaves were built outside Christiansborg in Osu.

30. Protten to Hagerup, March 26, 1765, Ad. A259, G. B. Journal Litr. A, p. 12, Generaltoldkammeret, Vestindiske-Guineiske Sager, RA.

31. Guinea correspondence, April 22, 1765, and two undated letters from 1765, A219, Guineisk Brevjournal Litr. A, pp. 30, 34, 35, Generaltoldkammeret, Vestindiske-Guineiske Sager, RA.

32. Romer, *Reliable Account,* 86–87; Hans Debrunner, "Notable Danish Chaplains on the Gold Coast," *Transactions of the History Society of Ghana,* 2 (1957), 22–24.

33. Debrunner, "Notable Danish Chaplains," 22–23; Norregard, *Danish Settlements,* 167.

34. Feldtmann to Guinea Company directors, Oct. 23, 1769, Guineisk Kompagni, Kompagniets Kobenhavnske Arkivalier, No. 14–15, Kystdokumenter 1768–69, letter 23, RA.

35. Diary of Esau Quist, Oct. 21–23 and Dec. 15, 1766, Guineisk Kompagni, Kompagniets Kobenhavnske Arkivalier, No. 12, Kystdokumenter 1767–76, RA; Fiskalens Journal på Christiansborg, Dec. 15, 1766, Guineisk Kompagni, Hjemsendte arkivalier fra Guineakysten, no. 174, RA. On Oto Brafo, see Carl Christian Reindorf, *History of the Gold Coast and Asante* (Basel, 1895), 102.

36. Jacob Meder to Brethren's Directorate, Sept. 12, 1767, in "Neue Guineische Akten, 1767–73," R.15.N.8.1e, no. 65, UA. On Bargum, see Norregard, *Danish Settlements,* 120–130.

37. Romer quoted by Jacob Meder in letter to von Schweinitz, Dec. 1, 1767, Neue Guineische Akten, R.15.N.8.1e, no. 76, UA.

38. Meder to Jonas Weiss, Jan. 16, 1768, Neue Guineische Akten, R.15.N.8.1e., no. 78, UA. Among the many works on Christian antislavery views during the second half of the eighteenth century, see David Brion Davis, *The Problem of Slavery in the Age of Revolution, 1770–1823* (Ithaca, N.Y., 1975), and Lamin Sanneh, *Abolitionists Abroad: American Blacks and the Making of Modern West Africa* (Cambridge, Mass., 1999).

39. Meder to Jonas Weiss, Jan. 16, 1768, Neue Guineische Akten, R.15.N.8.1e., no. 78, UA.

40. Michael Cröger to Friedrich Neisser, April 30, 1768, Diaspora der Brüder-Unität, Dänische Staaten, Brief aus Kopenhagen, R.19.E.10.a.4, no. 90, UA.

41. Letter to secret council from fort employees, July 31, 1769, Kompagniets Kobenhavnske Arkivalier, No. 16–17, Kystdokumente 1770–71, Guineisk Kompagni, RA; Norregard, *Danish Settlements*, 122, 166.

42. Probate auction protocols, Jan. 11, July 30, and Nov. 20, 1768, Kompagniets Kobenhavnske Arkivalier, No. 16–17, Kystdokumenter 1770–71, Guineisk Kompagni, RA.

43. Jonathan Briant to Friedrich Neisser, March 17, 1769, Diaspora der Brüder-Unität, Dänische Staaten, Brief aus Kopenhagen, R.19.E.10.a.5, no. 112, UA; Reindorf, *History of the Gold Coast and Asante*, 223–224; Adam Jones, ed., *Afrikabestände im Unitätsarchiv der Herrnhuter Brüdergemeine* (University of Leipzig Papers on Africa), Mission Archives, ser. 11 (2000), 71–72; Norregard, *Danish Settlements*, 130.

44. *Gemein Nachrichten*, 1770, week 13, item 6, UA.

45. Letter from Christiansborg council to Guinea Company directors, July 25, 1770, Kompagniets Kobenhavnske Arkivalier, No. 16–17, Kystdokumenter 1770–71, Guineisk Kompagni, RA; account book (omkostningbog), 1769–1770, Hjemsendte arkivalier fra Guineakysten, No. 194, Guineisk Kompagni, RA.

46. Gersdorf letter of Oct. 13 [1773] quoted in Guinea Co. Directorate to Lorenz Praetorius, Feb. 24, 1774, R.15.N.8.3.31, UA.

47. Christiansborg council to Guinea Company directors, Aug. 19, 1776, Kompagniets Kobenhavnske Arkivalier, No. 21, Kystdokumenter 1775–78, Guineisk Kompagni, RA; Norregard, *Danish Settlements*, 131–142.

48. Wöchentliche Nachrichten aus der Unitäts Aeltesten-Conferenz, Week 29, July 22–28, 1781, p. 84, UA.

EPILOGUE

1. Description taken from Leif Svalesen, *The Slave Ship Fredensborg* (Bloomington and Indianapolis, 2000), 211–217.

2. Hans Werner Debrunner, *Presence and Prestige, Africans in Europe: A History of Africans in Europe before 1918* (Basel, 1979), 109.

3. J. C. S. Mason, *The Moravian Church and the Missionary Awakening*

in England, 1760–1800 (Woodbridge, Suffolk, and Rochester, N.Y., 2001), 16–17; Beverly Smaby, "'No one should lust for power . . . women least of all': Dismantling Female Leadership among 18th Century Moravians," in Michele Gillespie and Robert Beachy, eds., *Pious Pursuits: German Moravians in the Atlantic World* (forthcoming).

4. For details of Oldendorp's life, see his *Lebenslauf,* or autobiography, in Oldendorp, *CM,* 633–640. Also see the introductory remarks by Ingeborg Baldauf, Hartmut Beck, Gudrun Meier, and Horst Ulbricht in Oldendorp, *Historie,* vol. I, 9–25.

5. Oldendorp, *Historie,* vol. II, parts 1–3.

6. Ibid., vol. I, 639–675.

7. Oldendorp, *Geschichte der Mission der evangelischen Brüder auf den caraibischen Inseln S. Thomas, S. Croix, und S. Jan* (Barby, 1777). The first English edition, published in 1987, was Oldendorp, *CM,* while a four-volume edition of Oldendorp's original manuscript was published in 2000–2002 as Oldendorp, *Historie;* see the Prologue, n. 7.

8. Sylvia R. Frey and Betty Wood, *Come Shouting to Zion: African American Protestantism in the American South and British Caribbean to 1830* (Chapel Hill, N.C., 1998), 1.

9. Oldendorp, *CM,* 625–626; Mason, *The Moravian Church and the Missionary Awakening,* 142; G. Oliver Maynard, *A History of the Moravian Church, Eastern West Indies Province* (Port-of-Spain, 1968); Richard Price, *Alabi's World* (Baltimore, 1990).

10. Frey and Wood, *Come Shouting to Zion,* 80–117; Albert Raboteau, *Slave Religion: The "Invisible Institution" in the Antebellum South* (New York, 1978); Mechal Sobel, *Trabelin' On: The Slave Journey to an Afro-Baptist Faith,* 2nd ed. (Princeton, N.J., 1988).

11. Frey and Wood, *Come Shouting to Zion,* 80–117, quotes on p. 106; John Saillant, "Antiguan Methodism and Antislavery Activity: Anne and Elizabeth Hart in the Eighteenth-Century Black Atlantic," *Church History,* 69 (2000), 86–115; Mary Turner, *Slaves and Missionaries: The Disintegration of Jamaican Slave Society, 1787–1834* (Urbana, Ill., 1982). Moravian influence on these developments is discussed in Mason, *Moravian Church and the Missionary Awakening,* and Andrew Porter, "Church History, History of Christianity, Religious History: Some Reflections on British Missionary

Enterprise Since the Late Eighteenth Century," *Church History,* 71 (2002), 571–572.

12. Among the many authors who have explored this theme, see Frey and Wood, *Come Shouting to Zion,* passim; Sylvia R. Frey, *Water from the Rock: Black Resistance in a Revolutionary Age* (Princeton, N.J., 1991); Turner, *Slaves and Missionaries;* Douglas R. Egerton, *He Shall Go Out Free: The Lives of Denmark Vesey* (Madison, Wis., 1999); Margaret Washington Creel, *"A Peculiar People": Slave Religion and Community-Culture among the Gullahs* (New York, 1988). For an example of proslavery Moravian writing, see August Spangenberg, *An Account of the Manner in Which the Protestant Church of the Unitas Fratrum, or United Brethren, Preach the Gospel and Carry on their Missions Among the Heathen* (London, 1788), 41–43.

13. Henry Louis Gates, Jr., and William L. Andrews, eds., *Pioneers of the Black Atlantic: Five Slave Narratives from the Enlightenment, 1772–1815* (Washington, D.C., 1998).

14. Mason, *Moravian Church and the Missionary Awakening,* 114–142; James Ramsay, *Essay on the Treatment and Conversion of African Slaves* (London, 1784), 164. On the larger context of religion in the abolition movement, see Robin Blackburn, *The Overthrow of Colonial Slavery, 1776–1848* (London and New York, 1988), 131–160; David Brion Davis, *The Problem of Slavery in the Age of Revolution, 1770–1823* (Ithaca, N.Y., 1975); Seymour Drescher and Christine Bolt, eds., *Anti-Slavery, Religion and Reform* (Folkestone, Eng., 1980).

15. Hugh Honour, *The Image of the Black in Western Art,* vol. IV, *From the American Revolution to World War I,* part I, *Slaves and Liberators* (Cambridge, Mass., and London, 1989), 62–63.

16. Daniel P. Hopkins, "The Danish Ban on the Atlantic Slave Trade and Denmark's African Colonial Ambitions, 1787–1807," *Itinerario,* 25 (2001), 154–184; Christian Degn, *Die Schimmelmanns im atlantischen Dreieckshandel* (Neumünster, 1975); Svend E. Green-Pedersen, "The Economic Considerations Behind the Danish Abolition of the Negro Slave Trade," in Henry A. Gemery and Jan S. Hogendorn, eds., *The Uncommon Market: Essays in the Economic History of the Atlantic Slave Trade* (New York, 1979), 399–418.

17. Lamin Sanneh, *Abolitionists Abroad: American Blacks and the Making*

of Modern West Africa (Cambridge, Mass., 1999); James W. St. George Walker, *The Black Loyalists: The Search for a Promised Land in Nova Scotia and Sierra Leone, 1783–1870* (New York, 1976); Saillant, "Antiguan Methodism and Antislavery Activity." On the multi-directional nature of Afro-Atlantic linkages, see also Robin Law and Kristin Mann, "West Africa in the Atlantic Community: The Case of the Slave Coast," *WMQ,* 3rd ser., 56 (1999), 307–334; Deborah Gray White, "'Yes,' There is a Black Atlantic," *Itinerario,* 23 (1999), 127–140. See also Jean M. Humez, *Gifts of Power: The Writings of Rebecca Jackson, Black Visionary, Shaker Eldress* (Amherst, Mass., 1981); Nell Irvin Painter, *Sojourner Truth: A Life, a Symbol* (New York, 1996); William L. Andrews, ed., *Sisters of the Spirit: Three Black Women's Autobiographies of the Nineteenth Century* (Bloomington, Ind., 1986).

18. Neville A. T. Hall, *Slave Society in the Danish West Indies: St. Thomas, St. John and St. Croix* (Mona, Jamaica, 1992), 208–27.

19. Interview with the author, May 20, 2001. On these aspects of the Virgin Islands' history, see Isaac Dookhan, *A History of the Virgin Islands of the United States* (St. Thomas, 1974); William W. Boyer, *America's Virgin Islands: A History of Human Rights and Wrongs* (Durham, N.C., 1983); Maynard, *History of the Moravian Church, Eastern West Indies Province.*

SOURCES

MANUSCRIPTS
Denmark

Rigsarkivet, Copenhagen (RA)
  Vestindisk Guineisk Kompagni (VGK) (West Indies and Guinea
    Company)
    Kompagniets Kobenhavnske Arkivalier (Company Copenhagen
      Archive)
      Documents concerning the Moravian Brethren on St. Thomas,
        1737–49
    Generaltoldkammeret, Vestindiske-Guineiske Sager
      Documents from Guinea, 1760–71
    Guineisk Kompagni (Guinea Company)
      Kompagniets Kobenhavnske Arkivalier (Company Copenhagen
        Archive)
        Coast documents, 1767–78
    Lanslister St. Thomas, 1726–40 (St. Thomas Property Lists)

Germany

Unitätsarchiv, Herrnhut (UA)
  Danish West Indies Papers (R15.Ba, Bb)
    Letters and Reports, 1726–45
    Zinzendorf's Stay in St. Thomas, 1739
    General Reports, 1731–42
    Minutes and Letters, 1740–45

Reports, Diaries, and Letters from the Start of the Mission in St. Thomas

Official Documents from the Mission to St. Thomas, St. Croix, and St. John, 1741–47

Reports and Letters from St. Thomas, St. Croix, and St. John, 1731–42

Letters from Negro Brothers and Sisters, 1737–65

Visitation and Travel Diaries from the Danish West Indies, 1732–42

Miscellaneous Mission History Documents, 1734–99

Report of the Wedding of Matthäus Freundlich with the Mulatto Rebecca, 1739

St. Thomas Diaries, 1732–1743

Diaspora of the Brethren, Danish States (R19)

Letters from Copenhagen

Dienerblätter (Missionaries' Pages)

Rebecca Protten, Christian Protten, Friedrich Martin, Susanna Nitschmann

Gemein Nachrichten (Unity Reports), 1760–70

Guinea Mission (R15.N)

Protten's Diary, 1737–41

Protten's Miscellaneous Letters, 1735–60

Protten's Travel Diary, 1756–61

Protten's Papers, 1762–64

New Guinea Acts, 1767–73

Correspondence, 1765–75

Herrnhut Congregational Records (R6, R27)

Church Book, 1722–58

Congregation Diary, 1751–62

Jüngerhaus Diary, 1747–60

Catalogues of Married Choirs, 1754–60

Synod Minutes and Reports, 1739–60 (R2)

Wetterau Congregational Records (R8)

Herrnhaag Diary, 1742–50

Herrnhaag Elders' Conference, 1742–50

Marienborn Diary, 1742–51

Marienborn Elders' Conference, 1742–51

Catalogue of Communicant Brothers and Sisters, 1745
Hourly Intercession Schedules, 1742–50
Marienborn and Herrnhaag Conferences, 1742–50
Emigration Tables, 1750–51
Wöchentliche Nachrichten (Weekly Reports), 1781

United States

Moravian Archives, Northern Province, Bethlehem, Pa. (MA-NP)
Johann Valentin Haidt, "Treatise on Art"
West Indies Catalogues
Virgin Islands Mission, Church Register 1737–50

U.S. Virgin Islands

Enid M. Baa Library, St. Thomas
Von Scholten Collection
Hugo Ryberg, typescript, "A List of the Names of Inhabitants,
Danish West Indian Islands, from 1650–1825"

PUBLISHED PRIMARY SOURCES

Capitein, Jacob Elisa Johannes, *The Agony of Asar: A Thesis on Slavery by the Former Slave,* trans. and ed. Grant Parker (Kingston, Jamaica, and Princeton, N.J., 2001).

Caron, Aimery P., and Arnold R. Highfield, trans. and ed., *The French Intervention in the St. John Slave Revolt of 1733–34* (Occasional Paper No. 8, Bureau of Libraries, Museums, and Archaeological Services, St. Thomas, 1981).

Carstens, Johan Lorentz, *St. Thomas in Early Danish Times: A General Description of all the Danish, American or West Indian Islands,* trans. and ed. Arnold R. Highfield, originally published in the 1740s as En almindelig Beskrivelse om alle de Danske, Americanske eller West-Indiske Eylande (St. Croix, 1997).

Christian den Femtes Lov (Copenhagen, 1693).

The Christian Monthly History, IV (1744).

Oldendorp, Christian Georg Andreas, *Geschichte der Mission der evangelischen Brüder auf den Caribischen Inseln S. Thomas, S. Croix und S. Jan* (Barby, 1777).

———— *Historie der caribischen Inseln Sanct Thomas, Sanct Crux und Sanct Jan. Kommentiere Edition Des Originalmanuskriptes,* vol. 1, ed. Gudrun Meier, Stephan Palmié, Peter Stein, and Horst Ulbricht (Berlin, 2000); vol. 2, parts 1–3, ed. Hartmut Beck, Gudrun Meier, Stephan Palmié, Aart H. van Soest, Peter Stein, and Horst Ulbricht (Berlin, 2002).

———— *History of the Mission of the Evangelical Brethren on the Caribbean Islands of St. Thomas, St. Croix, and St. John,* ed. Johann Jakob Bossart, English trans. and ed. Arnold R. Highfield and Vladimir Barac (Ann Arbor, 1987).

Pannet, Pierre J., *Report on the Execrable Conspiracy Carried Out by the Amina Negroes on the Danish Island of St. Jan in America 1733,* trans. and ed. Aimery P. Caron and Arnold R. Highfield (Christiansted, St. Croix, 1984).

Rimius, Henry, *A Candid Narrative of the Rise and Progress of the Herrnhuters, Commonly Called Moravians or "Unitas Fratrum"* (London, 1753).

Romer, Ludewig Ferdinand, *A Reliable Account of the Coast of Guinea (1760),* trans. and ed. Selena Axelrod Winsnes (Oxford and New York, 2000).

Spangenberg, August Gottlieb, *Leben des Herrn Nikolaus Ludwig Grafen von Zinzendorf und Pottendorf* (Barby, 1773–1775).

———— *An Account of the Manner in Which the Protestant Church of the "Unitas Fratrum," or United Brethren, Preach the Gospel Among the Heathen* (London, 1788).

Trutenau, H. M. J., ed., *Christian Protten's 1764 Introduction to the Fante and Accra (Ga) Languages* (London, 1971).

Winsnes, Selena Axelrod, ed., *Letters on West Africa and the Slave Trade: Paul Erdmann Isert's "Journey to Guinea and the Caribbean Islands in Columbia (1788)"* (Oxford and New York, 1992).

Zinzendorf, Nikolaus Ludwig von, *Büdingische Sammlung* (Büdingen, 1740–1745).

———— *Hauptschriften: Ergänzungsband* (Hildesheim, 1965).

———— *Materialen und Dokumente: Band XXIV. Herrnhut im 18. und 19. Jahrhundert, drei Schriften* (Hildesheim, 2000).

———— *Texte zur Mission* (Nürnberg, 1748; republished, Hamburg, 1979).

ACKNOWLEDGMENTS

Governments and authors have a way of accumulating unseemly debts. Authors, however, at least have the advantage of being able to recognize them. I only hope that the many people and institutions who helped make this book possible understand the depth of my gratitude.

This project emanated from a short talk I gave in April 2000, at the invitation of Emily Clark and Mary Laven, at a conference on "Women of the Atlantic World in the Age of Religious Reform and Revival" at the University of Cambridge. Little did I know that this would start me on a serious effort to understand Rebecca Protten's origins and follow her trail across the Atlantic. Several years later, having visited the fort on St. Thomas where Rebecca was imprisoned, seen her daughter's eroding gravestone in Herrnhut, and studied records of her West African years in Copenhagen, I thank Emily and Mary for the invitation that became a quest.

I thank the staffs of the Unitätsarchiv in Herrnhut, Germany, the Moravian Archives in Bethlehem, Pennsylvania, the Rigsarkivet in Copenhagen, and the Enid M. Baa Library in Charlotte Amalie, St. Thomas, for their assistance in making their magnificent collections available to me.

Several institutions provided financial support at critical stages of the project. Archival research was made possible by a Humanities Scholarship Enhancement Grant from the University of Florida and a travel grant from the Deutscher Akademischer Austausch Dienst, or German Academic Exchange Service. I completed much of the writing at the National Humanities Center in 2001–2002 through a fellowship from the National Endowment for the Humanities. I am grateful to the Center and its staff, particularly then-director Bob Connor, Kent Mullikin, and the terrific team of librarians, for creating such a congenial and productive environment. Thanks, too, to the many other fellows in residence for enriching my time in that magnificent facility with friendship and lively conversation.

Early on, my friend Woody Holton gave me a chance to try out some of my ideas in his class at the University of Richmond. Woody and his students, along with Doug Winiarski and Carol Summers, made the discussion one of the liveliest and most instructive I've had about this project. Since then, I've spoken about Rebecca's world at many conferences and colloquia, and I thank the organizers of those sessions for the opportunities to do so, as well as the commentators and audiences whose responses enriched my thinking.

Working at the unlikely intersection of the Danish, Dutch, and German Atlantics reminded me of the far greater agility with which Rebecca navigated between cultures and languages than I can. Translations of Dutch documents by Marjoleine Kars, Sanneryn Jansen, and Ron Dorrestein, many of them in difficult handwriting, opened numerous doors for me. During my visit to Copenhagen, Louise Sebro's adroit skills in research and translation made accessible a collection of Danish records essential to the story.

Many people have offered helpful comments on the text. I'm especially grateful to Ira Berlin and Jon Butler for reading the entire manuscript, and to Sylvia Frey and Doug Winiarski for reading the majority of it. In addition, selected chapters or versions of parts of the work were read by Holly Brewer, Lil Fenn, Chuck Grench, David Hackett, Woody Holton, Jessica Harland-Jacobs, Gregg Roeber, Leah Rosenberg, Carol Summers, Fredrika Teute, Luise White, and David Wills.

Many others contributed in different ways. On St. Thomas, the congregation of New Herrnhut Moravian Church welcomed me, and Rev. Glenvil Gregory, Yvonne Francis, Lynne Mulraine, and James Francis took the time to answer my questions. In Germany, my cousins, Uwe and Ulrich Hoppe, led me on a freewheeling adventure to the remains of old Herrnhaag. Dan Reboussin and Peter Malanchuk of Smathers Library at the University of Florida recommended several useful citations. Robert Lopez prepared the maps. Chris Schultz sheltered her brother-in-law for a year. Others who gave advice or help of various kinds include Craig Atwood, Kathy Brown, Bernard Gadagbui, Myron Jackson, Betty King, Sheryl Kroen, Vernon Nelson, Mark Peterson, Paul Peucker, Shane Runyon, and Dan Thorp. As always, thanks to Peter Wood for everything else.

The enthusiasm and advice of Joyce Seltzer at Harvard University Press have helped shape the book in important ways. Thanks, as well, to David Lobenstine, formerly of the Press, for his early support of the project and thoughtful editorial suggestions, and to Rachel Weinstein. The text has been improved by Mary Ellen Geer's sharp copy editing.

I would not have been able to complete this book without the support of my family. In particular, my father, Werner Sensbach, spent countless hours transcribing and, in many cases, translating the documents that form the core of my research, many of them written in archaic and often colloquial German script that can be a punishing job to decode. Our long conversations about the story we were unearthing really made him a collaborator on the project, and there is something of him on nearly every page. And my wife, Beverly, probably did not anticipate the level of personal sacrifice she would be asked to make in support of my work when vows were exchanged years ago. Her grace and humor remind me every day why we spoke them in the first place.

INDEX